D1443036

BLUE IN A RED STATE

ALSO BY JUSTIN KREBS

538 Ways to Live, Work, and Play Like a Liberal

BLUE IN A
RED STATE

A Survival Guide to
Life in the Real America

Justin Krebs

THE NEW PRESS

NEW YORK
LONDON

Requests for permission to reproduce selections from this book should be mailed to:
Permissions Department, The New Press, 120 Wall Street,
31st floor, New York, NY 10005.

Published in the United States by The New Press, New York, 2016

Distributed by Perseus Distribution

LIBRARY OF CONGRESS CATALOGING-IN-PUBLICATION DATA

Names: Krebs, Justin, author.
Title: Blue in a red state : a survival guide to life in the real America / Justin Krebs.
Description: New York : The New Press, 2016.
Identifiers: LCCN 2015031077 | ISBN 9781595589729 (hardback) |
ISBN 9781595589699 (e-book)
Subjects: LCSH: Liberalism—United States. | Right and left (Political science)—United
States. | Liberals—United States—Biography. | Political culture—United States. |
BISAC: POLITICAL SCIENCE / Civics & Citizenship. | POLITICAL SCIENCE /
Political Ideologies / Conservatism & Liberalism. | POLITICAL SCIENCE / Political
Ideologies / Democracy. | POLITICAL SCIENCE / Government / General.
Classification: LCC JC574.2.U6 K753 2016 | DDC 320.51/30973—dc23
LC record available at http://lccn.loc.gov/2015031077

The New Press publishes books that promote and enrich public discussion and
understanding of the issues vital to our democracy and to a more equitable world.
These books are made possible by the enthusiasm of our readers; the support
of a committed group of donors, large and small; the collaboration of our many
partners in the independent media and the not-for-profit sector; booksellers, who
often hand-sell New Press books; librarians; and above all by our authors.

www.thenewpress.com

Composition by dix!
This book was set in Adobe Caslon

Printed in the United States of America

2   4   6   8   10   9   7   5   3   1

CONTENTS

INTRODUCTION

Lisa in Waukesha, Wisconsin, has two Facebook accounts. One reflects her liberal politics; the other is for acquaintances and family members to whom Lisa shows only her cat photos. Christina, in Milford, Massachusetts, has a sign in the back window of her car proclaiming support for a Democratic candidate. But as soon as she parks in the company lot, she puts it facedown on the backseat. Byron has lived in the same small town of Pomeroy, Iowa—population 662—his entire life. He brings his partner to family dinners but has never actually said to his conservative sister that he's gay.

Lisa, Christina, and Byron are "blues in red states"—liberals who live in conservative communities that exist in every state, Republican- or Democratic-leaning, across America. They and people like them are constantly reminded they aren't quite like everyone else: from the churches they do or don't attend, to their purchases and media preferences, to their loyalties at the ballot box. On a daily basis, liberals who have made homes, formed friendships, and participated in the civic life of conservative towns and cities are confronted with unsettling reminders that they're different, and they've found myriad ways to take that truth in stride.

On some occasions, it's best to say as little as possible. Chris in

Cincinnati, Ohio, is quick to talk liberalism—except when he's hanging out with his ice hockey team. Spike in Sandia Park, New Mexico, and Dean in Pawleys Island, South Carolina, are both white men in their sixties who often hear offhand right-wing comments from people who assume they are conservative, and then have to determine whether it's worth speaking up. Diane in Fairbanks, Alaska, occasionally talks politics with her neighbors but never lets it get too heated—she's always mindful she might need that neighbor to dig her out of the next big storm. Some might call this strategy "passing"—going undercover, by conscious deception or simple omission, to blend into conservative surroundings, staying quiet through sticky moments, or deftly navigating around political minefields in one's neighborhood or workplace.

But in some instances, it becomes too hard to stay quiet. Susannah in Kalispell, Montana, has had to interrupt the conversation of her quilting group when it's veered too far to the right—whether debating government policy about wolves or discussing Native Americans. Rita, in Pawleys Island, South Carolina, mentioned to one of the members of her water aerobics club that the prayer before their post-practice lunch made her uncomfortable (at their next lunch, the women prayed while Rita was in the bathroom). Lenzi in Austin, Texas, asked her law school classmates not to use the word "retarded"—and was reprimanded by her professor as a result. Byron doesn't like to stir up any controversy in his bar but found he had to say something as regulars muttered racial slurs. Coming out as a liberal happens when it's important to stand up for liberal values even momentarily, in situations where remaining silent would feel complicit. Here and there, liberals living out of their element sometimes feel a need to lean into their politics—boasting a yard sign on a conservative block, offering a divergent point of view at a cordial meal—and then lean away just as quickly for the sake of civility and stability.

And at other times, there's no choice but to make a scene. When Desmond visited a comedy club on a trip home to Tuscaloosa, Alabama, he was so stunned by the performer's homophobic comments that he piped up in the middle of the set. Dan in Idaho Falls, Idaho, questions his children's science teachers about evolution—letting them apologize for teaching "that theory" before he reveals he's a scientist who is in favor of a reality-based curriculum. Such moments call for unapologetic pride in one's political perspective. At these junctures, liberals living in conservative areas wear their true colors, launching the long-shot local campaign, marching in pride parades, striking up conversations to convince their conservative acquaintances, calling out homophobia, racism, or sexism, or even running for office.

At the same time, liberals often cope with and find comfort in their conservative surroundings by seeking out their tribe. Dan of Idaho Falls has started an atheist society. Desmond discovered a local theater group while growing up in Tuscaloosa. Even in the most isolated moments, Joe of Brandon, Florida, can still consume progressive blogs and podcasts. Chris of Yankton, South Dakota, streams left-leaning radio shows daily.

However, whether they find their kindred spirits in small clusters or online, when these liberals walk out their doors, they come face-to-face with—and need to learn to confront, conform to, or otherwise navigate—their right-wing reality: TVs in local venues are tuned to Fox News. Co-workers can quote Rush Limbaugh. Anti-Obama comments are rife, made as a casual matter of fact, often ignorant and sometimes crossing the line to racist. Neighbors and colleagues assume that everyone attends church, and some are suspicious of those who don't. The same assumptions are made about gun ownership.

In these settings, being liberal can be challenging and it can be frightening. As one woman in Oklahoma City confessed, before she found other liberals she could talk with who gave her confidence, she would have been too nervous to "come out of the closet as a liberal." And this isn't just liberal paranoia: a conservative Mormon in Salt Lake City, Utah, explained that she had become disgusted with the venomous rhetoric of the Republicans in her state and it pushed her to meet some liberals. When she finally did, she recounted in total seriousness, "The first thing I learned was that they didn't want to kill babies."

No wonder so many liberals, in such areas, feel out of place. But as many of them have discovered, they don't have to give up their politics or give up their homes. Like all of nature's creatures, they can adapt: they learn when to push their politics and when to put politics aside in order to form meaningful connections with neighbors despite differences. They learn to tap into values that run deeper than party affiliation. They find ways to share community happiness, which is key to daily survival, through a mix of coping, cajoling, and conquering, a balancing act of fight and flight, and knowing when it's worth engaging, or when happiness relies on disengagement.

A few blues in red states ultimately find they cannot exist comfortably as lone outposts of liberalism and choose to leave. They pick up from their conservative settings and find their way to college towns and state capitals, coastal metropolises and diverse big cities, where many liberals feel more naturally at home. But for the many liberals who stay put, the key to happiness is not in choosing which type of liberal to be—but in developing a rich array of coping mechanisms, "code-switching" among all the approaches. Knowing when to escape inward and when to escape outward, when to find strange bedfellows, or when to let good fences make good neighbors, helps even the most true-blue liberal survive and thrive in deep-red pockets of America.

In an increasingly crowded, urbanized, and multicultural country, blues in red states provide lessons in coping and civility that can benefit all of us. How can we talk meaningfully and respectfully to our neighbors, even when they differ from us? How can we find common ground sturdier than daily turmoil? How can we communicate thoughtfully and share our values, one conversation at a time?

We live in an era when Facebook and other social media increasingly tell us what we want to hear and share with us content that affirms—rather than challenges—our beliefs. More and more of the media we consume is nationally accessible—conservatives in Vermont can listen to Glenn Beck and Sean Hannity as easily as liberals in Texas can find Amy Goodman and Rachel Maddow. Whether one clicks over to the Drudge Report and RedState or to Alternet and Daily Kos, Americans can choose online news and opinion that make them feel at home.

And yet, the virtual world has its limits—and we find ourselves interacting on a daily basis with people whom we can't always choose as easily as we click on a link, and can't shut out as quickly as we close a browser window. Liberals in conservative areas forge relationships with people of different political views all the time. Sometimes, they are able to persuade someone to accept a more progressive perspective. Sometimes, they find common ground over lifestyles or values that run deeper than politics. And occasionally—though rarely—they even find themselves agreeing with a conservative point of view.

These liberals keep up the pressure for progress in the most intimidating surroundings. They voice unpopular but necessary views. They live side by side with many Americans who don't strongly identify with any political label and are the most potentially persuadable. And they also put a friendly face on "liberalism"—making it harder for conservatives to demonize them, just as liberals need to remember not to demonize those with politics at the other end of the spectrum.

●　●　●

My own life geography has been solidly blue: I was raised in a Democratic small town in New Jersey; attended college in Cambridge, Massachusetts; then made my life in New York City. I live close to independent bookstores and movie theaters, our neighborhood has curbside composting, and my wife and I belong to a food co-op. I'm a white, heterosexual male. It's been easy being a liberal.

Then a little more than a decade ago, a friend and I started a club called Drinking Liberally. It was 2003, during the dark days of the Bush administration. Our nation had just entered a war we shouldn't have been in, Americans were being warned by the White House to "watch what you say," and there was a sense that we lacked liberal leadership and liberal community. So we started gathering at a bar each week to talk politics with fellow progressives—to learn, share, vent, and organize.

The idea took off and within a few years Drinking Liberally was everywhere. It quickly made the leap from progressive areas, where it was a fun social networking opportunity, to conservative areas, where it was a lifeline for liberals who otherwise felt politically isolated. It has grown into a network of hundreds of chapters. As exciting as Drinking Liberally was to my friends and me, it was even more critical to folks in red states who needed to know they weren't alone.

Over the decade since, I've had the chance to visit the more than seventy-five chapters of Drinking Liberally, which now exists in almost every state. From thousands of conversations, I've seen that, despite regional differences and habits, there is a core to liberalism that runs nationwide. Those who call themselves liberal in America today believe that we're all better off when we live for one another than we are when we live only for ourselves. That's the simplest value at the center of our politics—and it resonates as clearly with self-identified liberals in rural Kentucky as it does with those in the Boston suburbs.

It's also the central value that has the potential to define our politics, strengthen our society, and create a better future. If we're going to spread that liberal value, we won't do it by talking only with other liberals. We'll do it by talking with conservatives, moderates, and the large slices of regular Americans undefined by political leanings, in Texas, Idaho, Montana, South Carolina, and Arkansas—one conversation at a time.

We've heard about red states and blue states so often that we accept the division as fact. And it's true: an increasing number of states have one-party control over both houses of their legislatures. There are fewer toss-up Senate and congressional seats. Even on a local level, as detailed maps of recent presidential elections show, every American is most likely to live in a solidly Democratic or Republican neighborhood.

And yet, in most places, the story is more complicated. Montana can elect a Democratic governor, and Massachusetts can elect a Republican. A woman in Grapevine, Texas, can be attacked by conservatives when she runs for town council—then work as a private citizen with those same conservatives to enact government transparency laws. A coalition in Pawleys Island can unite the left and right over sensible development and planning. Democrats can help elect a Republican mayor of Idaho Falls, then work with her to push for expanded nondiscrimination laws. A group of hard-core progressives and hard-core reactionaries can sit down in Waukesha for "Détente Dinners." A liberal retiree who spent his life in the air force can spend years in a regular book club with Republicans, Libertarians, and Green Partiers. A state legislator in Arkansas can help Democrats elect an insurgent Republican head of the state assembly in order to pass Medicaid expansion. A man in Yankton can belong to a church where he supposes he knows the politics of fellow parishioners but never asks—and then is surprised to run into them at a political gathering for a cause they share. These stories are among the many I heard in a series of conversations that took place in 2014.

The truth is more like what a certain keynote speaker at the 2004 Democratic Convention in Boston noted: "The pundits like to slice and dice our country into red states and blue states. . . . But I've got news for them, too. We worship an awesome God in the blue states, and we don't like federal agents poking around our libraries in the red states. We coach little league in the blue states and, yes, we've got some gay friends in the red states. There are patriots who opposed the war in Iraq, and there are patriots who supported the war in Iraq." As then–U.S. Senate candidate Barack Obama summed it up, "There's not a liberal America and a conservative America; there's the United States of America."

BLUE IN A RED STATE

Lisa Muxworthy

I'm very outspoken. However, not in certain areas.
We don't put signs in the windows of our condo. We
want to have cordial relationships with neighbors.

As proudly liberal as Lisa Muxworthy is, she does have some friends with whom she doesn't talk politics. Some are more conservative. Others are liberal but burned out from years of constant outrage in Wisconsin. There are also a number of friends from childhood whom she doesn't want to alienate further, as well as relatives around the country who have a limited appetite for Wisconsin politics. So Lisa created a second Facebook account. On one account, she posts politics. On the other: "I just have a place for cat photos."

She knows her sister lost Facebook friends after becoming politicized by the Wisconsin 2010 collective bargaining fight. Lisa's sister refused to create a separate account. Lisa's husband, Paul, will also post liberal items on Facebook even though his gym and work friends might see them. For Lisa, though, the separation made life easier. She needed someplace where she didn't feel like she was in the trenches.

"I'm part of the small minority that stays here and refuses to leave," Lisa Muxworthy says about her residency in Waukesha, Wisconsin, between Milwaukee and Madison, an hour from the state's famously liberal college-town capital, and half an hour from the state's largest city, with its socialist past, diverse population, and brewing tradition. Yet Waukesha, in some ways, couldn't be further from either.

"Honey, I need some Madison," Lisa and Paul will say to each other, and they'll hop in the car and head over. In recent years, they've made the trip to join protests against Governor Scott Walker's attacks on collective bargaining. They've participated in the Solidarity Singalongs inside the massive and monumental capitol. At other times, they just go for a meal or a stroll— a change of scenery.

"Every time I drive into Madison, when I drive past the Dane County line, I suddenly feel I can breathe," explains Lisa. "I know it's stupid, I know that it doesn't make sense, but when I'm there, I walk differently. When I drive home, I feel I'm buttoning up again, like against the cold. In Madison, I can let loose, say what I want. I'm not going to flaunt who I am here as freely."

Lisa, white and in her forties, is a liberal activist and blogger. In a heartland state that has been at the heart of America's political battles over the past few years, it's not unusual to find people of her passion and her politics. It's just unusual to find them in Waukesha.

Lisa isn't completely alone. Waukesha County does have the third-highest Democratic vote tally in the state. She didn't realize how many Democrats there were until Walker "dropped the bomb," as she describes it, on collective bargaining. In the immediate aftermath, she was surprised to learn how many of her neighbors shared her views.

But they are still vastly outnumbered. The state's Republican hub is in Waukesha. It's not a city that elects Democrats. And it's a place where the frequently opinionated Lisa feels like she needs to watch what she says.

"I'm very outspoken. However, not in certain areas." She sounds a little bashful as she admits it. "We don't put signs in the windows of our condo. We want to have cordial relationships with neighbors."

Her downstairs neighbors are an older couple and the wife is hard of hearing. The woman leaves on Fox News all day and has the volume turned so high that Lisa is forced to hear it constantly. "I can't stand it. I have to put on the overhead fan to drown it out."

Lisa doesn't talk politics with those neighbors or with almost anyone in her building. Occasionally, though, her views slip out—and sometimes she discovers a pleasant surprise.

"A new couple moved in," she recalls, "and I see the guy outside with his dog. I stop and say hi, and he asks me if I ever hear the noise coming from our older neighbors. 'Oh, that's Jo,' I explain. 'She can't hear and cranks that damn Fox News.' I caught myself as soon as I said it and waited for his reaction. He suddenly grins. 'You're a Democrat! Hell, yeah!' he shouts. We slap high fives and he adds, 'Thank God, we share a wall with one of us.' "

Lisa doesn't put stickers on her car either. "When I got my first new car, a convertible, I knew it would cost way too much if there was damage." Her sister, a teacher, has had political bumper stickers since the Walker fight began, and people will drive by and shout at her. At the local supermarket, Lisa watched as some-one shouted, "You lost!" at her sister. She thought they meant that she had lost some groceries. Instead, they were referring to her "Recall Walker" sticker. "I don't want to deal with that when I drive."

Over the years, Lisa's blogging has earned her more than enough online vitriol. She doesn't need it in her everyday life as well. "I don't like that about myself," she admits. "It's a contradiction. But in my home and my car, I want to feel safe. It's about minimizing risk."

Lisa's sister, like many teachers, felt personally targeted by the attacks on collective bargaining. It changed her life significantly. She hadn't been very political beforehand, but then everything changed. Her union job was the steady income in her family and accounted for her family's health insurance, yet her husband constantly bashed unions. Now they are divorced.

Lisa's marriage is on firmer political ground. Her husband grew up in Canada. "They're socialists," she half jokes.

Lisa wasn't political growing up. She moved around several times in early childhood, ending up in Wisconsin at age nine. Both of her parents were teachers, and both were Democrats. She remembers her father, during the Reagan years, marching around the house ranting to her and the rest of her family, "World's going to hell in a handbasket."

Lisa has heard people say that you become more conservative when you get older. While it hasn't happened to Paul or to her, it did happen to her father. That said, she sees another culprit besides age.

"He had an operation, during which he lost oxygen to his brain. After that, he became a Republican." Was Lisa kidding? Does she really equate conservatism with losing one's mind? "He had dementia and that's when he started listening to Rush Limbaugh. We joke about it, but it's true."

Lisa doesn't remember being part of heated debates growing up. She became politically active when she went to Madison for college. After she met Paul, she moved to Waukesha. The plan was to move to Austin, but "life got in the way." Life in Waukesha is significantly less expensive than in Madison or Milwaukee, and Paul's job pays more in Waukesha than it would in the city. So they stayed.

When they first arrived in 2007, it felt different. "Politics wasn't as contentious," Lisa says, almost nostalgic. "Things have changed dramatically over the past several years."

She used to go to barbecues where conservative friends would tease her about politics, knowing she was a Democrat. "Look at what your buddy Doyle is doing," they'd joke, referring to the Democratic governor. "We'd laugh it off," she remembers. "Wasn't a big deal."

"After Walker dropped the bomb," she explains, using that same phrase again, "it changed everything."

In some ways, the change was good. Suddenly she realized she wasn't alone. "All the Democrats and liberals came scurrying out of the woodwork, looking to combat Walker's agenda. There are more of us than we thought. But people are suffering from that agenda—it's not a good thing."

There may be more liberals, but Lisa is still reminded on a regular basis that she's in the minority in Waukesha. In 2012, as you drove into Waukesha, you were greeted by a giant Romney/Ryan sign. On the highway, churches posted conservative messages on their billboards. For an atheist like Lisa, it was a frequent reminder that she wasn't in Madison anymore. In cafés, she'd hear people complaining about Obama. Bumper stickers had anti-Obama messages, especially aimed at Obamacare, and the messages got more ferocious over time. Fox News was almost always on the televisions in local businesses.

Lisa and Paul pick their moments for everyday protest. "We belong to the Wisconsin Athletic Club. Most of the people are Republicans. They know we're liberals. Whenever we go to the gym, the TV is always set to Fox. We change it to MSNBC. We do it at the car dealership as well."

At places like the athletic club, they rub shoulders with more conservative neighbors. Some know that Lisa is the rare liberal. Others just assume they are Republicans—especially since Paul is clean-cut and works in banking. It's not uncommon for Obama bashing to be part of casual conversation.

Lisa doesn't always fight back—it's too tiring. "Whether I voice my own views depends on so many things. It depends on my mood. On whether I think it might make a difference. On whether I need to go someplace quickly. You learn how to feel people out, who might be volatile and who might not be. You don't engage the people who just want a fight . . . though sometimes I snap."

Even for a political animal like Lisa, she doesn't want to have to be a liberal advocate at every step of her day. "Politics 24/7 is hard," she admits. "We need time when things aren't political. Need to talk about the weather now and then."

Lisa and a few other liberals also decided they needed to do something to lower their political temperature. "It's hard to sustain this level of animosity toward people who don't agree with you. I think it's ridiculous to have any animosity." So they hosted a series of "Détente Dinners." Three or four liberals, three or four conservatives, and a libertarian or two would get together for a meal. "A lot of old-school people miss the days when you could talk about politics, then have a beer together. Some of them want to bring that back, and we gave it a try." They chose some large topics to discuss: reproductive rights, gun control—and made a commitment to listen to one another.

"At first I thought someone was going to get shot; I was scared," recalls Lisa. "But we needed to do this. I needed to know that these people were not bad people. And they're not."

The first dinner had a rough start, and Lisa acknowledges that the liberals weren't making it easier. The liberals were talking but not listening. Lisa worked hard at listening. And she learned a lot.

She came to a conclusion: "They aren't bad people. They just think differently." On Facebook and Twitter, she hears that "conservatives don't care," but she doesn't think that's the case. On popular liberal blogs, such as Daily Kos, Lisa thinks many contributors make the left-right differences too simplistic. "They'll write, 'Those people, they're racist.' Well, maybe some are. But some aren't. Sometimes they want the same thing and just believe there's a different route. It's not that they aren't thinking—they just come to different answers."

The dinners would lead to casual conversations as well, and they'd even forget why they were there as they caught up about work, lives, kids. Although the dinners petered out, Lisa's lessons from the experience have stayed with her. "If I thought these people were awful people, I couldn't stay here. But I know that's not the case. It makes me feel better about living here to know how they got where they are."

Just because she can be civil, though, doesn't mean these dinners have changed her mind. "I never get convinced." She laughs aloud. "I know better."

Lisa wishes others—on both sides of the spectrum—would remember to turn down the political volume at times. She has a friend whose father was in the hospital—and in between posts about his father's health, the friend was posting about union politics. "Finally someone commented: 'Knock it off and be with your father.' It's just exhausting. During the recall we were on high alert and constantly angry. It's hard to keep that up. Some organizations—Democratic and Republican—try to keep that up. But sometimes people just want to have their lives."

Of course, even everyday life can be hard for a liberal in a conservative area. Even when you're not talking politics, your liberal values are part of you. In Waukesha, that's not an easy lifestyle to live.

"There are restaurants here that pride themselves on the fact that they don't have vegetarian options," Lisa observes. "I've seen signs boasting, 'There's no tofu here.' Or: 'No vegan crap.' Like it's manly for a diner not to have tofu."

Lisa drives a Mini Cooper. In Madison, she's surrounded by Priuses. In Waukesha, SUVs. "I can't see around these big tanks," she complains. "I feel like, 'These goddamn gas guzzlers; they want to dominate the road.' OK, I realize they maybe just want to keep their kids safe. But that's how it feels."

She remembers when she moved to town, Waukesha was resisting a smoking ban in restaurants. "People would say, 'Thank God we can smoke here. It's a free country.' I felt like we couldn't go out."

Lisa and Paul are members of Costco, as are many of their liberal friends. They know that it pays a living wage, which makes it a more progressive alternative to Sam's Club. She says that Costco has more organic fruit, more tofu, more of the "liberal" options than its competitor. Recently, a member of her political social club admitted quietly that she also had a Sam's Club membership.

Lisa laughs at that confession. "Paul and I will often say that we're being bad liberals. Sometimes, in the winter, it's cold and it's icy and I'll drive to our mailbox. . . . I'll think about the awful emissions—I can't believe I'm doing it—'I'm such a bad liberal!' "

Even more than the Costco, Lisa points to the Good Harvest market as a sign that there is a taste of the liberal life even in Waukesha. "You go there and people have dreadlocks; they are driving Priuses with Obama stickers. I get my fair-trade coffee and free-range meat. Feels like I'm in Madison."

At other times, they just sigh and recognize that they are strangers in a strange land. Paul's workplace had an office party on a lawn next to a firing range. On one side of the grassy divide were kids playing and there was a face-painting station. On the other side were the sounds of firearms. Lisa's father was a hunter, but she never took to it. She and Paul felt like they were the only ones alarmed at the gunfire. A couple of years before, an eight-months-pregnant woman was hit, not fatally, by a stray bullet from that range. "Yet over here, they are so comfortable with guns, they think nothing of it." Lisa shrugs. "Paul and I are the weirdos."

Paul and Lisa are also atheists, which makes them stand out. At Paul's work, nobody had said they were celebrating Christmas at the office—it was just assumed. When everyone brought a present for a gift swap, Paul was the only one empty-handed. Rather than saying he didn't know, he took the opportunity to announce that he was an atheist. "That ended friendships with several colleagues," says Lisa. "They thought, 'Who is this weirdo that doesn't believe in God?' Now I make Paul have several wrapped gifts in the car if he ever needs them. And he has gotten better at office politics."

Being an atheist is about as hard as being liberal in Waukesha. At the supermarket, each spring, Lisa will be handed a coupon for Easter ham. "There are so many assumptions: that I celebrate Easter. That I eat ham. Sometimes I say something. Sometimes it's not appropriate, or I'm not in the mood, or it feels too alienating to speak up."

Sometimes, though, Lisa doesn't just go with the flow—but leaps in and swims with it. That's how it felt when she campaigned for a candidate in the recent mayoral race. What made it unique: she was supporting a Republican.

There was a Democrat running, but he was someone who Lisa felt had politicized an office that shouldn't be politicized, that "he didn't have a firm grasp of the role, didn't work hard, and that he was a jerk." So she chose a Republican—in fact, the more conservative of the two Republicans—because she thought he knew what he was doing. Some members of the local Democratic Party chastised her for going to the election night party of the Republican. And for the first time, a particularly right-wing activist retweeted her. "For once, we agreed." She chuckles. "But I'm not going to vote for someone if they're not the right person."

It's the same way she felt when people assumed she'd vote for Hillary Clinton because they are both women. "WTF! I don't vote for women because they are women. I won't vote for Democrats just because they are Democrats!"

Lisa's die-hard liberalism isn't the same as it was when she lived in Madison. In some ways, it's sharper for living in a conservative area. In other ways, the desire not to be pigeonholed, the exhaustion of being outnumbered, and the dose of political pragmatism have just made it a different political flavor than when she was in the liberal oasis of a university town.

"Waukesha kicked my ass," she declares, recalling the culture clash of moving there. "I was a smug liberal from Madison. I thought I knew better than everyone. But the Democratic Party here is blue-collar and didn't accept me immediately. They made me work to earn their respect. It took work, it took time, and I did," she says with pride.

"I'm a better person now living here than in Madison. I don't judge the way I used to." She pauses, reflects, and laughs. "I'm not perfect. Of course I still judge. But I'm not so quick to jump to conclusions."

"Also, I think I'd be bored living in Madison," Lisa sums it up. "I like a challenge."

Spike Murphree

SANDIA PARK, NEW MEXICO

I like the soft sell. You can bring a person around to a liberal and/or Democratic point of view with a soft sell rather than a hard sell. A sign on your yard can put them off rather than recruit them. . . . I told my family, I don't read stickers. If someone has something to say to me, say it one to one, face-to-face.

During Spike's time in the service, the air force was never as completely Republican as people expected, he recalls. "There were always Democrats in the air force—women in particular, though not always." If they seemed like they weren't there, it's because they often kept their views quiet. "It's not how much you talk; it's how you vote. Conservatives barked a lot. Democrats voted."

Spike remembers examples of that conservative bark from throughout his career. There was one incident during the 2000 election that he felt crossed a line. A colleague forwarded something "off the Web, off the Internet, something very pejorative toward Al Gore and Joe Lieberman, with a strong implication of support of the other ticket. This was sent out—you know how people get carried away, send jokes—and it was beamed out to everyone on staff where I worked. I thought about that, and I wrote a letter-style e-mail to my commander about it."

Spike was careful not to advertise his own views too frequently, and he felt the need to be just as careful how he phrased this objection. He wrote to the commander, whom he had known for nearly a decade. "He and I had fought together in the Gulf War in '91," he recounts. "We were comrades-in-arms. I thought he would trust me for that." Spike recites the e-mail as though it had been written only a few days before. " 'Dick, I think we need to avoid this sort of thing. If junior enlisted as well as NCOs see an officer supporting a particular candidate, that can be seen as a commander's undue influence on subordinates in an inappropriate way. Dick, you know me, I'm a flaming liberal and you're not so much, but that's not what is the point here. In fact I have a soft spot for Ralph Nader and I know he's going to lose, so I don't have an axe to grind. This isn't the bitterness of a bitter loser. This type of thing is not the way officers should comport themselves. This is not just for politics, but for social policy as well. You don't send an e-mail saying you're a die-hard Roman Catholic and anyone who uses protection is a sinner. If it's true for social issues, it's true for a political campaign.' I signed it, 'Respectfully your comrade-in-arms, Spike.' "

Spike's objection—which, he dutifully notes, may have been voiced by others on his team as well—worked. "He sent out his own e-mail in response to that saying to everyone—in general terms, in a very good way—if you have ideas you'd like to discuss, then keep it to your circle. Either face-to-face, by word of mouth, or if you want to communicate by e-mail with your circle, that's fine. But don't go sending out blanket e-mails to everyone." Spike approved of this response—because it spoke to a bigger concern he had as well. "This is government e-mail. Since when did the

U.S. Air Force become a wing of the Republican Party or any party?"

Given his background and his profile—a white military veteran in his midsixties living in Sandia Park, New Mexico—Spike has been mistaken for conservative more than a few times. Sometimes, he'll hear a right-wing comment from someone who assumes he shares the speaker's point of view. He takes those remarks as he takes most challenges: in stride.

"It depends on the issue and on my mood," he remarks. "When I was on a liaison tour in the army, I had doctrinal issues with the army commander—so our mantra was to pick your fights. You don't slay every dragon every day."

The dragons he's working on now are the Republicans running against his preferred Senate and House candidates. In recent years, he has joined the Democratic coordinated campaign. "I'm what they call a neighborhood team leader," he explains about his role in the 2014 election. A typical Saturday during that election season might have found him recruiting a local coffee shop to become a "makeshift headquarters" for area volunteers. Not quite an air force operation, but a campaign nevertheless.

Coordinating plans, recruiting allies, working toward a unified vision, and pouring his energy into it are tasks that Spike is comfortable with. Over decades of service in the air force, these were skills he honed. He also found himself regularly working with people of all kinds of backgrounds and all manner of political views, starting as early as the Air Force Academy.

"The service academy had drawbacks, especially when it was all male," he admits. "But a good thing about it was the geographical quota. You may have been from inner-city Boston, and your roommate would be a rural Alabaman. You would learn about each other. When you share the same foxhole, you become more tolerant."

That tolerance serves him well in the community where he

now lives and where he so actively canvasses. He's in a small town outside Albuquerque. As Spike explains it, the metro area is divided into three districts: the city, the Northeast Heights, which are on the Albuquerque side of the mountain, and then his area east of the mountain. His is a community that is politically mixed but more conservative than the city. Maybe it's because of the town's makeup or maybe it's in Spike's nature—either way, he found many friendships with locals on both sides of the aisle and beyond.

One example is his book club, which spans the political spectrum—something that "happened quite by accident," Spike explains. It had started as a "Great Decisions Book Club," coordinated through the Foreign Policy Association, which was "founded in 1918 to encourage America to get involved intellectually with the rest of the world following the isolation after World War I." As Spike speaks, his style is thoughtful and professorial, poking beneath each rock he finds. "Since World War II, one can argue we became overinvolved via Mickey Mouse business in South America and so forth."

As the club has evolved, it's often engaged "dark-horse topics you don't normally hear about. For example, the arctic ice cap is melting—will it be easier or harder for navigation?"

The group gathers every eight to ten weeks and has for ten years. When it started, the members were "neighborhood acquaintances, not friends necessarily. Since we've come together for discussions over ten years, we've become friends. We try to bring in outsiders to keep us from getting too narrow in our thinking," he adds.

As folks have moved out and others have joined, the group has ended up with a rich diversity of political thinking. There is one man who isn't a registered Republican "but tends to vote that way. He's more of a libertarian than a social conservative."

Other members have crossed over the party line in the other direction. "There are two Republicans in my group who are Obama Republicans. You've heard of Reagan Democrats. These are Obama Republicans. They were very unhappy with the poor judgment" of the Bush administration. "The Fox News stuff that's over the top turned them away even more."

Spike highlights Sarah Palin as an example of the more fringe right-wing thinking these friends distance themselves from, commenting about remarks Barbara Bush had made about Palin. "The ones in the club are Barbara Bush Republicans and voted for Obama." Often, though not always, these Republicans are more liberal on social issues, while conservative on other topics.

Another member took an online test that determined he was a "militant moderate." That wasn't so surprising—"He's not affiliated with either party. He's not a registered Republican or Democrat. He's also very disillusioned. The war in Iraq is one of the things that bonded us."

Feelings about that war unified most of the members of the book club. "Conservatives nationwide and libertarians, let alone liberals, were disillusioned with Iraq," Spike says, noting the opposition by such Republican figures as Ron Paul and Pat Buchanan.

"Another uniting issue was the bank bailout. When the banks misbehaved, it created a lot of distrust of banks," he observes. "When someone gets down on Wall Street, down on banks, is that libertarian or liberal? Turns out to be both."

He pauses and edits himself. "I should say progressive. Some traditional liberals still kind of regress to trusting big money and big business."

Thinking through the book club membership, he recounts, "Three-quarters of the group said the bailout was necessary but didn't like it. Twenty-five percent said, 'I don't like the banks;

the bailout wasn't a good idea.' Hatred of big banks misbehaving was unanimous. How to handle it is an intellectual issue. . . . You don't need to get angry about it."

Not getting angry has been part of what keeps the group together—and what has helped Spike form long-term friendships with people whose opinions differ sharply from his. In this regard, the club offers a road map of how to interact in politically mixed communities. "Everyone knows we have different opinions. I honestly can say most of us have changed over the years. We're more willing to listen, more mellow. . . . We've come to know each other. When you do that, often you'll listen better. We listen better now. Over the years, you do mellow." He laughs recalling one comment. "One member said, 'At the time when I graduated college, I thought I knew everything. Now in my sixties and retired, I realize I don't.' "

Spike considers himself "an old-fashioned liberal," a label he doesn't use casually. "A quick history lesson," he begins. "After World War II, ironically, it was liberals who wanted to get involved overseas," from the Marshall Plan to a "muscular foreign policy." But once you fast-forward to the 1960s, "the liberals split." Spike views himself as part of the camp that continued to push for international engagement and intervention, at a time when many liberals joined the antiwar movement.

That division, explains Spike, has shaped how liberals—and Americans—have thought about overseas involvement in the decades since. "Old-fashioned liberals escalated the war in Vietnam; new liberals called us on the carpet." As a result, liberals for a time may have become "gun-shy, overly cautious."

In some ways the Iraq War saw the cycle repeat—chasing many Americans back from their eagerness to engage in overseas actions. "I've mellowed," Spike admits. "My observation, from my book club: we have liberal, libertarian, conservative, Democrat, Republican—everyone seems to be burned out with overseas involvement. Not putting boots on the ground in Libya, Syria, Iraq, et cetera, seems to be the majority American consensus. That's where I am now." He sees this debate playing out among the Democratic leadership. "Say, for Hillary Clinton, she may believe in a more assertive foreign policy, diplomatic or military, whereas President Obama wants to withdraw and retrench. I tend to agree with President Obama as opposed to Hillary Clinton. But I would vote for either of them."

Spike traces the roots of his political orientation to his upbringing. "Growing up, I was in a traditional liberal Democratic family, which meant you're against—this is the 1950s, post–World War II—racial segregation, for the Cold War."

He recalls hearing stories that "the Tuskegee Airmen escorted my father's group in World War II. He wasn't politically active, but he was in favor of integration."

His mother was more explicit in her politics. "My mother was in the League of Women Voters all her life. She worked on integrating her little Texas town, Dickens. Many of her relatives had racial prejudices. She rebelled." Again, Spike touches on a history lesson to pinpoint the nature of his mother's liberalism. "When women's liberation came around, my mother was full for it. She was the Betty Friedan type. She was married with children. She felt you could be married with children and be a feminist. The movement split," he recounts, with some of the more radical feminists declaring, "marriage is slavery. My mother was a more traditional feminist, but she still respected the young women coming her way."

From this liberal background, Spike found himself coming into his own in the 1960s, just when the consensus around international military action broke apart. During the Cold War, some of our "overreacting on foreign policy did us more harm than good. Come the 1960s, it was full speed ahead on integration and racial equality, but we were diverging on foreign policy."

At times, he agreed with each perspective—but never fully subscribed to either in a conventional way. "In the beginning, I trusted everyone's judgment escalating the war in Vietnam. Then in 1968 came the My Lai Massacre, which became public in 1969. In 1970, the Kent State shootings. Students not even protesting were accidentally shot and killed. That's when I began to say that this particular involvement was hurting the USA. When we turn our guns on the enemy, it's one thing. When we turn guns on ourselves, it's beyond the pale."

While those incidents may have chased a generation of liberals away from lives in the armed services, and even some into dodging the draft, it had the opposite effect on Spike. "Interestingly enough, three weeks after Kent State, I entered the Air Force Academy. I was convinced we needed a variety of people in the armed forces, a variety of people—not conservatives—so another Kent State wouldn't happen."

The academy didn't make Spike more conservative. In fact, much of his experience there reflected the kind of diverse meritocracy he believed America was becoming. "From the early 1960s to the mid-1970s, public schools and universities were finally integrating. That included service academies. We had black cadets. When you go through basic training, you bond, regardless of ethnic background or race. When black classmates would challenge a policy at the academy or air force–wide, we'd listen," he recounts.

"It took a while, but Jackie Robinson's teammates would listen to him when he told them, 'The team we're playing today, they are particularly bad' " in terms of race. "This is just hypothetical, but probably true," Spike explains. "We had our own Jackie Robinsons, young men that we trusted."

He remembers one man in particular: Charlie Stalworth— a boxing champion in air force competitions and a "good informal leader in our squadron. If something untoward was going on informally with cadets or with the administration, Charlie and his fellow black cadets would bring it up. And we listened. If Charlie Stalworth says something is fishy here, then something is fishy. Let's fix it."

In other ways, though, cadets were more conservative. "In terms of foreign policy, they had a tendency to be hawks," as did Spike himself. "Some cadets overreacted to antiwar protests. Some GIs coming back from Vietnam weren't treated well; they were blamed for things they didn't do." This led many of his fellow cadets and those he served with throughout his career to retrench to the right of the American political spectrum.

Spike continued beyond the academy, and he stayed in the armed forces through 2002. Over the years, he would hear conservative comments but also met a good number of liberals. Politics, though, wasn't foremost on anyone's mind. "Day to day, your main concern is operations. Doing your job. Think of a medical doctor or medical nurse. You get into an operating room, you know your job and you do it well. Social issues as well as political issues have to wait until you're out of the operating room." That was largely how it felt in the armed forces. "In that life, you have your nose to the grindstone so much, you don't have time to think about other things."

Which isn't to say that Spike stopped following politics, or never found the time to share his views. "Generally you kept political opinions to yourselves. If you happened on a fellow liberal, you'd vent a little bit. If a conservative finds a fellow conservative, they'd vent a little bit."

He does wish there were more liberals who would choose to engage in the armed forces rather than retreat from them—because the armed forces are institutions that will continue to evolve and can be forces for positive change.

"In the mid-'70s, a lot of officers left the army, disillusioned. Norman Schwarzkopf and Colin Powell didn't leave. They said, let's make it better, let's make the officers reflect the American population," explains Spike with a touch of admiration. "They were my role models in that respect."

Spike entered the air force at a time when the relationship between liberals and the armed forces was particularly complicated. In many ways, over his career, he feels as though it's improved. "After World War II, every GI was honored. A generation later, after Vietnam, it was reversed. A generation later now, while policy might be criticized, while you might have the feeling that the GIs were in Iraq for the wrong reasons, you'll say the GI him- or herself is sacrificing a lot and deserves better. It's come full circle."

Even when he has seen areas for improvement in the air force, he's always felt that liberals should stay in the service in order to make those changes. "It's like your favorite team—Yankees, Dodgers, the Cubs in my case—when your team is down, you don't desert them. You try to fix it. You stick with them in good seasons and bad seasons, and you try to fix it."

No longer serving, Spike still has occasion to interact with his old colleagues—and now politics can come up a little more frequently. "I have my fortieth reunion in October. I'll be preparing my arguments in advance." He laughs. "I'm determined to be thick-skinned. In my response, I'm not going to be as wise as Gandhi or reasoned and respectful as Martin Luther King, but I'm going to try."

For example, he knows that a number of his fellow veterans will argue about wanting a smaller government. "When they complain about government spending, I'll say I've run into Tea Partiers who want to cut military funding including the VA. Are you for it or against it?" he asks in preparation. "I'll put them on the spot but not embarrass them."

He looks back into history for an example he knows his colleagues will understand. "The GI Bill—I tell that to libertarians in particular, but also to conservatives. The GI Bill was expensive. It cost money. But it was an investment. It was fair and good for individual GIs, and it also helped build a middle class that was strong and well educated. Look at it from a business, libertarian perspective. The American taxpayer invested money into people, into education, and the country as a whole came out better for it. When we invested in the interstate highways, Eisenhower needed to justify it with military reasoning. The benefits have been enormous. The Saint Lawrence Seaway was federal investment—it made trade better. Federal investment can enhance capitalism."

He acknowledges that these arguments may go only so far. "I have some classmates who became frumpy old men. You either mellow or you harden."

Many people have a mix of views, Spike has observed, and if you listen to them and meet them where they are, you can find agreement. He recalls one colleague: "Male, hetero, married, Roman Catholic, family man—a conservative lifestyle." But as conservative as he was in some ways, "he was liberal when it comes to the separation of church and state, even though he's Roman Catholic. He was annoyed with the Protestant 'religious right.' " Spike and this man would discuss the problem of religion in the public sphere. " 'If we want Christian law embodied in American law, which Christians?' " he recalls the colleague saying.

Spike also enjoys a healthy rapport with his conservative mother-in-law. "She's an Iowa Republican—but she's disillusioned with the Republican Party, and she became an Obama Republican. Iowans are hardheaded; they like common sense." They spar on some issues but on others find common ground. "When I told her I didn't think making abortion illegal is 'pro-life,' she jumped in and said, 'That's right!' " This response surprised him. "I suspect in the '40s she had some contemporaries who tried to have abortions illegally, did this at the risk of their own lives. Having a law against abortion doesn't stop it."

For his mother-in-law, women's equality is not antithetical to her conservative worldview. "She's a very conservative Christian but doesn't want to be discriminated against as a woman. In her version of Christianity, women are treated equal to men in salvation. They should be treated equal in life as well." Tying it back to his experience in the air force, he adds, "There were black cadets I knew who were very religious and conservative but very liberal on race issues."

Spike is a member of the League of Women Voters—"in honor of my mother"—and a member of Emily's List, "partly at my mother's urgings." He's also been an ACLU member since the late 1990s. His direct involvement in Democratic politics is more recent. "I always voted. I have always spoken up if I thought someone was out of line." In 2008, "I decided I wanted to get more involved, particularly in local politics. I had moved around in the service. Now here I am in New Mexico as a permanent resident. I have to get to know this area. Campaigning, I've come to know the area so much better—the people here, who they are, what they do. I've grown in that respect. I've influenced people, but they've really influenced me."

Spike and his wife live in one of the more conservative areas near Albuquerque, but that just gives him more opportunity to start dialogues with right-leaning people and, perhaps, convince them. "I had an argument over health care with a woman assuming I was conservative. I said, 'Your parents paid for your medical care growing up, so that's what you think everyone should do.' But my sister-in-law was diagnosed with arthritis at seventeen, her parents couldn't afford the coverage, she had to go on Medicare. I used reason and respect. She said, 'I agree, but that's the exception.' It was a small victory. I made a dent. . . . There are a lot of exceptions, but I didn't get that far."

He finds unassuming opportunities to engage people as well.

"There's a retired medical doctor on our corner, born in Argentina, moved to the U.S., married an American, all his kids are American. He's independent, he votes. We talk about things when we're walking with our dogs. I said, 'My sister is gay and Democrats help gays and that's why I'm voting Democratic.' Since so many people have friends or relatives who are gay or know someone who knows someone, they're more respectful. I could tell that made a difference. I just stuck a sign out that said Tom Udall"—the Democratic senator running for reelection— "so now he might be reluctant to talk. But I snared him with a stealth approach." Spike laughs.

In general, Spike avoids lawn signs. "I like the soft sell. You can bring a person around to a liberal and/or Democratic point of view with a soft sell rather than a hard sell. A sign on your yard can put them off rather than recruit them." He's similarly skeptical of bumper stickers. "I told my family, I don't read stickers. If someone has something to say to me, say it one to one, face-to-face, not tattooed on their arse."

Living in a conservative area is a challenge that gets his energy up. "There are many closet liberals in rural New Mexico and near-rural areas where we live. They are there. They are also highly motivated liberals because they are surrounded by conservatives. They can be extra motivated to make a difference. It helps us recruit and campaign better out here."

That's not to say that Spike wants to be viewed as a one-note liberal. "I am not knee-jerk antibusiness—small business or big business. There's nuance; it's more complex. This comes not only from listening to conservatives or libertarians but from my reading." He's had nuanced conversations with book club members and fellow campaigners about the minimum wage because he tends to believe a big increase might hurt, while a small or medium rise would help individuals and the overall economy.

"I have people in my campaign who are die-hard for raising the minimum wage. Someone in my book club, a conservative Democrat, is against it. I strike a middle ground."

He sees this as another example of the effects of listening, and of mellowing. "Maybe I've been listening to libertarians. I've mellowed in my opinions. It's not like the road to Damascus for Saint Paul. There's still right and wrong, but there's more than one way to be wrong. Not raising the minimum wage is wrong. Doubling it is wrong."

The key—whether campaigning door-to-door, engaging in a stealth conversation, or returning to an air force reunion—is to take it all in stride. "Don't let it get under your skin. Don't shout when you have a disagreement. Don't get angry. If someone says something and it bothers me—let me look in the mirror and see if Spike is too thin-skinned. If I can't take a little criticism or hear someone I disagree with, maybe I'm too thin-skinned. I will let it pass—when I look back, maybe I should have said something. There's always the next time. I will have an answer ready next time."

Rebecca Lehman
and Chris Flowers

CINCINNATI, OHIO

*There was a time you could only claim you were a
Cincinnati native if you could identify your high
school and your parish. If you're from Cincinnati,
you know your parishes.*

Chris and Rebecca have a problem: one of their favorite ice cream
stands, a few miles out of the center of Cincinnati, is owned by
loyal Republicans. "It has a framed picture of W," Chris recounts,
referring to President George W. Bush. "It felt like we ventured
into a different world."

"But it's so good!" adds Rebecca with a touch of longing.
Then, in all seriousness—voicing a question she and Chris have
discussed before—she asks, "So what do we do? Do we support a
small family business? Or do we go to Dairy Queen?"

There is no simple right or wrong answer to that conundrum,
or to a number of the choices Rebecca and Chris make as they

balance liberal political values, community spirit, practicality, and convenience. But they are used to a balancing act as residents of Cincinnati, whose professional and social lives—she is a social justice educator, he is a museum IT manager, and both were preparing to become Peace Corps volunteers in Moldova—have often taken them across the Ohio River into the more conservative neighboring state of Kentucky.

The greater metro area of Cincinnati, the southernmost of Ohio's big cities, isn't confined by state lines. The towns of northern Kentucky are intimately involved with Cincinnati's daily life. The Cincinnati airport is actually over in Covington, Kentucky.

Yet the Ohio River, which snakes between the two states, has long represented a dividing line greater than its actual breadth. It was the barrier between slave state and free, over which many slaves found their freedom or died trying. It's not insignificant that one of Cincinnati's best-known museums is the National Underground Railroad Freedom Center. Not that far across the river is the Creation Museum, an elaborate and popular series of exhibits maintaining the Earth was formed in accord with the literal words of creation in the Bible. The rooms that show Adam and Eve side by side with dinosaurs are far from the most unbelievable part of the tour.

All of which is to say that there is a real difference between living in Covington or Newport, and moving across the river to Cincinnati, as Chris did a few years ago.

"The cost of living in Kentucky was a little lower," Chris explains, which is why he first settled in the suburbs of Covington when he moved from Colorado. White and forty, Chris was originally from Indiana, so it wasn't the Midwest that surprised him. "I didn't realize when I chose that it was the most conservative town in the most conservative county in the area. There were only Republicans on my ballot for the most part. There was one time a Democrat won only because the Republican candidate lied about his military record."

Though he had lived in conservative areas before, this experience surprised him. "I had campaign signs defaced or stolen. You didn't know who you could talk to. People were virulent about their views. There was a lot of anger from the right." In many ways, "it was not safe to talk about your politics; it was not accepted."

Chris was working in Cincinnati and also forming bonds with other lonely liberals in Kentucky. During that time, Chris became involved in progressive political groups on both sides of the river, and it was through one of these organizations that he met Rebecca, a white Ohio native in her thirties. She gave him the excuse to cross the Ohio, and they now reside together in a Cincinnati neighborhood near the university.

While it proved far easier to find like-minded neighbors, to support businesses with liberal views, and generally to feel at home politically, Cincinnati is still a far more politically mixed city than liberal bastions like Brooklyn and Berkeley. "There are times I feel I'm in a bubble of progressive people, and don't interact with conservatives," describes Chris. "Then it's suddenly back in our face. There are great things happening in this city: in terms of public transit, the new streetcar, we're preserving major historical buildings—the music hall, the old train station. You see these really good things. Then you'll hear in conversation, 'Why should we pay for this? I'll never use this streetcar. It's in an unsafe part of town. Nobody goes there; you'll get shot.' "

These complaints are often racial in their subtext, reflecting attitudes in a city with a history of divided communities and racial tension. When Chris hears these views, he knows that Cincinnati still has deep divisions.

Rebecca identifies a different sort of division that she and

Chris are part of. "We segregate politically," she says. "We live near the university. It skews liberal. When I move out of the city center, I'll run into conservative values. A couple miles west or east, it shifts: socially, politically, economically."

Living near the university often makes it easier to live their liberal values—but not always. The ice cream parlor with President Bush's photo is only one of the many establishments that cause them to question how they are voting with their wallets. Rebecca and Chris are conscientious consumers and try to make their purchasing choices reflect their values . . . which isn't always that straightforward.

When he lived in Kentucky, Chris recounts, he just "assumed every business is supporting a conservative. We would try to choose places that support our politics. We want to support that kind of business in Kentucky."

It was difficult on that side of the river. "We stopped going to a coffeehouse in Covington that supported a very antigay Christian group. Other than that surprising revelation, it was a very open place; it had a seemingly progressive vibe. It shocked me— I stopped going there."

Just as often, practical considerations can make it difficult for Chris and Rebecca to live their values. "We don't have solid public transit infrastructure here. So we have to have a car," Chris apologized. "There are places we can't get without a car. We may not prefer it, but it's part of our lifestyle."

They don't shop at Walmart—and, in fact, don't have one too near them—but they are frustrated with their supermarkets. "We don't have a lot of grocery choice," laments Chris. "The Kroger company is based here in Cincinnati, so they have a monopoly on food. They are also the number one employer of people on public assistance," which is one measure of large companies underpaying their employees.

"A natural foods store is the closest grocery," interjects Rebecca.

"But we have to make better choices. . . . We tend to shop late at night," when the natural grocery, and other small businesses, are often closed. "We do sometimes go to Whole Foods, though we don't agree with the owner's politics," she admits, referring to CEO John Mackey's outspoken views, including his public opposition to the Affordable Care Act.

They have had the unpleasant experience enough times of discovering that a business they liked put a Mitt Romney or Rand Paul sign in the window that it makes them a little nervous when they find new places they love. For example, they have begun to frequent a new meatball shop called Packhouse. "I'd be surprised and not surprised," Rebecca says, to learn the owner is conservative. On the one hand, "You don't tip there—everyone earns a living wage—and they give bonuses for people who work during the busiest times. But I have this fear that he's going to say something. It's a subtle fear—but he always describes the rationale as a business imperative rather than a values thing. He might say, 'That's my bottom line and that's the most important.' " And it might turn out that he, like many small business owners, votes Republican.

At which point, they'd have to make a decision: "Do you want to support someone doing something that you value?" asks Chris, referring to the progressive, pro-worker business policies. "It's tricky."

"It's only been open a few months," Rebecca chimes in.

Chris shares a story about a place he used to volunteer: "a social enterprise pizza parlor—it was training people with real job skills. It had an association with the Catholic Church, which has its own problems." That said, "The nuns were great."

Rebecca's experience with nuns has been just as positive. "Catholicism is often cited as driving conservative values. But people I work with are Catholic and extremely progressive. Nuns on the Bus–type folks. There are campus ministers doing great interfaith work, even if more conservative groups aren't into working together."

If Rebecca, who is outspoken in most settings, had any reservations about topics she could bring up with the nuns at work, that hesitation quickly evaporated. "Sister Leslie started talking about Schweddy Balls," an innuendo-laden Ben & Jerry's ice cream flavor inspired by a *Saturday Night Live* skit. "Anything goes."

"She's the coolest nun around," agrees Chris.

Neither Chris nor Rebecca is religious. Chris grew up in a Jehovah's Witness family in Indiana. "We don't discuss politics at all," he says of his parents and sister.

Chris thought of the area of his childhood as very conservative and deeply religious. "Now they are one of the counties issuing same-sex marriage licenses," he muses. "Maybe I didn't know it as well as I thought."

His town was one of many that lost its major industries. In that transition, conservative values took hold. Many of his neighbor families "were transitioning from United Auto Worker jobs to being unemployed. They were just doing what they could."

Rebecca grew up about thirty-five minutes from Cincinnati. While she says her family didn't talk politics, the dinner table conversation heavily influenced her perspectives. "My family believes you live your values. In our everyday lives, they role modeled values." Rebecca remembers her family getting involved, from joining protests to serving as clinic escorts. "I joke about how early I understood what abortion was because I saw hanger signs at protests." She and her sisters still "talk more values than issues. We don't talk about referendums. We talk social politics, race, class."

Though they don't participate in organized religion, Rebecca and Chris are surrounded by it. "There are churches everywhere in Cincinnati," says Rebecca. "Within a couple blocks of our home, there are several churches."

Chris continues, "There was a time you could only claim you were a Cincinnati native if you could identify your high school and your parish. If you're from Cincinnati, you know your parishes."

This type of localism goes hand in hand with a network of fifty-two neighborhoods that make up the city. Many of the neighborhoods were once independent villages, and even after joining the larger city, they retained their previous ethnic identities, as well as limited forms of self-rule. "People didn't leave these communities for a long time. You'll have grandparents, parents, kids, grandkids, all living within a mile of each other, within a city of 2.1 million people," explains Chris.

There are some very good qualities that come from these neighborhoods. "You get something like small-town values; you know your neighbors. You look out for each other, take care of each other. You have pride in your community. These are good things."

"And good festivals," adds Rebecca, "that really celebrate the communities."

Perhaps predictably, these neighborhoods have also experienced tensions in any time of transition: as the city became more diverse and the neighborhoods integrated, and more recently, as waves of gentrification have led newcomers to navigate relationships with the established communities across the city.

As diverse and cosmopolitan as the city may be, these traditions can give it a conservative feel. Rebecca recalls that within the city, though outside downtown, she might get asked, "Where are you from?" But it's not an innocent question. " 'You're obviously not from here' is the subtext. I don't dress in proper feminine codes for bars, I don't meet expectations, I wear very trendy glasses." She laughs.

Although Chris knows there is conservative rhetoric in the air, it sometimes surprises him where he hears it, including at work. "I'll hear something conservative from people who volunteer at the museum. They believe in a museum but also are conservative in their values. I'd assume that wouldn't go hand in hand."

These conservative tendencies stretch into electoral politics. Even though the city often elects Democrats, "people think they are more liberal than they are," argues Chris. "Ohio and Kentucky Democrats are very moderate nationally. They don't have liberal values."

As an example, he speaks about a former congressman who "swept in on Obama's coattails. He got into Rebecca's face, red-faced over abortion. He is a Catholic Democrat and he believed very strongly in antiabortion politics."

"Not just abortion," Rebecca leaps in. "He's anti–access to reproductive health, anti–birth control, anti–sex education." When Rebecca brought up these issues with the congressman in person, "he said, 'Why do you want to kill my children?' He put his hand on [his children's] heads. 'I think we're done, Mr. Driehaus,' " Rebecca recalls saying.

Another example is the new mayor. "He won the Democratic primary but fought against every progressive action of the previous administration: the streetcars, bike paths, zoning regulations on parking, changing how money is allocated to the communities. He's very middle-of-the-road," states Chris. "But for mayor, the primary is where it matters."

Chris and Rebecca sometimes vote for Charterites, a progressive third party. There are no Republicans, though, who ever attract them. Have they ever voted for a Republican? "No, not to my memory," answers Rebecca. "Possibly when there was no other name on the ballot," admits Chris.

Which is not to say they aren't friends with Republicans. Rebecca has friends whom she met through her university work, some of whom are former students, and while they get along socially, she knows they have very different political views. "We get together with [conservative] friends over food and other things. But not politics."

Chris is part of an ice hockey team made up entirely of Republicans. His captain has a "Stop OSHA" bumper sticker. "Your ice hockey team has a no-politics rule," explains Rebecca.

Chris doesn't find it hard to follow the no-politics rule because he thinks that restraint is endemic in the region. "It's the midwestern culture of politeness," he offers. "Once we identify differences, it's not polite to discuss them. Even among friends, it becomes not a point of discussion." He continues, "We're good at compartmentalizing things around here. There is no time we don't hang out with conservative friends. We just don't talk topics we don't agree on."

You might expect that this becomes harder during presidential cycles when all eyes turn to Ohio. Nationally, as rhetoric heats up, Ohio is in the spotlight. Yet for those living in Cincinnati, it can have the opposite effect.

"Election fatigue can temper political conversations." Chris sighs. "There are so many ads, so many visits. By October, we're tired of it. People have made up their minds. And they don't want to talk about it."

"Fatigue is the right word," agrees Rebecca. "Why would we want to talk about it? Meeting politicians isn't even a mark of pride. New people in town will say, 'You saw Obama live?!' Yeah, like, five times!"

"We are so jaded," confirms Chris.

The election season will sometimes be when unknown loyalties are discovered. "Occasionally a professor will have a Romney sign or a Rand Paul sign. That will surprise us. There was one in an office with a window near the garden we were sitting in, and we all came out—like, really?"

Still, what a change from Kentucky. "You might have an angry conversation in Cincinnati," Chris says. But it felt different across the river. "In Kentucky, it often felt like you could only talk politics if you were right wing. In Newport and Covington," considered more liberal Kentucky cities, "there is still an entrenched view that there is no room for compromise. There are not very many moderate conservatives."

On the progressive side, there are issues over which both Chris and Rebecca find themselves disagreeing with national Democrats. While it isn't an issue he breaks sharply on, for Chris, "The minimum wage conversation is off. It should be increased, but a fifteen-dollar-per-hour minimum wage doesn't necessarily work in a small town where housing might be two hundred dollars per month," he articulates, thinking of where he grew up. "I don't feel like there is one number for the whole country. There is a different cost of living between New York City and New Castle, Indiana, my hometown. We're drawing the line in the wrong spot."

For Rebecca, who works in racial justice training, there is plenty to find fault with in major-party politics. She's frustrated "by race-blind or identity-blind conversations rather than race-conscious and gender identity–conscious." And as someone with a life partner who has intentionally decided not to marry, she thinks the LGBTQ rights movement has focused too much on the wrong issue. "We both believe everyone should have the right to marriage, and we think it's the least important right. Look at murder rates of trans women; look at the rates in the school-to-prison pipeline. It's hard to get excited about the marriage example."

Overall, Rebecca knows she stands apart politically. "I don't think I stick to a liberal or progressive line—my values are rooted in community uplift. We all do better when we all do better. And 'we' is very expansive—not just a locational we or family we." She reflects for a moment. "Conservative friends may also believe we do better when we all do better—they just define 'we' narrower and 'better' in a more capitalist way."

"For conservatives, it's not 'we'—it's 'us' and 'them,' " elaborates Chris. For him, the reason he is liberal is "big picture. Decisions I make don't just affect me. They affect the community and people around me. When my friends, my family, my community, my neighbors do better, I do better. We're all in this together. While I do make a lot of selfish decisions, I try to keep this in mind, and I feel better when I make decisions that look after the greater good."

Both of their beliefs are put to the test by living among conservatives—and ultimately strengthened by that experience. Living in Ohio, Rebecca explains, means they are "regularly surrounded by people from different perspectives. It becomes harder to dehumanize conservatives. They have values, just different values. They are not idiots. Don't write them off. We're bound to have to deal with them—to be in classes together, work together, play on sports teams with them. That's a benefit of being out here."

They also see ways they could push their own liberal friends and allies—in day-to-day life and on a policy level. "I would love more of our climate conversations to deal with food. I eat a lot of almonds, and that's really wasteful. I should pay for it. Or for burgers." And for meatballs from their new favorite spot?

"We eat the quinoa-and-carrot meatballs." Chris chuckles. But, he acknowledges, quinoa's popularity in America has its unforeseen consequences: poorer residents of the South American nations where quinoa is produced can no longer afford to consume their own grain. So, if you're making sustainable and ethical choices, even ordering the vegetarian meatball "has its own problems."

Diane Fleeks

FAIRBANKS, ALASKA

The person you are screaming at about Obamacare might be the same person who notices your house caught on fire. If your house catches on fire, you might go bunking at their place. . . . Because we are a smaller community, we may be different. We live in extreme environments. Extreme things can happen. We have very cold winters. It's just not worth blowing up.

"We live in a relatively small community," explains Diane, an African American woman in her fifties. Fairbanks is the second-largest city in Alaska, and the population hub of the state's interior. To Diane and many of the other residents who have been there their whole lives, it can feel like a small town.

That influences how Diane thinks about politics and, as a Democratic chair for her region, how she advises others who are running for office. "Things can get passionate on the campaign trail, I tell them. But after election, you're still going to run into these people at the grocery, postal box, the watering hole, your church. It's not worth blowing up your life and your relationships." Plus, she adds as a savvy bit of political insight, "you'll probably be running for office more than once."

Diane knows plenty of folks on both sides of the aisle and finds herself offering the same advice to all audiences. "I tell this to folks running on the Republican side. They get fired up, get a couple drinks in them, start talking" in more argumentative and confrontational tones. "I say, 'Listen, listen, listen'—I hate to be the old lady in the room, but I guess I am—'think this through. If you want to blow up your life, your choice.' "

It's not that Diane doesn't feel invested in political campaigns or believe their outcomes matter. As someone who grew up around politics and as a longtime party organizer, Diane has Democratic campaigns in her blood. However, there is something to living in a small community—especially in a somewhat isolated one—that makes her think about the relationship of politics and everyday life a little differently.

"The person you are screaming at about Obamacare might be the same person who notices your house caught on fire. If your house catches on fire, you might go bunking at their place," she calmly articulates, in what sounds like a lesson she has taught before. "Because we are a smaller community, we may be different. We live in extreme environments. Extreme things can happen. We have very cold winters. It's just not worth blowing up."

Alaska is far away from the contiguous forty-eight—in its geography and in its lifestyle. It is a sprawling state with a low population. It may seem like a Republican stronghold, but the state also has very recently sent Democrats to the Senate. In the past few years, Sarah Palin may have been Alaska's best-known export, but her polarizing national presence is not a genuine reflection of the political temperature of Alaskans.

In addition to both being lifelong Alaskans, Diane and Sarah

Palin had something else in common: they both wanted to get rid of Palin's predecessor. Palin as a candidate, explains Diane, "pissed off the old boys' club. When she ran, she was portrayed as anti–old boys' club, anti–big oil, and someone who could work in a bipartisan way with Democratic leadership." Even as governor, Palin did not lead crusades over the social issues she later became associated with as a vice presidential candidate.

Palin rose to the statehouse in part because her predecessor had stepped on "the third rail of Alaskan politics," as Diane puts it: oil and gas revenues. "He cut a sweetheart deal. 'Thou shalt not give our money away.' It's a huge part of our economy." Crossing that line ruined his reputation and cost him reelection, Diane believes. Alaska relies heavily on its resource wealth. "Fairbanks gave up most of its taxes during the go-go days of the Trans-Alaska Pipeline. We were soaking in money, thought it would be forever, and we ditched all our taxes except property tax and sin tax. The state got rid of the income tax. We got rid of the sales tax. Now we're paying the price for it."

With frustration, she adds, "We've pissed it away. Now there is very little left for our children. For the first time in state history, our state is running a deficit."

Oil and gas revenue is the type of issue that can unify Alaskans. Another—to the chagrin, perhaps, of liberals in the rest of America, is drilling in the Arctic National Wildlife Refuge— or ANWR. "That's a third rail. It splits Democrats. You won't get elected to any office in the state if you close down drilling in ANWR. It's a nonstarter. School board. Borough assembly. City council. Service area commission." That's not to say everyone agrees. "There are people in the state who are firmly, strongly, staunchly against this—the environmental conservation folks. You learn how to deal with it. Alaska Conservation Voters have been sponsoring campaign training for the Alaska Democratic Party. You'd think the Alaska Conservation Voters wouldn't play nice with mainline Democrats, but there are other issues they can agree on."

With a sense of history, Diane reflects, "However, none of this is new. This has been going on for generations now."

As an example of Alaska's particular set of issues, she adds, "If you want to get people worked up, talk about salmon fishing. Our constitution says we have equal access to salmon. Many folks were here before we had a constitution. They were hunting and gathering, what you'd call subsistence living. Then you have commercial fleets going after the same salmon. And you have sportfishing." As a result, there is a constant tug-of-war among the various interests—including tension between individuals and industrial fisheries.

"We can get up in arms on that pretty fast. . . . It's a long-term issue. It bogged down statehood for a while. This is our resource, our fish, you know—it's never going to make the national news. It can all blow up in very nativistic ways. . . . That's a little difficult to explain. I probably just sounded like a total whackadoodle myself, but this can set people off. It's Alaskan identity politics."

Sometimes the matters that animate Alaskans the most are the ones that separate them from the rest of the country politically, or just seem so particular that the rest of the country doesn't understand. "We've had our government come to a standstill over burning wood," recalls Diane.

On energy issues, it can be hard for Alaska liberals to see eye to eye with liberals elsewhere. A liberal from California might be surprised where an Alaska liberal stands on certain conservation issues. "We'd come back with: explain how to heat my house."

Home heating is one of the issues that cross party lines for residents in Alaska's interior. "We have very specific concerns that may not be shared down in Anchorage or in Juneau or on the western coast. The biggest: our basic standard of living. Heating a house is astronomically high. We don't have any heating oil refinery here. There has been a big push to reduce the cost of home heating oil. It can cost nine hundred dollars to heat your home in a bad winter month. . . . This is one of our biggest, hottest issues."

It's an area where Democrats and Republicans find themselves on the same side. "I've seen conservative businessmen go after our governor at a chamber of commerce" meeting over this issue, recalls Diane.

She also recalls campaigners who came from out of state to help elect a Democrat to the senate—and how out of touch they were with what Alaskan voters had on their minds. The campaign staffers would encourage Alaskan Democrats to run on the same issues as Democrats everywhere. "They would try to tell us our politics aren't any different. No. This is not just Alaska exceptionalism. I grew up here; I've always lived here . . . and we do have issues that are very much ours—stemming from where we are on the map."

While Alaska may be on the edge of most maps of America, it is the center of Diane's America. She is fifty-five and grew up breathing, thinking, and knowing Alaska. "It's a pretty easy place to be a kid. Not the most complicated part of the world."

It was clear from the start where she would fall on the political spectrum. "I learned my politics the old-school way, sitting up and listening to my dad and his friends talk politics in a bar, smoking cigarettes. . . . It was an old-school liberal community. My dad was on the civil rights commission—he was very much small-*d* democratic. He cared about minority rights, education, proper use of resources, including how you take care of your elders." As part of Alaska's African American population, Diane's father was well-known as a Democrat. She has become as familiar a face in the local political scene.

Fairbanks's African American population is 9 percent, higher than most non-Alaskans realize. Diane points to several waves of migration. Many black families came out with the gold rush. Others were part of the military, stationed at army and air force bases in Alaska, and decided to stay. "When we became a state, federal jobs opened up and that's why my family was here. My folks decided the best thing they could do was come back to Alaska and make a home." As Diane notes, by 1960 there was already a well-established black community. "The local chapter of the NAACP predates statehood."

This is just one of the many pictures of Alaska most Americans don't imagine. "Whenever people talk about Alaska, the images they have are white, or of natives. Nobody talks about the history of African Americans in the state, or the history of Asian Americans, which is similar. Nobody talks about the expanding Hispanic community."

In many ways, Diane thinks Alaska is particularly suited to new residents. "In a smaller community, it can be easier to start a church and hold on to cultural traditions. Through your community, it can be easier to find work." Noting some of the area's diversity, she highlights, "There are thirteen Thai restaurants and food trucks. Three are within walking distance. More and more are actually owned by Laotians. Go figure. . . . Fairbanks is pretty diverse. Twenty-seven languages are spoken in the school district."

Immigration isn't as charged an issue in Alaska as it may be in other conservative states. "One of the things about being a fairly young state: everyone who is not a native came from somewhere else. You can walk yourself off the cliff pretty fast with that one."

Alaska followed Hawaii's lead in a proposal to make the native languages the official ceremonial language of the state. Diane recalls that one conservative legislator "kicked up a fuss about his Norwegian parents and how they gave up their language. 'Your parents weren't sent off to separate schools; yours weren't acculturated by force. The fact that you weren't speaking Norwegian

had more to do with your parents than with the government,' "
Diane says, recounting the backlash to his objections. "By the
time it was voted on, he quietly changed his vote."

Not everyone supported the measure. "The only guys who
didn't were my legislator, who is a whackadoodle, and the one
from the next district, who is head of the whackadoodles. . . .
Your views on immigration depends on how whackadoodle
you are."

Fairbanks has had both conservative representation and more
progressive representation. Diane sees it as a mixed city that
way. "Outside of the interior, you'd claim that Fairbanks is very
conservative," she admits, but if you live here, it can look different. "We have the most progressive borough mayor in the state."
Alaska, she explains, is divided into boroughs, not counties.
"He's been here for a long time. A lot of people knew him. A lot of
people knew his family. And he ran an excellent campaign. He's
a pretty fair, honest guy. He doesn't hide his progressive credentials, never runs away from them. He's someone who can sit down
and talk to anyone."

That skill is important in a town where you kind of know
everyone. There are conservative politicians Diane can respect.
"In terms of true old-school conservatives, yes. But the whackadoodles, no. We have our fair share of the crazies." She has voted
for Republicans in her life as well, mostly in municipal, nonpartisan races. Even though there is no party affiliation next to a candidate's name in those elections, "you kind of know. Somebody
knows them. You make a few calls." As for partisan races, Diane
"could count on one hand" the number of Republicans she has
cast ballots for. "They were people I knew."

She does have her share of conservative friends. "We talk politics. We already know where each other stands. 'We're thinking
this; what are you guys thinking about it?' There is not a lot of

persuading, not a lot of 'Hey, you're wrong, let me prove how wrong.' "

Diane recently had a large party where, she estimates, half of her guests were "old-school Republicans"—as she carefully distinguishes them from Tea Partiers. "Except for folks who are going to be die-hard ideologues, your conservative friends are likely to dig out your driveway; you are going to go to weddings together; you are going to their house for a barbecue."

Diane had "one very good neighbor for years and years and years. He and I were on opposite sides of the spectrum—but every time something new came up, he'd call me and ask about my opinion. Did I change his mind? Probably not. We would literally have across-the-picket-fence conversations—about marriage equality—I would try to convince him that it could benefit people we knew. Did I change his mind? No. But at least we talked about it."

With her conservative friends, Diane "gets where they are coming from. They are just wrong."

Familiarity helps the conversation—which may be why picket-fence conversations are more civil than so much of the discourse Americans hear on cable news, on talk radio, and online. "Look at the comments in our online newspaper: when they couldn't comment anonymously, people calmed down."

That said, not all Alaska conservatives are the reasonable kind. "Extremists are extremists. I've been around a long time, and I'm not going to go into situations where I'll get into a screaming match with someone who won't listen. I'm out in public—I'll be at a Democratic Party booth at the state fair. When I'm there, I'm fair game. Ask me anything. I'll even go work a booth in the North Pole, which is über-conservative. Folks will walk up—for the most part, we'll have a relatively sane conversation. If they absolutely have their heels dug in, they'll walk past. There are only a handful of incidents when someone rolls up in my face and starts in. I think that's the same for everybody."

While it puts her in the minority, Diane embraces the word "liberal." "I tend not to use the word 'progressive' because it feels like running away from being a liberal is not going to gain you anything. I realize people use the terms interchangeably, but really the whole point of 'progressive' is to dance around 'liberal.' I am a liberal. I never adopted the *p*-word."

As few liberals as there may be in Alaska, Diane is far from alone. There is a Democratic Party that is alive and active—and a national movement she knows she's part of.

"For the most part, we stand for abortion rights; we fight against the war on women; we are concerned about affordable health care—many folks were skeptical, but now more people are getting insurance cards, so that's died down. We're all on the Internet. We're one of the two most wired states, so we see all of this same stuff. We agree with it."

She knows Alaska liberals may be quieter on some social issues. "We stand for the same social issues—our Democratic platform says all that. Individuals just are not going to storm over to our representatives in the same way. We're not holding demonstrations." On gun ownership, the kind of issue that one might imagine would make Alaska Democrats wary of the national party, Diane actually thinks it is the moderate Republicans who are nervous. "Open-carry folks have our more outspoken gun-rights folks getting nervous. There is an open-carry movement—started with the whackadoodles—and now we have idiots carrying handguns into borough assembly meetings because they can."

These fights, like so many, Diane has seen before. "I'm not older than Methuselah, but I look at folks in their twenties and early thirties, just now figuring out that they haven't invented the world. Issues like food security or leaving the smallest footprint . . . renewable energy, all of that. Folks might think they have just come up with this. . . . That's fine. . . . I appreciate your enthusiasm. . . . You are actually borrowing from a pretty old tradition and a lot of what you think is new is elderly. That's OK. I was the same at your age. I'm not mad at you.

"I think I was pretty center. Then, starting with Reagan, I ended up on the left wing. I had nothing to do with it—I didn't change."

Dan Henry

IDAHO FALLS, IDAHO

*Other than my parents, I don't have very close con-
servative friends. I have a friend from high school
who I battle with over Facebook. I set out to get a
few conservative friends on Facebook and did get
three—at least, we can talk together. But they have
to be very reasonable Republicans. One of them I do
see regularly. . . . We like interacting, but we don't
really socialize.*

Dan Henry is a convener of Idaho Falls' local atheist society, a
founder of the Snake River Freedom Coalition, an antiwar protester, Obama supporter, and ACLU board member. He is also a
Republican.

"Everyone knows that I'm a registered Republican," Dan explains, his earnest voice not betraying the undertone of mischie-
vous glee he must be feeling. "The GOP was scared liberals were
crossing over to vote in their primaries. So now they have closed
primaries. Democrats have open primaries. But there are never

contested Democratic primaries—all the action is on the Republican side. So in order to have an effect, several of us are registered Republicans. We joke about it. I like to skew their statistics. Sometimes I'll vote for a crazy candidate if I know that they won't win—or I'll vote for the more sane candidate of the two, if I think that one has a chance of winning, since a Republican is always going to win in the end."

Joining the Republican Party—even for his idiosyncratic reasons—is one of the few ways Dan has conformed to life in Idaho Falls. Otherwise, as a liberal and as an atheist, he is in the distinct minority. "There's something similar in nature between being liberal and being atheist here. People here are surprised when they meet a liberal. They are surprised when they meet an atheist. I'm not sure which is harder. Could you be elected as an out atheist or as an out liberal? Neither stands a chance."

Dan doesn't mind this minority status—and, in fact, relishes it as important. "Surprising people can help make them start questioning—they might start to challenge the way they were raised and indoctrinated. Having a group stand up and declare themselves different makes other people think a little bit."

One of Dan's current passion projects is pushing the city council to adopt a broader nondiscrimination policy. And he's by no means alone. His wife, Hollis, who grew up in the area, is active in the campaign. So are high school students who are part of the gay/straight alliance. Members of the Unitarian Church have stepped up to participate, as has the town's liberal Methodist chapter. Some local Lutherans are helping out as well.

Most noteworthy is that a number of the town's politicians are on board, including the female Mormon mayor of Idaho Falls. Although local politicians are elected on nonpartisan ballots, everyone knows she is a Republican. She's been a delegate to the Republican National Convention. And this is Idaho Falls. Everyone is a Republican.

While respecting a person's sexual orientation is becoming more common across America, respecting—and protecting the rights of—people of different gender identity remains more controversial. "Transgender" is still an unfamiliar term to many Americans, and one that many politicians would rather not utter—2015, in fact, was the first time a president said the word in a State of the Union address. This makes it all the more surprising that one city currently wrestling with legislation to protect against discrimination based on sexual orientation and identity is Idaho Falls.

Idaho has its liberal pockets. Boise—the capital and the home of the university—has the college-town feel you see across America: more diverse, relaxed, and inclusive than the rest of the state. There are slivers of land where the rich and famous—some of them quite liberal—keep their summer homes or ranches. Even Pocatello, the town of fifty thousand about an hour south, toward Utah, is viewed by Idaho Falls residents as their more progressive neighbor.

Idaho Falls is not one of those liberal enclaves. It's a conservative hub in a red swath of one of our country's most Republican states. The town is heavily Mormon, with a Mormon temple near the town center, and is characterized by the quiet, pleasant conservatism often associated with that religion. No Democrats get elected in Idaho Falls. Not many people of color come through.

In this landscape, Dan stands out in many ways. He's tall. He's outspoken. White and in his fifties, he has an interracial family with three adopted children. He plasters his car with provocative bumper stickers. He doesn't hesitate to speak up when he wants to assert a progressive point of view, or just be a little contrarian.

Born at Fort Benning in Columbus, Georgia, educated at UC Berkeley, he is a transplant to Idaho Falls. In that, he's not alone. One of the city's largest employers is a nuclear research facility. Many of the town's newcomers arrive to work at the facility—often coming from bigger cities and coastal universities and bringing more liberal perspectives. (As a result, liberals in Idaho Falls are much more enthusiastic about nuclear power as the clean energy of the future than most liberals elsewhere.) These researchers, scientists, and project managers run headfirst into the town's conservative nature—which sometimes quiets their politics or, at other times, as Dan has seen, inspires them to team up with other like-minded liberals and speak their minds.

For a long time, Dan assumed that most of the city's liberals were transplants, but he is pleasantly surprised that it's actually a healthy mix of the transplants and native-born, many of whom are locals who have left the Mormon Church. In leaving the heavy trappings of that religion, they often leave behind its more conservative politics as well.

"You can get the impression that it's monolithic here," Dan says, "but it's not. There are liberals of all ages. They may be inactive or hidden, but eventually they come out."

His wife is a case in point. "Hollis's family is here; they are extremely conservative," Dan relates. "They send horrible right-wing e-mail jokes. She has battles with them."

She is as active as Dan in local political campaigns. In addition to the nondiscrimination effort, they both worked to help elect the mayor.

"My wife and I helped on her campaign because the alternatives were horrible," Dan explains. The mayor may be conservative, "but she's a reasonable person . . . a good Republican . . . the kind you can work with and compromise with. Other conservatives might call her a RINO"—the commonly used right-wing critique that a moderate is "Republican In Name Only." When Dan and Hollis heard her say that she would support nondiscrimination measures, they started supporting her campaign. During their time as volunteers, they never had the experience of working alongside people they didn't feel comfortable with.

Dan had the chance to get to know her campaign strategist, a longtime Republican, but "an interesting guy" with whom Dan shared a series of political conversations. And their liberal friends never gave them flack for supporting a conservative candidate.

After all, the mayor is publicly in support of nondiscrimination in a state that's so conservative that the state legislature won't even hold a hearing on the issue. On the other hand, the mayor has also dragged her feet on taking local action, insisting that it's the state's responsibility . . . and maybe being wary of being viewed as too liberal. Pocatello, down the road, passed a similar ordinance already. But everyone knows that Pocatello is no Idaho Falls.

One courageous advocate for the bill is also a reminder of how entrenched conservative upbringing can be. The advocate, a friend of Dan's, is transgender. She was raised Republican. She came out publicly about her sexual identity in order to testify on the issue. What mystifies Dan is that in spite of how the GOP looks at her now, "she still defends Republicans. She defends their fiscal policies. She's convinced that Republicans are better with money."

In other instances, though, religious and political transformations go hand in hand. "I've noticed that when people abandon theology and become atheist, they have to start answering questions about where their values come from," explains Dan. "As they question that, many of them turn out to be liberal." There are also quite a few, he admits, who become libertarian—and it can be challenging to engage them politically. "Atheist libertarians—they just don't like being told what to do."

Dan has his liberal pals and a few libertarians—but not very many conservatives in his circle of friends. "Socially, we have a limited circle of people . . . but they tend to be the best people," he playfully boasts.

It's hard, he has realized, to have deep friendships with

conservatives. "It's hard to say why. There just isn't a comfort level. Other than my parents, I don't have very close conservative friends. I have a friend from high school who I battle with over Facebook. I set out to get a few conservative friends on Facebook and did get three—at least, we can talk together. But they have to be very reasonable Republicans. One of them I do see regularly. He does musicals." Dan pauses, then adds, "We like interacting, but we don't really socialize."

Dan's kids are a different story. His son Matthew has a good friend who is Mormon—or "LDS" as Dan says, using the common abbreviation for the Mormon church's proper name, the Church of Jesus Christ of Latter-day Saints. They have sleepovers and the friend has taken Matthew to church. "We are flexible," explains Dan. "It's fine if our kids want to explore religion. They can go to church when invited by friends."

The openness isn't always reciprocated. Dan believes that the Mormon community is polite and friendly, but only to a point. When he first moved to Idaho Falls, he remembers Mormons who befriended him until they realized he wouldn't convert; then they distanced themselves. He saw the same with his kids—they would play with children who were Mormon, but as the kids got older, their friendships drifted apart. The Mormon children, Dan says, are told not to associate too closely with people not of their faith.

Dan wants his children to find their own routes—and that includes their pathway through politics. "At election time, the schools engage in discussions about politics and the kids'll come home asking, 'Mom, Dad, are we Democrats?' Or they'll announce they're liberal"—he laughs—"and we say, 'You don't know that yet! You can't declare yet!'"

However, it must be hard for the kids not to declare when their father declares so boldly. On his car, Dan has an array of bumper stickers: a Darwin fish, a rainbow flag, an Obama sticker, and swag for different candidates during political seasons. He knows this makes him stand out. "It happens occasionally during campaigns," he recalls, "that you'll get a finger or two when you have Obama stickers."

His wife has stickers on her car too, though that wasn't always the case. When she worked in real estate, she didn't want her politics to be identifiable to buyers. While Dan says that it shouldn't have mattered, he acknowledges the reality: she never wanted to make a bad impression.

Dan has also been willing to bring his questioning spirit to his children's schools. "In Idaho, they teach evolution in seventh grade. So when each of the kids was in seventh grade, I'd go to the parents' night and ask the teacher how they teach evolution. I didn't indicate my leaning—and they'd sometimes assume I was against it. They'd explain it apologetically: 'We teach it in the spring, it's one module, we touch on it, we don't spend a lot of time on it.'"

Dan continues, now assuming his own voice: "'Wait a minute, it's the foundation of all biology. What do you mean you don't spend much time on it?' Sometimes the teachers seem to regret that evolution is downplayed. But they've learned that it has to be minimized. The state demands it. Or maybe it's not even an active decision, but they learn through experience and they know they have to keep it to a minimum or else hear from angry parents."

There have been other instances where Dan has been reminded that conservative politics may enter the classroom. He recounts one example of a history teacher he liked. "My daughter came home and said, 'Mr. Owens hates the government.'" Dan chuckles. "What? I can imagine where that came from. Little things slip . . . maybe he made some comment. There are these little clues that some teachers are real conservative."

On one occasion, a book was removed from the list of recommended reading for a tenth-grade English class. The book—Sherman Alexie's *The Absolutely True Diary of a Part-Time Indian*—talks about masturbation. It was enough for parents to protest and have it removed from the curriculum. It wasn't banned completely, though, and was still in the school library. "I just read it with my son," Dan announces. "It's a really good book."

Dan knows that other parts of Idaho might feel more welcoming. "Pocatello has college-age kids. They can even elect Democrats. We've elected one Democrat to state office in the twenty-five years I've been here. He served one term."

Continuing on the comparisons, he adds, "We're behind Boise and even Pocatello by years. We want a Costco to compete with Sam's Club. Or movie theaters—Boise has an independent movie theater. Pocatello does single-night runs of independent films and documentaries. Someone tried a club to watch single-night runs weekly at our local theater. It didn't last. We can't sustain that sort of thing."

Although, he notes, Idaho Falls isn't the last in line. "It all goes away by Rexburg. You go up there and they say, 'Recycling—that's a socialist plot.' On Facebook, someone from up north asked if he should move to Idaho Falls or Rexburg. Don't dare move to Rexburg! There are no bars. Everything shuts down at five p.m. Nothing is open on Sundays except a few chains on the highway."

Dan also knows that Idaho Falls has its strengths. "We complain more than we should," he admits, "to impress people in blue areas about how tough our life is. The fact is that we stayed here—because of our jobs but also because of our quality of life. It's low stress, low crime, and low population density here."

Dan may have no allegiance to the Mormon Church, but he does recognize a positive way it has influenced his life. "There are good qualities in Idaho Falls, and they are part of the good qualities in LDS. There is family-values-type stuff that isn't annoying. It really does translate to good living conditions for raising kids. Maybe it's all a rationalization, but it does feel like you have more control over your kids' experience."

Dan contemplates for a moment, then continues. "We tell ourselves it's a great place to raise kids. Whether it's real or not, I don't know. There are lots of other things I wish my kids experienced."

They talk about moving. At times, Hollis is tired of being where she grew up, tired of being in the minority. They talk about Washington State and Portland, or about retiring out of the area eventually. But Dan's not sure. "It's stressful being here," he asserts. "But my personality is that I don't take it personally. You should live where you're doing the most good. Moving someplace blue would be giving up."

John Turner-McClelland

LITTLE ELM, TEXAS

Transplants may feel they are more liberal than native Texans, but it's not true. There are liberal Texans. We're only twenty years removed from being a Democratic state. It's not really as hard-core Republican as people think.

John McClelland is a liberal organizer in the heart of conservative Texas. He's an atheist in a religious area. He's the elected chair of the local taxation board. He's a transplant from New Jersey by way of North Carolina. He's a married man—he and his husband wed in New York shortly after same-sex couples received legal recognition.

He's also a recovering Republican.

"When I was young, I probably voted more about the economic issues than social issues. And it didn't hurt that I was a member of the Young Republicans. I joined because there was a cute guy at the table," he recalls with a laugh. "That's actually the only reason

I joined. Otherwise, I wouldn't have been a Young Republican but probably would have voted the same way."

John cast his first presidential vote for Bob Dole in 1996. "It was more of a vote for Jack Kemp; Bob Dole happened to be there. I was not a huge fan of Bill Clinton," he explains.

Though he knew he was gay at the time, he didn't have qualms casting a Republican vote. "I didn't see the homophobia in the media aside from the Jesse Helmses of the world. You get a lot more access to that now, even though they were more explicitly homophobic then. In addition, it was an era when the Democrats weren't much better—the days of DOMA [the Defense of Marriage Act] and 'don't ask, don't tell.'"

That was the last time, though, John gave the Republicans his presidential vote. "I was a Republican in the mid-'90s, but I never voted for Bush," he says proudly. "In a partisan race, I will no longer vote for a Republican; I learned my lesson on that. George Bush and Rick Perry did that."

Bush and Perry were putting a more frightening face on the Republican Party, while John found himself moving to the left on social and economic issues—both for personal reasons. "At the same time I was coming out of the closet, a lightbulb went off. Obviously there are gay Republicans, but it's not a concept I subscribe to or understand. That was a large part in my mind changing. The other being unemployed when I moved to Texas. George Bush was sending everyone rebate checks. Everyone got four hundred dollars allegedly. Mine was, like, twenty dollars. I thought, 'If I didn't have to eat, I'd actually frame this.'"

John moved to Texas from North Carolina but is originally from New Jersey. "Like most people who get brainwashed by Fox News these days, I had it in my brain that we would be rich and successful, and liberals were bad," he recounts, explaining his childhood Republican leanings. "That's what I saw living in New Jersey as a little kid."

There were no political discussions in his house, but his earliest political memory involves his grandmother. "She was a lifelong Democrat. I do remember going with my grandmother to cast a ballot, voting for Mondale. I remember asking her, 'Why are you voting for Mondale when he's going to lose?' Even then, watching TV, I was very aware he was not going to win."

Her answer to her seven-year-old grandson: "That she was a Democrat. That's all she said. At least she took the time to bring me so I could see what a voting booth looked like. That was all she said of it."

His grandmother's influence didn't rub off. "I thought of myself as a Republican. My uncle was Republican. I thought I'd be like him. I thought I'd be a salesman, then CEO of a small company, earn six figures. It didn't happen, especially because I came out of college at the end of 1999, right when the recession hit, and no job."

John's family moved from New Jersey to North Carolina in 1987, and he stayed there through college and a few years beyond. "Even though Democrats controlled the area where we lived, it was a very conservative state," he explains. "We were living there with Jesse Helms still in office. Even the Democrats there were conservative." That environment just reinforced John's Republican identity.

A few years after college, John was underemployed, unhappy with North Carolina, and ready to move on. "I moved to Texas because I couldn't stand living in North Carolina anymore. It's a good place to live if you were a student or retired. Being a gay man, there wasn't a large pool of gay people there to begin with. I was fed up with work, fed up with Chapel Hill in general, so I picked up and moved where I had a friend. I thought, 'I don't want to move to a city where it's expensive,'" which ruled out conventional gay-friendly cities like New York and San Francisco. "I could've ventured back to New Jersey and tried to stake a claim. In the end, it was here or New Orleans. I think I chose the right one. I moved out here in 2001. It's now been thirteen years."

Part of the draw was that despite Texas's reputation, the Dallas area struck John as far more dynamic, diverse, and tolerant than where he was coming from. "Dallas is gay-friendly—more so than you would think. I was surprised. There was a thriving gayborhood—people were able to walk down the street holding hands. This is Dallas? This wasn't a concept I'd ever seen, especially in the South. Nobody was saying anything, nobody driving by and throwing things at them."

The move to Texas coincided with John's continued political evolution. By 2000, he was no longer a Republican—"I felt Bush and Gore were the same in how they answered questions in the debates, so I cast my vote for Nader, the only one who had something to say"—but he became more of an activist in the years that followed.

"I got a job, Bush was in office, Perry just started the governorship, and a shit storm went on from there: 9/11, Afghanistan, the Iraq War. Toss in Rick Perry going along with the Bush and Rove initiative of bringing a marriage ban to Texas. It all culminated around the same time," he recalls.

As John explains, in Texas a ban on same-sex marriage "already existed on the books as a law. They went ahead and tossed in a constitutional amendment—in 2005—right after Bush was reelected. That topped the cake. Kerry losing, throw that on the next year, I wanted to explode."

He became more politically active as he found himself moving into more conservative neighborhoods. For a while he lived in Addison, on the city's northern edge. Now he's in Little Elm, twenty-five miles north of Addison. "It's definitely exurban," he describes. "Dallas is the center of attention. The area I live in you wouldn't call a suburb. It's the outskirts of suburbs. Basically where everyone can get cheap housing, but you can still have cows and horses down the street."

John moved for the affordability. He discovered an area that's been undergoing its own changes. "Little Elm was a very small town until a decade ago. Then they started letting developers go crazy. It's probably twenty-five thousand people. Looking at it, you wouldn't say it's a big town, but you wouldn't say it's a tiny town. We have more than one stoplight. If you go five miles north of my house, it's a one-stoplight situation."

The area's growth means that many transplants, such as John, are slowly changing the local makeup. "It's overwhelmingly white but also has middle-class African American, Hispanic, and Asian families," he says. "A lot of people have moved into Texas from other areas. If you're looking for somewhere cheap, you come up this side of the city. You get Californians, people from the Midwest."

These newcomers may also someday change the area's politics. "The young families are typically more liberal," notes John. "We're kind of on the cusp—if anywhere were to change to the blue side, it would be an area like this. But now it's still pretty conservative in how we vote." As an afterthought, or a way of explanation, he adds, "We're not that far from Oklahoma."

John also adds a caution: don't assume transplants are liberals and locals are conservative. "Transplants may feel they are more liberal than native Texans, but it's not true. There are liberal Texans. We're only twenty years removed from being a Democratic state. It's not really as hard-core Republican as people think."

However, Republican politicians continue to dominate John's area—in part because they are often unopposed. "Where I live, unfortunately, doesn't do a good job of putting down-ticket Democrats on the ballot."

As a result, John ends up with Tea Partiers representing his area. "I was helping a neighbor run for state representative against a Tea Party guy in his first term. I got [the Tea Partier's] newsletter—yes, they are allowed to send out a newsletter from their legislative office during election time." He groans. "It was about his 'Merry Christmas Bill' that he got passed."

The Merry Christmas Bill was in response to the trumped-up outrage that in "some situations in some schools there were teachers reprimanded for saying 'Merry Christmas.' So now a bill passed that allows 'Merry Christmas,' 'Happy Hanukkah' "— John pauses and thinks for a moment—"that might be it, without reprimand."

That was the representative's proudest accomplishment, but not all that he highlighted. "He talked about an antiabortion bill and something else ridiculously crazy. Then his priorities for next session: border control because 'Obama can't do the job' and, oddly enough, term limits—'ten years is enough in office.' I hope it's just two for you." John chuckles.

This particular representative holds the seat for the "brand-new district created by a wonderful redistricting process that was highly illegal," John explains, but he's not the only conservative by a long shot. "All the state reps in the county are Republican. All the local officials are Republican. But my neighbors, numbers-wise, are probably not."

It's not that all the politicians are right-wing, John believes, but that the political game pushes them to the right. "The ones on the county level I don't think really are like the Tea Party, but they play along to stay in office. Some have been challenged by the Tea Party and managed to stay elected." There are some true ultraconservatives, John admits, who "have made their way into city councils, local school boards, but more of it is on the state and congressional level. My congressman, Michael Burgess, is most famous for saying that a fetus masturbates in the womb. And therefore it's a human. He's a gynecologist, so I guess he knows this," says John with a sigh and a dose of irony.

The conservative consensus around him has turned John from a moderate into a progressive. "I came to the left more socially first, then economically. Of course I am way to the left on both now."

That said, despite his strong feelings, John also has a portion of his life where he keeps his politics in check. "I try not to be too far to the left on economic issues because I'm a nonpartisan elected official—in our special taxing district." Having given this spiel often—probably to voters and friends alike—John continues, "CliffsNotes version: these districts were set up for rural areas to get water and sewage. Developers found a way to use these entities to develop gigantic planned urban developments out in the middle of nowhere, essentially. They are having a way to get bonds to pay for their infrastructure—the developers are getting back seventy percent of what they put into development, with the debt saddled on people who live here."

John is now the president of the board of directors of the taxing district. It wasn't the first time he tossed his hat in the ring. "One of my majors was poli-sci. I always had that interest; I was always serious about local-level politics. I had looked at running right after I got out of college. Then when I moved to Texas, I didn't do anything with it. I was just trying to work, to survive. 'Hey, I'm poor, I'm going to run for senate'—it's not something that crosses most people's minds unless you're a little bit crazy."

He ran for other offices and did not win. Then he ran for this position: with few people following and no opposition, there was no election. "If there's no opposition, they save money by not holding the election," John explains. "It happened both times— in 2010 and this past May. Three seats were up. Three people filed."

The role is more governance than politics. "It's the boring stuff: passing bonds, approving garbage contracts, getting deputies out here to patrol, telling someone they can be late on the water bill this month."

Serving in this capacity has made John realize that the old wisdom about partisan divides disappearing on the very local level is true: "There is not a liberal/conservative way to approve a garbage contract. We're probably more conservative in a way. We have to have a balanced budget. We can't go spending on social projects, which isn't what we do. We typically try to take the lowest bidder on services."

Yet, there is also something very liberal about the role: John finds himself articulating the role of government and the value of the public good. "Things will come up. Constituents realize what their taxes are—they'll ask, why do we have this tax, what do you spend it on?" John gets animated as he retells this common exchange. "This is what we spend it on: if you'd like to have a fire department and police and your trash picked up and water, you should pay that bill."

Then he adds with his usual droll understatement. "We're having the fire hydrants painted now, not a whole lot else. It's a master-plan community, so we don't have a lot of leeway. We would have the authority to create parks, but we don't have the space—and they're there anyway—they were master-planned in."

While party politics may not play a role in the taxing-district work, John knows the affiliations of everyone he serves with. "Four of us are Democrats, one Republican, oddly enough. Two of the Democrats are originally from California. The Republican is a moderate, an older gentleman. He told me he wouldn't vote this year—probably because of the insanity in his party. Good to know there are some waking up to Tea Party antics."

There were a few times in his various campaigns when John felt he was being attacked over his sexual orientation. The attacks weren't direct; rather, his opponents would take opportunities to highlight his affiliation with the Stonewall Democrats, the gay Democratic club. But the comments were always veiled—and these were years ago. He has felt a change in Texas, and by and large people aren't concerned about his orientation.

It's true at work as well. John let his colleagues know he was gay from the beginning. "I work for Evergreen Shipping, all your nice containers to get cheap Chinese goods. The person training me asked right away if I had a girlfriend or if I was married. So I told her. Set it straight. I had a boyfriend," John recounts. "She accepted it and most people I told that to where I work had the same reaction."

John's workplace is politically heterogeneous. "Oddly enough, the department I work in, at the time was fifty-fifty liberal and conservative," says John. "One of the guys I worked with was more liberal than I—not a native Texan either."

John is vocal with his political views among friends. He is more restrained at work. "It depends if I'm passionate enough to argue and work at the same time," he says of debating when he disagrees with a co-worker. "I'll try to tell them my viewpoint. If they argue, I'll argue. If they ignore me, I'll let it go—hopefully it will sink in. A lot of them are on Facebook; they see what I post. Whether they like it or not, they're still Facebook friends."

One of the issues that divide his colleagues is immigration, a hot-button topic in Texas. "Immigration comes up quite a bit. I work with a lot of non-American-born people. One was born in Peru. One in the Philippines. One from Mexico, who grew up in Chicago." Their backgrounds, though, don't make them more liberal on these issues. "They have problems with people coming across the border, when they had to go through a long process to come through legally. The woman from the Philippines has had problems getting visas for her family, and they have to go through a legal process. I think they see it from that side."

When it comes to the issue closest to John's life, however, just about everyone—his colleagues, his neighbors, his friends—stands with him. He acknowledges the possibility that in 2005, when Texas passed the constitutional amendment banning same-sex marriage, he may have known some people who voted for it, but "none that I know of would admit it."

The only public confrontation that John remembers was at a march against the amendment in Austin, where the KKK was planning to meet the protesters as they approached city hall. "I get there, at the front of probably two thousand people, marching toward them on one bridge, a thousand people coming down another street to join us—and there are five Klan members. They had to be protected; we weren't allowed to be anywhere near them. There were mounted police, police in the river, police in helicopters, police on buildings—making sure we didn't rush them, which wasn't going to happen."

John fondly recalls that experience. "Even that was hopeful to me, though the outcome [of the referendum] didn't work out—that so many people would go out of their way to support not having a marriage ban."

Since then, Texas in general and his circle have become even more tolerant. "According to the last poll, a plurality of people polled agree marriage should be legal—marriage or civil unions—the naysayers are in the minority," boasts John. "That's in stark contrast to nine years ago, when [the anti-equality] amendment passed with sixty-seven percent of the vote."

John is married but couldn't be married in Texas. "I met Jimmy two months after I moved here. We were together ten years before we were officially married," he says. They were married in New York. "I was leaning toward not doing it at all until it was legal in Texas. We had discussed it before. Neither of us had said, 'Hey, would you marry me?' Then that did happen one day. Him asking me. I was, like, "Um, OK."

John chuckles at the proposal and at what followed. "What are my options now? Where do we go? New Jersey was not an option at the time. We discussed Canada, but looking at cost and dealing with going to another country was crazy. We picked New York because it had just become legal the same month he asked me, and since I have family in New Jersey."

John returned a married man, but in the eyes of the state of Texas it was more complicated. Most rights are not acknowledged. "The state doesn't recognize it. When we came back after getting married, we had to go through a process. Do we change our names? In New York, we got married for twenty-five bucks and changed our names on the form. Here they didn't recognize that. So it was a legal name change through the court. Two hundred fifty per person. At least we didn't have to pay a lawyer—a friend did it as a gift, so there were no attorney fees. That was the only way they were going to change anything else. At the time DOMA was still in effect; Social Security was not going to change our names. For our drivers licenses—not unless we had a legal name change. They put it on the site: 'Out of state same-sex marriage licenses: not valid. We will not recognize them.' Now they have to follow a court order for our legal name change."

There is one challenge that same-sex couples face in some states that John and Jimmy don't need to worry about in Texas. "We don't have to file separately because there is no state income tax. That's why everyone likes to move here. This past filing season was the first time we did a joint return for federal taxes."

While the state government isn't tolerant, the people of Texas are a different story. "Most people are accepting when you tell them you're married," remarks John. "Of course, maybe they just don't say anything to your face—whether they believe it in their hearts or say it behind your backs is something else."

When he does hear something negative, it's from someone on the political extreme. There was one comment on a neighborhood website he remembers: "If you want legal rights of marriage, you have an option—you should marry a woman . . . then you'd have all of these rights." John tries not to take that kind of remark too seriously. "It's just a Tea Party spouting point. It's not someone I personally knew, but it was someone who lived in the neighborhood—it was a neighborhood message board. It's easier to talk shit about your neighbor online than it is face-to-face."

By and large, that rule holds, which makes life in Little Elm civil and comfortable. "No one goes out of their way to be vindictive," John observes. Then, after a moment, he amends that claim: "There are people who do—who go out of their way to make people miserable. And not be the good Christians they should be," he adds sarcastically.

None of which is to say that he has found universal agreement among his peers. "I do know people who don't agree with it. I have a friend who still doesn't," he admits. "He grew up Mormon, fancies himself conservative, now a moderate. He didn't agree that marriage between the same sex should be there—though wasn't opposed to civil unions."

In an evenhanded tone, John continues: "I would be fine with civil unions if the same laws applied to all couples. He was fine with that too. Common ground. If your religion believes it, that's fine, that's the church. I'm not going to a Mormon temple to get married. I don't think most people would do that."

The Mormon friend and John could find agreement and remain collegial. At his workplace, on his taxation district board, and in his Texan exurb, that's what John strives for. He also believes that such neighborly connection actually could be the core to a theory of change. "That's what I hope for—when they interact with someone they see as a friend, they realize," he begins. "If something's further away, you disassociate—but something you're dealing with on a daily basis or in your own family, you may or may not subscribe to that same view. Some people do, but if it's closer to home, you tend to think about it more."

Susannah Casey

KALISPELL, MONTANA

People describe Montana as a small town with really long roads. We've been here thirty years. You pass people on the highway you recognize.

Susannah is a mother of two grown daughters, and a retiree from an eclectic professional life that included work as a carpenter, an entrepreneur, and a bird enthusiast. In her sixties, she now has time to devote to avocational interests. She has led donor tours for the American Bird Conservancy for birders from around the world who want to come to Montana. She helped conduct a hunter/harvester survey for the state's parks department. She quilts.

"I've been sewing all my life; I like working on fabric. It helps with the long, hard winters," she explains. "I joined a quilt guild. Ninety-five percent of the members are Republican, but we don't discuss politics."

The civil silence on political conversation was broken at a retreat that Susannah attended with seven other quilters. "It was eight people in a cabin at a really nice facility—two nights, three days. On the first morning, we were having breakfast together. I only knew one other person; the others were from east of the mountains. They started talking and soon they were ripping apart wolves. Wolves are a big issue."

Susannah didn't want to debate the treatment of wolves and hoped the conversation would pass. She left the room, but when she returned, "They were up to 'those fucking environmentalists.' I raised my hand—I do that; I had to learn to be more tactful— and said that I understood there were some things we shouldn't talk about: religion, politics, abortion. I would respectfully ask to put wolves on that list."

She recounts the incident with a little boast. "It was hard for me to stay there, but I did. I got over it. I'm proud of myself."

Over the years, Susannah has become even more involved in the guild. There have been times when she has heard people use racist terms, especially referring to Native Americans. Sometimes those terms have been intended as slurs; sometimes they have just been used in uncomfortable ways. One friend in the guild is part Native American, which not all members know and which heightens Susannah's discomfort. On these occasions, Susannah doesn't stay quiet. "I raise my hand; I say there are lots of ways to look at things and that we need to have empathy," she recounts.

"I have to say something. At this point in my life, if I don't say something, it would eat me up. I'm learning to be more dip-lomatic, and learning to say things that don't scream out I'm a Democrat—I'm trying to ask people to think of things in a dif-ferent way."

There are plenty of opportunities to challenge the thinking of her neighbors and fellow citizens in and around Kalispell, Montana. Kalispell is near Glacier National Park, and the town swells with visitors in the summer. In the winter, the dwindling population still receives its fair share of skiers. Susannah lives in nearby Summit, where she moved thirty years ago from Denver. She is originally from eastern Ohio, her husband from New Jersey—but Montana is their home, where they raised two daughters and where they have dug into community life.

When they moved to Montana, they weren't aware of how conservative their new home was. In fact, Susannah recalls, it did not seem as conservative then. "At the time, we had Democratic county commissioners from time to time. Historically, back in the mining days, this was a Democratic state. And we have gone a little bit purple—we've had a Democratic governor and two Democratic senators . . . but I think that's really going to change."

Their area, in particular, has been changing. While Susannah describes it as having "blossomed economically," the more sinister development is a recent population shift. "It's changed acutely in the last seven to ten years. More of the neo-Nazi types from Idaho have focused on our county. We attracted the number one neo-Nazi from Florida."

She sighs. "We've gone from being a wholesome kind of place to having this little faction."

The good news is that they haven't taken over. "The neo-Nazi numbers are small," she explains. "We have a community college that has grown dramatically and is pretty progressive. A neo-Nazi tried to run to be on the board. He was defeated handily—which was encouraging."

There have been discouraging moments as well. "Missoula," the more progressive college town, "welcomes diversity. Here we have few Hispanic people," admits Susannah, who describes herself as "boringly white." "When we get immigrants, they get mistreated. We had some Ecuadorean people who worked in the ski lodge industry. There have been stories about them being mistreated. A friend had a deli and she had an Indian employee. People were just rude to him. They're not afraid to be rude to people who don't look like us."

Susannah remembers when a company came out to do cable installation, a supervisor asked whether she should be worried about her black employee venturing into more rural areas. "I would," Susannah recalls telling her. "In public . . . people aren't going to make fun of you. But if you're out in their neighborhood . . ." She trails off.

Then there are the local elections. "I have to vote in the Republican primary," confesses Susannah. "We have an open primary system at this point. The Democrats are running unopposed for the most part—but the Republican is going to win. The primary is the only time when we can affect who will be in office. If we have three conservative Republicans running for county commissioner, one of them will be elected. We have to get in there to have any impact."

She continues, explaining how a liberal approaches a Republican primary. "What's my strategy here? If we get the Tea Party guy in and he's so bad, will people figure that out and change course? I generally try to get the lesser of the evils."

Sometimes, she admits, the lesser of the evils can be OK. "There are some Republicans who have been good moderates. Best you can say about any [of the Republicans] is that they are slightly more moderate. And most of the moderates," she adds with regret, "are retired."

There are a few issues on which she has found common ground between liberals and conservatives, often around conservation.

"With bird conservation," she begins, referring to a community she's been involved with for years, "you don't find out too much about other people's politics. . . . Politics don't come out too much at conservation meetings."

She recalls one exception: "There was one longtime member

who had been in the legislature, and he was Republican. But the Republicans in the 1980s, even 1990s, are so much a different animal than Republicans of today. They've gotten way more conservative. The Tea Party keeps pushing them. The party has gone further and further to the right."

She has also found kindred spirits among hunters. "A majority of people in Montana hunt. I did a hunter/harvester survey for our parks department. I was impressed. I was scared that people would be angry—it was the hunting season after a hard winter on game animals. I interviewed hunters—and I was positively impressed. Some of them chose not to take down a deer or elk that was not in good shape."

She reflects on the experience and on all the hunters—who one might presume to be conservative—she had spoken to. "Hunters get a bad rap. One bad apple spoils the bunch. We've had poachers, but they are not the same as hunters. Most hunters are pretty respectful. They do it as a family. It's not a bad thing. It's a good family tradition."

Susannah includes her own family in that group. "We're gun owners. My husband hunts." However, that does not make her sympathetic with the gun-rights activists around the country. "Every time they talk about taking our guns away, we want to say, they are not coming after your hunting rifles; they are coming after your AK-47s. That's how we think about it."

Looking at the actual impact the last few years has had on the industry, she notes, "Obama is the best thing that ever happened to gun manufacturers. Gun ownership—it's over the top." There has been so much propaganda claiming that the Obama administration would try to take guns away from gun owners that it has led to spikes in sales. Even after tragic shootings in Aurora, Colorado, and Newtown, Connecticut, gun stores reported an increase in sales of high-capacity weapons—as though buyers were rushing to make purchases before new laws came into place.

And yet, federally, no new laws on gun safety were passed during those years. Susannah has seen this uptick in gun purchases locally. "We had a cute little gift store on Main Street; it went out of business. It was the economic downturn; people weren't buying gifts. Now it's Big Bear gun supply."

Susannah recalls recent news examples where castle doctrine—the right to shoot first and ask questions later—has led to unnecessary deaths. She also recounts her own anecdotes of being at parties with people who always carry guns. "It's a little creepy."

The reminders that she is in conservative country are everywhere. "The campaign materials I get at my door: they are Christian, pro-life, property rights, smaller government. . . . There aren't many people here who have a strong concept of what a central federal government does for them." She adds with pride, "We are on the side of the fence that looks at public lands as being awesome."

Over the years, she has been frustrated in attempts to make her environmental argument in her community. "When we first came here, I suppose I was naive. I spoke once at a county commissioner meeting. I was representing Audubon—and I made a comment about how it seemed economic factors were always outweighing environmental factors. This guy on the radio said about me, 'Maybe she lives in a cave.' This was twenty years ago. It's enough to make me say, 'Ooh, I don't want to be out there, don't want to be around these people."

Over that same period of time, though, she has found other liberals who remind her she's not alone. "For the most part, liberals look past it and maintain a positive attitude." She describes Citizens for a Better Flathead, a group that has advocated for a number of environmental issues. There have been fights to improve access to recycling. And for all the frustration, Susannah keeps active.

"Now that I'm getting older, I feel like I owe it to my children to at least speak out." Her two daughters both inherited their parents' values. One is a climate scientist living in California. The other is in Seattle, working for a nonprofit that does home visits as part of a Head Start program. "We are really proud of both of them. They are making a difference in the world."

Susannah says she never insisted they become liberal, though clearly they learned to share their parents' political leanings. "We didn't take them to church. We didn't tell them what to think— I think that's the only way to be a parent. We guided them; we did things with them. They appreciate we are liberals, and that we allowed them to think for themselves, and they learned to think about other people besides themselves."

Not going to church makes you stand out in this part of Montana. "There are so many churches," explains Susannah, "that there is an overall feeling that if you are not a Christian, you're not correct, you're not accepted."

That's not the only way Susannah is different. "I drive a Prius. I've been at an intersection, and people will drive around me and flip me off because I'm in a Prius. Get a life, people. There are better things to get worked up over than a hybrid car."

Other drivers just wear their politics on their bumpers. "It's acceptable to hate Obama here. You'll see trucks with great big signs that are just hateful. It's acceptable to broadcast your Tea Party views. The liberal people stay under the radar. . . . I have bumper stickers, but I don't go overboard." Susannah's bumper sticker says "One Human Family." "I'm sure that some people might take offense."

At the local athletic club and the local hospital, Fox News is always turned on. "If someone changes the channel at either place, people will start shouting at you," she says with a mixture of laughter and disbelief. "People who are conservative feel like everyone is that way. That's the most annoying thing about living here: the intolerance for any other kind of thinking."

As a result, with their conservative friends, Susannah and her husband "don't talk politics for the most part." Susannah mentions one conservative neighbor, an artist across the street. "She's the kind of person you can talk to about it. There are very few of those, with whom you can mention something and not have it turn immediately into a shouting match."

That said, Susannah feels that Montana is a great place to live—and plenty of liberals from other parts of the country may make the wrong assumptions about it.

"People outside of Montana might have misconceptions. Before we lived here, we had this feeling some people don't have computers, may live off the grid," Susannah admits. "There are some people who live up north near the Canadian border without indoor plumbing—maybe they have running water, but use outhouses—but that's a very small part of the population."

She expands upon the strengths of the area. "We have a lot of good liberal options. Montana is becoming a microbrewery destination. We have great brewers here. We are a destination beer-drinking state. We will probably never get a Trader Joe's because of our wacky liquor laws, but it's no big deal. We don't have a huge population for having a Trader Joe's or a Whole Foods. But we do have organic grocery stores. We have community-supported agriculture—we buy a share, get our vegetables. A lot of people do that; it doesn't matter if you are Democratic or Republican if you want organic food."

Overall, this is home. "We are in a great place. We don't want to leave. We thought about it for a number of years. We have friends in Corvallis, but you know what? They have a lot of conservatives there. You can think about Portland or Seattle, and you think, 'Wow, it's refreshing—everyone is liberal, isn't it great?' You're not a minority. You go there and it's refreshing to feel you're with a lot of like-minded people. You have to specifically find your friends here or you get discouraged. It can be depressing: you are so outnumbered, so many people so confident they are right and you are wrong."

But when she finds local liberals in Kalispell, they are as liberal as the folks in either of the left-leaning cities her daughters have moved to. "Liberals here believe in science. A lot of us are atheists or Unitarians, or belong to any of the churches open to gay people. There are the universal things that tie liberals together: human rights, women's rights, reproductive rights. Our liberals are in that group."

Susannah and her husband feel like they have found their community. "I feel sorry for the people addicted to Fox and focused on the negative," she notes. "Most of those people are unhappy. You have to take some consolation: I feel good because we liberals can't win elections but we're happier." That contentment also comes from the larger community she's cultivated—including people involved in wildlife and state parks, and just among fellow Montanans. "People describe Montana as a small town with really long roads," she notes happily.

Rita and Dean Smith

PAWLEYS ISLAND, SOUTH CAROLINA

*This is a small town. It's the South. It just wouldn't
be polite to get into an argument. . . . [Politics] is
something we just don't bring up unless you know
you're on safe ground.*

Rita and Dean Smith love where they live.

"It's a common thing with our neighbors—we'll say, 'How are
you doing?' and they'll say, 'Another day in paradise,' " describes
Dean.

This paradise is Pawleys Island, South Carolina. It's a coastal
town with plenty of retirees and snowbirds. "It's a lovely pace of
life," explains Rita. "The ocean is a bike ride away. People are
friendly. The cost of living is lower" than when they lived and
worked in D.C. "We don't have traffic alerts. The downside is we
have wacky-ass politics."

Rita experiences the conservative political leanings as part
of her routine activities. "My part-time job is teaching exercise
class," begins Rita. "President Obama was in the news and one

lady makes a comment—she goes on and on—I looked at her. 'Number one, I support the Democrats. Number two, this is not the place to discuss it.' Dang it if she didn't catch me later in the parking lot and go on and on again." Rita laughs at the memory but adds, "They assume they can make disparaging comments and I won't be offended."

Such assumptions come up around religion as well. "We also live in the Bible Belt," continues Rita. "So let's hold hands and pray," she says, voicing what she's heard countless times. She has a group of women she does water aerobics with and they'll go to meals together. When they do, someone always starts the meal with a prayer. "And it's not just pray, but pray to our lord and savior Jesus Christ."

Rita often lets it pass. "I put my head down, hold hands, and suck it up." At one point, though, she decided to say something to one of the women who often instigated the prayer. "I sent her an e-mail, very, very, very carefully worded. I said I don't feel comfortable—instead of saying grace, let's raise a glass. Good Lord, next time we went to lunch, when I went to the restroom, while I was gone, they said grace."

South Carolina may have pockets of liberals in Columbia or Charleston, but Pawleys Island is not one of those oases. "There are people who are local, they've been living here all their lives, and they're a product of growing up here," says Rita.

The rest of the area's residents are transplants—which, in this case, means retirees. "A lot of retirees from the Northeast are getting in touch with their fathers' politics," muses Dean with only a touch of facetiousness. "They are leaving behind their youth. Now they are old white folks."

Dean describes "pull up the drawbridge syndrome" as having taken hold among a number of these fellow transplants. "We have union people who retire here, on union pensions, and now retired into gated communities. They now talk trash about unions."

"Older retirees are mostly conservative," echoes Rita. Of course, there is a danger to assuming. Dean and Rita—white, retired, he in his sixties and she in her fifties, and happy residents of Pawleys Island—are an exception . . . and not the only exception. Dean explains that many of their close friends are from the North and brought their liberalism with them. "People are always surprised when they find fellow liberals," Rita continues. "There are more than two of us. You're always so surprised. We're just in the closet."

"There are a significant number of them," Dean agrees.

Dean and Rita see eye to eye on most things political. They share a passion for civic engagement and social justice, as well as for broader community spirit. And they share a delight in the life they've built in Pawleys Island.

"When Dean was a child," Rita recounts, "he used to come down here. Twenty years ago, we came down on vacation. Then we came down a couple times a year. Before we retired, we bought a condo and came down as often as we could. We were getting to know the area."

"We already had more friends down here by the time we retired than we had in D.C.," chimes in Dean. Both he and Rita had been federal employees with the Department of Energy.

"We wouldn't move back in a heartbeat," adds Rita.

"At first Rita wasn't sure," Dean notes. "Before we moved here, we were not sure how we were going to like it down here."

"It's a small coastal community," Rita interjects. "You're not moving to Podunk, Alabama—no offense to Podunk, Alabama. You get people from different parts of the country: Ohio, Pittsburgh, New Jersey."

"And international," says Dean.

Rita and Dean dove into the local life of Pawleys Island and stay busy in retirement. Dean serves on the local board of elections. In addition to teaching aerobics, Rita is on the board of the county's 4-H. They are dedicated to a local soup kitchen. They organize social, political, and volunteer opportunities for local liberals. They have both been involved in local efforts to preserve the qualities of Pawleys Island that attracted them there. And they take advantage of the area's easy access to outdoor exercise and exploration.

Through all of this, they've built up a community of friendships—and that circle is by no means exclusively liberal.

"We've got tons of friends who are Republicans, conservatives, some red-meat conservatives," asserts Dean. With their liberal friends, they talk politics. With their conservative friends, they tend to avoid the subject. "This is a small town. It's the South. It just wouldn't be polite to get into an argument. . . . [Politics] is something we just don't bring up unless you know you're on safe ground." So much of southern life, small-town life, and retired life is about being civil. "You just don't bring up things that would tick people off."

"We talk about other things," explains Rita. "You talk about your wife or husband, children, grandchildren." With political views, she adds, "I know you feel that way and you know that I feel this way. So it's just something you don't talk about."

"You know people for more than one thing," Dean continues. "In D.C., we'd know people because they were neighbors or because you work with them in the bureaucracy. Down here you know people four or five different ways."

"You meet more people through mutual friends," says Rita.

"It's a web of relationships. Where you live. Where you volunteer. If we were churchgoers, it would be through church," adds Dean.

"We love the interwoven relationships, the sense of community," Rita chimes in.

There are tensions within that community, though—especially because, Dean explains, often "people assume you're conservative and assume you're Christian."

"Rita and I both had it happen because we are who we are—white, retired, living in the South," recollects Dean. "People automatically assume we're conservative Republicans. They'll tell you racist things; the assumption is that because you look like me, you think like me."

Even while staying true to their values and being active in politics, they try not to pick political fights. Dean explains, "We're careful not to rend the social fabric," using a phrase that comes up again and again. They often discover that they share many community- and family-oriented values with people who choose different political affiliations—but they don't try to turn those people into liberals, or vice versa. Dean explains, "It's the South. It doesn't work that way."

Which isn't to say people don't know Dean and Rita's politics. "We go to the local watering hole. People there who know us might say, 'Here come the Democrat liberals,' and slap us on the back. And we have a drink with them," Dean says happily. "It's almost like an identifying thing. It doesn't become a topic of conversation. It's a random greeting."

Neither Rita nor Dean started life in a liberal household. "I came to being a liberal later on," Rita recounts. "My parents weren't political or politically active. . . . My grandmother, who was born in Italy, moved to the United States. She was a Roosevelt Democrat. A union-member Democrat. A staunch Democrat," some of which may have rubbed off on Rita.

"Rita's grandmother said that Democrats may have saved her life," interjects Dean. "She was doing Triangle Factory–type work—bad conditions—the unions and Democrats helped change that."

"But my father and mother generally voted Republican,"

resumes Rita. "Old-fashioned Republican. My father's been deceased many years. He was a lawyer—the rule of law was important to him. He was glued to the Watergate hearings, and Barbara Jordan became his hero. He thought she was marvelous."

Rita considers herself a "lapsed Catholic," but her years in Catholic school helped shape her politics. "I became a liberal somewhere in high school. Even though it was a Catholic high school, it was very progressive. The nuns were all about women's rights and empowerment. They didn't wear habits. I voted Democrat and considered myself liberal, which was easy to do growing up in Maryland."

Dean had more conservative influences in his youth. "I grew up in the Appalachian South in the mountains. I was in church a good deal. I was immersed in it. I never questioned anything." He sighs.

"Then I went off to college, and college changed me. I went in the fall of '67—I was there '68, '69, '70—I went from being literally a Goldwater Republican first semester of freshman year to a Mao Democrat the first semester of sophomore year."

Dean remembers those years fondly, with a little excitement and wonder. "A little bit of realizing how big the universe is in my science class changed me. All those things I had thought about were bound up in a small-town religious sort of thing. The universe is so big. Along with that came a political awakening. Then they started shooting people like me at Kent State. The war was hanging over me. I was 1-A for a while."

He didn't end up in the war, but this awakening did shape his career choice. "I wanted to work for government, so I wouldn't have to work for the man. Working for the government was working for the people. I kept those values."

Dean tried to pass those values down as well. "I raised two good atheist sons" from a previous marriage. "One who is a good liberal and good atheist is married to a strong Catholic. He rolls his eyes and keeps his mouth shut. His mother was Jewish; I was nominally Christian; we were both modern people. We gave them each a taste of both religions. They both decided not to do anything—they are perfectly happy being who they are."

Rita moved away from the church in her twenties, when she was in college. "I would still do Christmas and Easter to make my mother happy. A mother's guilt can reach across miles, even now from the other side."

Being nonreligious is about as unusual as being liberal in their community. They are content without a congregation, though they have relationships with some of the churches in the area. "We have a very liberal Episcopal church," says Dean. "It runs a free medical clinic in a separate building, an after-school program, a food bank."

"We are dedicated soup-delivery people for the soup kitchen," explains Rita. "It's a bunch of liberal Episcopals and a bunch of fallen Catholics."

While many of their volunteer activities are coordinated through local liberal groups and the Democratic Club—such as collecting school supplies and participating in trash pickup—other community events are where they meet some of their conservative neighbors and friends.

Rita is on the board of the county Habitat for Humanity. "There are about ten board members all across the spectrum. Two other liberals on the board. You've got both ends of the political spectrum. The director is a good liberal, but being executive director has to remain neutral, can't get politically involved. Because Habitat is a religious sort of organization, when we dedicate a home or a site, there's always a prayer. Fine, I can deal with that." But she never crosses over into political conversation with the more conservative board members.

Dean serves on the election commission and says, "I've got

close friends on the election commission who are Republican. We share everything except how we vote."

In part, regardless of your values, Pawleys Island is a hard place to be a Democrat. "We elect our sheriffs—we've only had twenty-five sheriffs over two hundred years. I run into our sheriff at the bar," relates Dean. "I was having a drink with him and he says, 'I was a Democrat for years and years, then realized I couldn't get elected as a Democrat.' Probably at heart, he's still a Democrat."

Dean is happy their different affiliations don't stop them from sharing a drink. Again, in a place like Pawleys Island, he sees no reason to let that stand in the way. "We're nonconfrontational. We want to protect the social fabric."

As much as they can tire of hearing right-wing rhetoric, they are also cautious about liberals who haven't adopted the lessons of keeping the peace.

"There are some people down here who wear their politics on their sleeve—they eat, breathe, and sleep politics," cautions Rita. "Those are the ones who will alienate their friends and neighbors. For us, it's part of our lives, but not all encompassing."

"The Democratic Club fell apart because one person was too hyperpartisan—that just didn't sit well with people who chose to move to a sleepy resort town," explains Dean. "Another guy moved in and resurrected the club. He's mild mannered, a retired Presbyterian minister. A good liberal—but doesn't get so hyper-confrontational. He's a southerner," he says, as though that's explanation enough.

Rita builds off that point. "The mean spirit you'd see on the Republican side"—specifically by the Tea Party on the national stage—"was being held by this particular Democrat. No, no, no, we don't want to be that way, we don't want to reduce to that level. They are not evil. They just vote differently. They are nice people. Don't demonize the other side."

Dean offers one example of a person whose values are in the

right place, but whose approach is out of step with the vibe of
Pawleys Island. "She's a dear, dear person, and she's taken on as
her life's purpose the elimination of plastic grocery bags. It's almost monomaniacal. When she brings up the subject, she's so out
of balance on this one thing—she ends up pushing people away
without knowing it."

He adds with a laugh that they'll say to one another, " 'If you
go to the grocery store and forgot bags, don't run into so-and-so!'
We appreciate people who are balanced, not hyperpartisan. It's
not mentally or emotionally healthful."

While they may disagree with people over national and even
state politics, as is often true, on the local level, they can find
agreement with the most unlikely allies. One of the reasons to
keep up good relations is that in a small community you never
know whom you'll end up working with. This was especially true
of a campaign called "Don't Box the Neck," an effort to keep big-
box stores out of the Pawleys Island area.

"We're a nice little small town and there was a threat of a big
box store. Walmart. There were various reasons we don't want
a Walmart. Well, this one store became a Pandora's box—the
outcry from the community was across the board," explains Rita.
"Black, white, Republican, Democrat—it was a coalition. Then
people started showing up at meetings."

"Thousands of people," adds Dean.

"There was a real sense of community. You move here for a
way of life. It doesn't matter how you feel politically."

"What happened was that Walmart didn't know it was getting into a community of retirees who were moving here for the
nature, the natural beauty," recalls Dean. These retirees had
resources and organizing skills. "Suddenly there were websites,
e-mail lists, T-shirts. We defeated this."

While politics often brings out local divisions, this campaign
united local residents. "We saw neighbors, friends, business

owners—the ones most affected—people concerned about quality of life," remembers Rita.

It had larger ripple effects as well, says Rita. "There was a Tea Party candidate for city council. The only opposition was another Republican. The Republican was involved in Don't Box the Neck and actively invited these people," meaning everyone who was part of the coalition, to be part of his campaign. "He's an old-fashioned Reagan Republican, which makes him look like a moderate down here. Democrats showed up and we beat this Tea Party guy sixty-eight, thirty-two; we beat him in every precinct."

There was another Republican who came to speak to Rita and Dean's liberal group. "He was the first Republican candidate to speak to us. 'We'll give you questions and be respectful,' I told him," says Rita. "He said, 'I'll be ready.' "

"A question was posed to him: why not run as a Democrat?" she continues. "He said, 'I'll be honest—it's hard to get elected as a Democrat.' We have some people in the group who say, 'I wouldn't vote Republican with a gun to my head.' Others said, 'You play with the hand you're dealt.' "

"Democrats turned out in that primary to defeat the radical conservative" by supporting him instead, declares Dean. "It gave us a voice."

This race wasn't in their district, but if given the chance, Dean and Rita would have had no qualms voting Republican. "We would have voted for him in a heartbeat."

That they have found Republicans they would vote for, conservatives they can collaborate with, and friends from all parts of the spectrum fits the life that Rita and Dean have carved out for themselves. Their friends back north are sometimes surprised they can take their conservative surroundings. To them, it just shows their friends don't fully understand.

"Maybe people think it's more confrontational down here than it is," ponders Rita. "There are no shouting matches. It's not in your face. You might have back-and-forth banter and local letters to the editors—but it's more polite. Sometimes it ain't easy to keep your mouth shut and to find people who think like you," but overall it has worked out to give them a community they cherish.

"Let's just say if folks in Congress had the attitude of people down here, a lot more would be getting done," speculates Dean. "The government just doesn't work anymore."

"You can find common ground and build on that," affirms Rita, returning again to Don't Box the Neck. "It wasn't a Republican or Democrat thing. It was common ground, quality of life. The gentleman who is the mayor of Pawleys Island had a reception. He's a Republican—but he talked about how we all came together."

"He also bragged about all the guns in his house," inserts Dean.

Rita dives in: "People in the North don't understand about this—they never had guns. People in the South hunt. I know people who are responsible gun owners. They're for hunting, for protection; they're responsible. So when you start talking gun control . . . everybody had guns."

"Those of us who spent the majority of our adulthood in metro areas understand that guns are not always a good idea," adds Dean. "It's one of those topics that's a conversation killer."

Along with guns, Rita knows that God holds a different place in southern and northern culture. She speaks of an effort by a Christian group to run a program in public schools. "A northern friend said, 'Could you imagine trying to pull that shit in Maryland?' Down here it's like, 'They took God out of schools.' "

"I've heard that out of the mouths of good Democrats," states Dean. " 'They took God out of the schools.' "

"It's one thing we do miss from the North," admits Rita. "You roll your eyes; it rolls like water off a duck's back."

There are other features of life in D.C. they miss. "The

restaurants," announces Rita. "Can't find Ethiopian, can't find good Thai."

"There are tons of good restaurants," Dean explains, but they're "all Italian or American. No diversity of food." What they miss tends to be "more cultural than political." In the population, "diversity is just black and white. Nothing else. No Asian, no Indian subcontinent, no former Soviet Union."

It can also just be easier living their values where they used to live. "When I go up to Maryland, you get five cents off for every bag you bring, and charged for plastic bags" at grocery stores, recounts Rita. "Ninety-nine percent of the people have reusable bags; very few come out with plastic. The reverse is true here. I don't see that awareness. There is a grocery store now that does the five cents off, and I go there now for that reason. If a Styrofoam cup falls out of your pickup truck onto the side of the road, good thing I'm there to pick up after you."

They do still recycle—and in doing so, they've run into one of their notable neighbors: Oliver North. "Saw him at Ace Hardware about a week ago, returning products." Dean chuckles. "Ran into him at the recycling center—recycling and driving a hybrid SUV," he says with knowing irony. "He saw me looking at him, gave me a little wink."

Rita recounts her reaction at seeing him: " 'War criminal,' I said under my breath."

Oliver North's notoriety was part of Rita's realization that, as a liberal, she was different from much of the country. "I knew something was horribly wrong when during the Iran-Contra scandal, on vacation in the Outer Banks, I saw some local little tabloid where Oliver North was touted as hero. What?! This man is a criminal! He broke the law! At that moment, I thought, what the fuck is going wrong with this country? This was during the Reagan years. Even people two years after me were Reagan conservatives. I was a child of the '70s. We were putting flowers in guns. In the Reagan years, people wanted to make a million dollars—that was the divide—and 'liberal' became a dirty word." That didn't stop Rita from being a liberal then, and it doesn't stop her now. In Pawleys Island, "people are proud to be conservative. But if you say you're proud to be a liberal, you might as well say, 'I'm proud to be a child molester.' "

Yet, this is now their home—and they are staying put.

"The good so heavily outweighs the bad," Dean offers simply. "We went back after we had been away six months or a year, back to friends in downtown D.C. We were riding the Metro—we looked around. Everyone going to work had a low-grade melancholy. They didn't even know they were unhappy. We'd been around happy people to know this was very different." When they got back to Pawleys Island, he says, "We wanted to get out and kiss our driveway."

"I hugged our palm tree," Rita says, laughing.

Boasts Dean, "In ten years, we've only had one snow. And that was gone in four hours."

Desmond Porbeni

TUSCALOOSA, ALABAMA/
NEW YORK, NEW YORK

I remember my first year in the city, I was on Forty-Second, in front of Ollie's. Someone screamed something horribly offensive. "Are you talking to me? Really? What?" It was the last thing I ever would have expected. I didn't deal with that sort of thing growing up in Alabama.

Desmond grew up in "one of those places where you know everybody is going to be in church on Sunday. And if you're not there, others are going to have something to say about it," he explains. The city was Tuscaloosa, Alabama—"home of Crimson Tide," he notes almost as a reflex, referring to the beloved and nationally competitive college sports franchise. He grew up with several generations of his family living nearby.

So when he chose to stop attending church, he knew that was a big decision. "Oh God, yes, I went to church every single Sunday of my life until I turned eighteen. At eighteen, I came out.

I remember this really sort of awful moment in Sunday school class. Someone I knew, who knew I was gay, started asking these questions—about whether gay people would go to hell. Really pointed questions, baiting me, staring at me across the room."

Desmond pauses, recalling. "You know, I don't have to do this anymore," he remembers saying to himself. "And I didn't."

But that meant he had to have two talks with his family: one about not going to church. And a second explaining why.

"For different family members, they reacted to different things. I came out to my mom. She did not take it very well. It took her some time to come to grips." Next to that revelation, "she didn't particularly process me not going to church."

But this series of announcements had the opposite effect on the older generation. "My grandmother didn't really seem to have any negative reaction to me coming out. She said something like, 'I knew that.' She made a joke, and it kept the conversation going. However, when I told her I didn't want to go back to the church she'd been in for fifty or sixty years, that really hurt her. A crushing kind of hurt."

He adds, "With the rest of the family, nobody really dabbles that much into anyone else's business."

Growing up gay in Alabama for Desmond meant being very aware of a dual reality. Tuscaloosa was a small enough community that everyone knew a bit about everyone else. But because it was the South, people were very adept at not speaking about some of the uncomfortable facts they knew.

It was a scary environment for coming out. "Football was king; hypermasculinity was the norm," he recounts of his hometown. "I grew up around people who I knew were gay, but they were married. They were beacons in the church community, and they lived lives pretending to be someone they're not—that's how their lives looked to me as an outsider looking in. That's what they did to exist in this world." That was true as Desmond grew up—and it remains the case now. "They are still doing it. People I personally know to be gay—intimately know to be gay—are married to women; they dated girls in high school. Just the way I did."

As a teen, Desmond explains, it was just easier to go with community expectations. "I grew up knowing that it would be better to date a girl, which I did, and then sneak around if you need to—rather than come out and say who you are."

And yet, as conservative as this environment sounds, it was actually one that surrounded Desmond with fellow Democrats and taught him to be liberal. After all, most black families in Tuscaloosa—and throughout Alabama and the South—were Democrats.

"I grew up in a very political family. My grandmother"—the same one who always suspected he was gay—"and other family members fought so hard to make sure I had the right to vote—and they made sure I never forgot it. My grandmother marched with Dr. King, participated in sit-ins. Anything you could think of to help, she was active in. It was always one of those things instilled in us, even as small children: 'You should vote, your ancestors couldn't, and others fought hard so you'd have the right.' "

Desmond laughs about how seriously he took these instructions. "Even in school elections, I remember telling everyone, 'You have to vote!' "

It wasn't just his family. Even in what many of us think of as deep-red Republican country, Desmond grew up in a community of Democrats. "Everyone in your church community was Democratic. Everyone in my family had the same political views, in general. Some people are more conservative than others when it comes to social issues, this or that. But I don't think it would lead anyone to not vote Democratic."

Of course, it was those views on social issues that made him feel excluded from the community in which he was raised. Among that community, "there's a split" over marriage equality.

"I don't think much has changed in the twenty years I've been away. More people have had to deal with coming out in their families, but I don't know it's caused sweeping change. The only gay clubs we had growing up have been closed by pressure from churches and the community."

Desmond's family belonged to a Methodist church. "Everybody in Alabama is Methodist or Baptist in general. We were probably one of the least conservative churches. Baptists tended to be more conservative—and other denominations like the Church of God, Church of Christ, were a lot stricter." And though the city, and even Desmond's neighborhood, was relatively integrated, church was not.

"Sunday morning is the most segregated hour of the week," he says with a smile, "or if you go to a black church, more like the most segregated three hours." Beyond his congregation, Desmond "grew up with friends of every race known to man that existed in Tuscaloosa." He recalls that he would occasionally go to a friend's church or bring a friend to his. "Nobody at my church was unwelcoming to white kids, or to me going to predominantly white churches. It was more like, 'We have a visitor, look at our special visitor,' in both churches. It was more like an alien walked in."

The division also existed along voting lines, for the most part. "I grew up in a neighborhood seventy percent black, thirty percent white—something like that," he describes. "You could definitely tell which house was which because of what sign was in the yard. It's very much a Tuscaloosa thing. In certain neighborhoods, you weren't allowed to put signs up—but most neighborhoods you could drive through: 'A white person lives there, black person lives there.' Every now and then you might be wrong, but you would pretty much nail it on the head."

Tuscaloosa is by no means the most conservative part of Alabama. "It's probably less conservative than other parts of

Alabama. Though that's not really saying a lot." He laughs. "I try to give it a little credit. In comparison to other major cities—I guess it's not a major city—but compared to Atlanta, even Birmingham, it's quite conservative. Compared to other cities in Alabama, though, it's more liberal."

He remembers some of the absurdity that came with the town's conservative nature. "Up until two or three years ago, you couldn't buy alcohol on a Sunday. It was funny growing up seeing people in line at two a.m. Saturday night, lined up to the back of the store—to get their beer, wine, et cetera—to make it through twenty-four hours."

That said, within a conservative environment, he found the avenues for a more progressive upbringing. Desmond went to Central—"the major high school in the area. It was pretty evenly mixed, as far as black and white goes. It was closest to the University of Alabama, and it was more diverse than if you went further out."

Furthermore, there were "pockets of people who are extremely liberal. I grew up as a member of the arts community. Lots of the arts community was vocally liberal, and the people who are out who are still living in Tuscaloosa tend to be part of that group. Also, a lot of the university professors, people of that nature, tend to be more vocally, outwardly liberal. I found myself becoming a part of that group—I always had sort of a home to fall back on. I always had a group of like-minded people around. That was a really, really sort of cool thing."

It wasn't just that Alabama was conservative that made it difficult for Desmond—it was also the small-town culture that made it tough when he didn't quite feel he fit in. "It's the sort of place where everybody knows everybody else. People don't tend to move away. If they do, it's not more than a state away. I wouldn't call it insular. People are just a little more comfortable being where they are, not, sort of, you know, going outward."

In that small-town environment, Desmond—whose friends now know him as a gigantic personality of good humor, vibrant warmth, and unbridled expressiveness—"tried to blend into the background. Back then, I was not one to go out on a limb. I was friendly and social, but I did not want to draw attention to myself. I acted in as straight a way as possible."

That included dating women, which he did right up until 1997—"right before I came out. I told her," he recounts, referring to the woman he was dating at the time, "and I don't know that she knew before then. But I sort of needed to get through what I needed to get through."

Desmond came out around the same time he graduated from high school, and then attended community college in Tuscaloosa briefly. Despite feeling he needed to get out, he also knew that there was safety in the town that was his only home. "I had received scholarship offers from a couple schools but didn't know if it was going to be enough. Financially, I didn't know what I was going to do. It was a time of turmoil. And I had lots of friends and friends' parents who were supportive. I knew if I was around, I'd be looked after."

Soon, though, he headed off to the University of Montevallo, where he found the opportunity to step away from the small-town neighbors who knew his whole life story—and for the first time was in an environment that was truly different and accepting. "Living on campus is the most liberal place you could imagine. Then you cross Main Street, and it's the most conservative place you could imagine. Off campus, you don't have anyone that is voting Democratic or any sort of liberal lean. . . . But at the school itself, you were pretty much being surrounded by some of the most liberal people in the state. You definitely had some ridiculously conservative people. But mostly, it was like a little oasis in the middle of Redneckville."

After college, Desmond went to Orlando for a year. And then

to New York, where it had been his dream to move for years. "I always knew Tuscaloosa was not the place for me. I remember in ninth grade or eighth grade, we had taken a trip to New York with some theater group. I came back, and in my history class, we were having some pro-Alabama conversation, and someone said, 'Why would anyone want to leave?' I remember being vehemently upset. 'I'm going to get the hell out of here!'. . . not saying 'hell,' of course."

He came to New York to pursue a life in theater and the arts. "Since the first time I came, I always loved it. And being an actor, it's the place you want to come." As he expected, life in New York turned many of the assumptions of Tuscaloosa culture on their head—not always in a good way, however.

For example, while he was finally in a place where it wasn't unusual to be out about his sexual orientation, "even being a gay man in New York is not necessarily the rosiest thing you can think of. I distinctly remember my first week, first couple of weeks, in New York, and I heard about a really, really bad gay bashing on West Fourth Street. A man was beaten badly. Welcome to New York."

As it turned out, Desmond recalls, "four years later, maybe five, I started dating this guy. It turns out he was the guy who was beaten up. It meant I really learned what he had gone through. He was very much affected by it, and in a way it made him double down and want to be more PDA-heavy than he probably was before," he says, referring to public displays of affection. "Strolling around Times Square, he wanted to hold hands. I've never been a big PDA person, but I think, 'OK, fine.' And people would heckle us and say all sorts of things. I was, like, 'Really? Here?' "

Despite instances like those, Desmond has found life to be very welcoming and a group of friends as rich and supportive as any he could imagine. "I have found community with my friends. A great group of friends, from all over the place, many of them in the arts." One part of Desmond's upbringing does stand out as distinct in this New York scene. "We are very similar in many ways, except for religion. I am one of the few Christians—though I can't say that I'm active. Some friends don't get it. But it's never been an issue. I'm not trying to beat anyone over the head, and nobody is trying to dissuade me. Everyone really respects what other people think. We'll have discussions, 'Why do you feel this way?'—and it's always respectful."

The ability to talk so openly about differences, especially potentially sensitive ones, is something he appreciates about New York. "I never got that in Tuscaloosa, and I can't imagine it—if people disagree on religious things, they tend to clam up about it." Here in New York, "I found it really, really cool to have those differences—and to find out why people believe what they believe."

That said, while Desmond considers himself Christian, belonging to a church—even an inclusive, progressive New York congregation—isn't part of his life on a regular basis. "I was away for so long, it's hard to ease my way back in. I went to Metropolitan Community Church in Manhattan a few times. For me, it seemed like it was more about being gay than being Christian. I thought, 'That's not necessarily what I'm here for.' I was glad people who are looking for more of a social outlet have that, but it wasn't necessarily what I was looking for. Realistically, I was looking more for the religious aspect than the social."

He's also visited Marble Collegiate a few times. "I heard that they had a good, accepting policy. They always have all sorts of people from all sorts of walks of life. I saw someone I knew as a drag queen a few rows in front of me at Easter. It's always been a positive place, but never stuck. I didn't go enough to feel a part of the community. I keep saying I'm going to go back . . . but it's fallen out of my system. I feel guilty for not going, but not guilty enough."

Desmond always imagined New York would be more accepting

than Alabama of him as a gay man. What he hadn't expected was that being a black man would come with its own hazards in this diverse metropolis. "I remember my first year in the city, I was on Forty-Second, in front of Ollie's. Someone screamed something horribly offensive"—a racial slur. " 'Are you talking to me? Really? What?' It was the last thing I ever would have expected. I didn't deal with that sort of thing growing up in Alabama."

"People are far more vocal in the South if they want to heckle based on sexual orientation than on race," he expounds. "If they are going to be prejudiced, they'll keep their racial prejudices to themselves. But they can get away with saying things to gays and lesbians in public without anyone having any issues. Even in high school, no one ever said anything to anyone else, no racial slurs. This was a high school my mother was one of the first kids to desegregate a generation before. Twenty years later, people may have had opinions, but they never said them. That's the southern polite way. They had to say them behind your back."

Thinking back to growing up, he had trouble recalling outwardly racist comments in Tuscaloosa. "Personally in my own experience, in my entire time living in Alabama, there was only one moment of a racial thing said—and I actually didn't hear it. Friends heard it. Since I've been here, I hear things quite frequently. I chalk it up to not really being about black and white. It's all sorts of people saying things about different people. We have so many different people in one place, and everyone far more vocal than in other places."

Desmond returns to Alabama three or four times a year. He still has family members and plenty of friends there. He has friends who had moved to New York then moved back to Alabama—because, he acknowledges, New York can be hard and "it's easier for them there for different reasons."

He described something hometown folks used to say about those who moved away, then came back to visit. "Friends used to say jokingly—or not necessarily joking—they'd have to sequester them for a while to 'de-Yankee-fy' them. I do sort of get that, after many, many years," he admits. "Now I'm far more likely to say exactly what's on my mind, say something is crap. In Alabama, you're more likely to nod and smile, gloss over."

Desmond recalls those first few years he'd come back. "I found myself in lots of political and social arguments when I was younger. I remember being at a comedy show four or five years ago in Tuscaloosa when I came home for Christmas, and the comedian making gay jokes, going on and on and on. He didn't say anything I found particularly offensive. I tend to think for the sake of comedy, if it's funny, it's funny. I was more offended that he wasn't necessarily that funny," he says deadpan. "He was going on about whatever he was saying—and he paused—'I have to be politically correct, I don't have any gay people here, do I?' So I raised my hand. Everyone looked at me. It destroyed him a little. 'I didn't mean to offend,' he said. He started asking me all of these questions, from the stage. Personally, I had no qualms, and my cousin thought it was funny. But her husband—if he could blink and make himself go anywhere, he would have. For me, though, I was ready. 'Let's go. If you want to play, let's play.' "

Desmond laughs at the memory of his younger self. "That's not how I would react today. I would try to consider who I'm with a little bit more."

He also adds that he's heard off-color comments from comedians in New York as well. In general, though, in New York or Alabama, he doesn't get offended. "Being from a performance background, I take everything with a grain of salt. What's their intention behind the joke? Is it trying to take something apart, or is it just a cheap joke? I try to analyze it before I make a judgment. Sometimes it's not meant to be offensive; it's meant to shock. Sometimes, it's just because the person is a jackass. So it's easier to say, 'All right, I'm done with you.' Then, typically my judgment is with my wallet, rather than anything else."

More recently, Desmond has had a companion on his trips home: his fiancé, Carl. Those visits showed Desmond some of the things he doesn't miss about home: "social things—I don't necessarily have to deal with here. For instance, if I'm at the grocery store, and Carl and I are sort of touching each other, not inappropriately, I don't really think about it here. There, I'm guarded and cautious. Also, just sort of the rhetoric you hear on the television—you get on the plane at JFK and LaGuardia, everyone is watching CNN, you get off the plane in Birmingham, everyone is watching Fox News. It's distinct." With a flourish, he adds, "And we're back!"

When Desmond brought Carl home, "the family on my grandmother's side was incredibly interested in meeting him. They wanted to find out what's going on with him and us. They went out of their way to be supportive."

That wasn't the only reaction, though. "My very, very conservative side of the family have not met him. I don't really have any dealings with them. There are no ill feelings—but my grandfather's side is more conservative than my grandmother's side." With some of those family members, Desmond has never even discussed being gay. "There's no moment when I have had to come out. They are my friends on Facebook; they've never made a comment. I'm not living life in the shadows. I'll post, 'Hey, if anyone wants to hang out while I'm home, let me know'—and they don't."

Now that Desmond and Carl are engaged, sooner or later that side of the family will likely have to admit that he's gay. Or maybe they won't. "I'm not really that close to any of them. I'd have no problems inviting them to the wedding, but I can't control how they would react to it. When Carl and I announced our engagement on Facebook, I used it as a litmus test. Looking back several months later, I don't think anyone on my grandfather's side commented at all—whereas several members of my grandmother's side commented."

Over the years, Desmond has also become more distant from his more conservative friends. He admits he has no conservative friends in New York, though some "conservative associates." As for his childhood friends with more right-leaning views, "I honestly don't spend as much time around them. The older I get, the more prone I am to say, 'You know what, we've grown apart.' It's not as though I don't love the person, or that we don't respect each other. But where they are in their lives, where they are going with their future, is different than me. We both believe in family, that sort of thing. And their view is a lot different than mine. I still have people who consider me a friend but don't believe I have the right to marry. It baffles my mind—how do you consider yourself to be my friend?! I don't wipe them out of my life, but I don't seek them out. It's a delicate balance."

As much as Desmond has found what he was looking for in New York, it's far from perfect. And the big city could learn a few things from where he grew up. "I miss the social interaction you have with people randomly. I'm a person who can talk to a brick wall. But in New York, most people you encounter who aren't already your friends don't want to interact socially. In the South, people make an effort to make sure people don't sit alone—something I find myself doing."

He would rather not choose one path or the other but take the best of both worlds. "I enjoy both—there are times I enjoy thoroughly wandering around without having to say, 'How are you? How's your mom? How's your uncle?' That's what I got growing up—everywhere I went, someone knew my mother, knew my grandmother. It can be a little annoying." Desmond pauses. "At the same time, now, you can go the entire day if you're not going to work or meeting friends and not have a conversation with anyone other than 'Yes, I'd like fries with that.' That's the difference. You can totally have the wonderful experience of anonymity. You can have the crappy experience."

Desmond hasn't tossed away all his old habits. He's just adapted them to his new life. "I try, as the old saying goes, to live the change you want to be. I actively try to do that. Whenever I visit Alabama, I try to let as many people know as possible, 'We're not all godless heathens sacrificing babies.' People who are New Yorkers, New Jerseyans—we're just like everybody else, we have families that we love, some of us have religious affiliations that we're true to, we're not vehemently opposed, for the most part, to the way things are in other parts of the country. You live your life and do your things as you want to do them. We will too. It's not either/or; it can be both."

The sword cuts both ways. "It's pretty much the same thing I bring to New York. Having lived in the South for twenty years, I know intimately there are a lot of people who are progressive thinkers, trying to bridge the gap between the way things were and the way things could be—it's not an absolute; nothing is absolute—there are people who are the most awful and offensive you can imagine, and people actively working from where they are, on a daily basis, to make their lives better and other people's lives better on any day."

As Desmond sums it up, bringing a little New York to Alabama, or Alabama to New York, is "the same thing coming from two different mind-sets."

That said, there's one way New York can't compete. "The food. I very much miss the food."

But it's not enough to lure him back. "I remember the day: October 26, 2004. It's now my tenth anniversary" since moving here, he boasts. Someone once told him that it took a decade to become a New Yorker. "So I'm a true New Yorker now. I survived for ten years . . . even though I now live in New Jersey," where they moved from Queens for Carl's new job. Even that may be a trait of a "true New Yorker."

"Honestly, I've felt at home," Desmond concludes. "I never thought I should be anywhere else."

Kathleen Thompson

GRAPEVINE, TEXAS

I have friends who live in Texas, but they are from other states. . . . I'll hear them critiquing national progressives on a number of issues. When you do that, I can always tell you're not from Texas. You come from a state where you don't know how good you have it.

Kathleen Thompson's two boys attend Vacation Bible School during the summer, a mixture of summer camp activities and Bible lessons. As Kathleen describes it, she speaks in an amused tone that suggests she has had to explain this program to northeasterners before. "In the Deep South, we have Vacation Bible School. All the churches have banners up. All the different denominations."

She picks them up each afternoon. One day was a special occasion. It was the anniversary of the filibuster by state senator Wendy Davis, a representative who held the floor of the Texas senate long enough to stall a severe, right-wing antichoice bill.

Davis's actions—now known simply as "the Filibuster" through-out Texas—caught the imagination of progressives around the country, fired up Texas Democrats, and catapulted Davis into political stardom as well as the gubernatorial race.

To mark the anniversary, Kathleen was wearing a burnt orange T-shirt—the color of the University of Texas, and a de facto hue of Texas pride—that bore a message of support for "Wendy," as the politician is universally known. "I wore it to work and to errands—and then to pick up the boys at Vacation Bible School. One woman who was picking up her kids said, 'We love Wendy too!' I was surprised."

Kathleen—a local organizer, civic activist, and loyal Democrat—is used to her shirts sparking reaction. It's just that the comments are usually negative. That exchange was proof that Texas is changing.

Kathleen recalls the 2014 gubernatorial race. "A lot of people said Wendy couldn't win, that it was too soon" for Texas to elect a Democratic governor. "But we had people calling the office every day. People would stop me. They'd say, 'We really like your shirt—we like Wendy too—we're going to vote your way in November.' They wouldn't have said that a year before."

Texas may seem like a deep-red state around the country—but Texans know that it's more mixed. It has a rich Democratic history, a large minority population, and increasing energy among progressives who are tapping into the sense felt across Texas that it's time to go in a new direction.

"Things are changing here," Kathleen says hopefully. "You can only bully people and beat up on people and get away with it for so long." She recounts how it felt when Davis entered the national spotlight. "It felt like Texas's time has come. What happened with the filibuster—Wendy performed this amazing multihour filibuster—so many people were there. People who thought that Republicans had overreached in this very bullying way. People just started screaming in the gallery. They couldn't take any more. It was a visceral response."

That incident sparked new energy among many Texans who were as mad as hell—and kicked off what Kathleen sees as a potential political transformation in her state. "Our [Democratic] state party had four employees. People started sending checks. By Election Day [2014], we were up to seventy. People were working around the state, canvassing around the state, working weekends, working weeknights. There were a lot of people who wouldn't call themselves activists, but they saw Republicans embracing junk science and started saying we're done with this party. Moderate Republicans got pushed out in any case. There's a resurgence of the Tea Party. It may not be doing so well nationally, but it's thriving in the Texas Republican Party. And that's going to drive people to our side all the more."

Kathleen's enthusiasm is palpable, sincere, and infectious—and you can imagine those qualities at play in her own campaigns. Several years ago, she ran for city council in Grapevine, a conservative town in the string of cities in between Dallas and Fort Worth. It was a consuming and frustrating race.

"It's a nonpartisan election that was made partisan," she recalls. Kathleen was not running as a Democratic operative. Her campaign was based on a series of local issues: a matter of sidewalk safety near the school, keeping the library open more hours. "We have money—we have the lake, the outlet mall, the airport, destination hotels," she argues. "We can make this town better for its residents."

However, "being a Democrat is enough to sink a candidate in Grapevine. It's not as bad as maybe Wyoming, which is eighty–twenty" in its Republican/Democrat breakdown. "It's closer to sixty–forty. . . . That was the way they could come after me.

Make it highly partisan. I got criticized by the local Tea Party and by the mainstream Republicans for voting Democratic in past elections. It was nonsense."

Her run attracted some big detractors. "The chair of the Tarrant County Republican Party came after me—on social media and on their website. It's a huge county. And the chair of the county and the local Tea Party and the local Republican precinct chair got into a frenzy because I vote Democratic. It's unfortunate and doesn't make any sense," she laments. "What I've done in Grapevine is totally nonpartisan. It has nothing to do with which box I check."

Kathleen didn't win the race but takes some comfort in knowing the issues she raised caught enough attention to live beyond the campaign. "I ran on and am still working on the sidewalk for the school—it was put in after the campaign. I campaigned on getting public records online. Neighboring cities publish their city council meeting minutes and agenda. In Grapevine, I'd have to submit state open records requests twice a month. Those records are now online," she says, pleased.

"I waged a campaign to tape and archive city council meetings. We were way behind neighboring cities with smaller budgets and smaller populations. So a group of us started going to city council meetings, videotaping them, putting the videos online, and talking to the local media about it—and about why a citizens group had to do this. A month ago, they started taping meetings."

In these postelection efforts, she found surprising partners. "The cycle for a city council race lasts a few months. Some people got worked up, calling me too partisan. Since then, some of these same people have been my biggest allies." Working with conservatives, she was able to push a nonpartisan local agenda.

Local residents on both sides of the aisle had reason to be behind these reforms and fed up with the incumbents. "Everything

I wanted to do that would cost money would also save money. Our city council members pay themselves outside the spirit and letter of the city charter." After a pause she adds as a matter of fact: "It's totally corrupt."

The local work is rewarding in a different way than state and national work. "After my family and my job obligations are taken care of, I try to split time between partisan and nonpartisan work," Kathleen explains. "A lot of people pay attention to the partisan world. Not enough pay any attention to the nonpartisan. They don't know names of school board members, their city council members. I know; I pay attention—and I would love it if more progressives would pay attention to what's happening on Main Street. Not every city council meets on Main Street, but ours does. What they do has more impact on our lives—on our kids, on our husbands—than what happens in Washington, D.C."

To be able to work with conservative allies, Kathleen had to let go of some of the frustration from her own race. But as she looked at her hometown, it wasn't that hard. "So much of the partisan rhetoric is really damaging when it comes down to neighbor to neighbor. There is always going to be more common ground if you focus on issues close to you, and it's better for everybody. We started a nonpartisan PAC to do all the things I ran on, and they are getting done. This is something that is nonpartisan, that people of all ages and ideologies have gotten behind. Too bad it took the campaign to get to where we are. We're going to live here for the foreseeable future with these kids. We want it to be the best community to raise them in."

Kathleen, white and in her thirties, and her husband, Jeremy, have lived in Grapevine for eleven years. She grew up one town over in Colleyville, a couple of miles from where she now lives. "My father's father has long Grapevine roots. My great-grandfather, great-great-grandfather, great-aunts and uncles, they are in the Grapevine Cemetery." She attended high school in Grapevine because Colleyville didn't have its own. "Basically I live where I grew up. It wasn't the master plan," she admits.

Her parents are Republicans, as are her grandparents. "They're not today's Republicans," she objects. "Know what I mean? Things are so different now. The mainstream Republican Party is gone."

Despite being Republican, her parents helped shape Kathleen's Democratic views. "My parents always talked about politics. I came from a Christian evangelical household that told me, 'I am my brother's keeper,' to look after people whether I know them or not, whether they are my neighbor or not. The party that I thought did that was the Democratic Party." She held leadership roles in her high school Young Democrats and ecology club and has been an organizer ever since.

And while they may disagree with the party she supports, her family didn't question whether she would make a respectable public servant. "My family was supportive because they knew that what I wanted to do, the goals I had for Grapevine were the right things for Grapevine."

Kathleen is active in her local religious community. Her family belongs to a Methodist congregation. "The Methodist Church is more progressive than some other offerings here in the South," she says, careful to note the difference between progressive values and progressive politics. "Its social doctrine is really more progressive than one might think. I wouldn't say it's a Democratic church by any means, or a liberal church. Lots of Republicans slam the Methodist Church for being leftist and liberal. Actually, we don't talk about politics at church. When we do, we talk about policies more than partisanship."

The values of her church reinforce her own progressive identity. "Taking care of our neighbors is a value. Not just sending people to foreign countries to help, but what we're doing in our

communities now to make sure people are taken care of here."
One example: their church community is active in supporting
programs that provide weekend and summer meals to children
who receive free or reduced lunches at school.

Kathleen points to the tension at the border with Mexico—
Texas's large, controversial border—as another area where you
can demonstrate how you take care of others. She notes that during the 2014 crisis of unaccompanied Central American children
gathering at the border, some in Texas were shouting at the children. Yet there were others—including elected leaders from Dallas County and other parts of Texas—who were making sure the
kids got food and shelter. "To me, that's why I'm a Democrat," she
announces with pride.

Of course, she is never far from knowing how many of her
neighbors don't agree with her. When she was running, compar-
ing her to President Obama was a common attack. "People would
say I brought Obama money to Grapevine. Oh my God! I wish
I had Obama money! On my campaign site, I blogged about what
I was doing while campaigning. Then someone would say 'You're
just like Obama, so many empty promises.' I had to say, 'I'm not
Obama, I am not running for president, why do people keep
bringing this up?' "

In 2012, she and a friend on her block both put up yard signs
for President Obama. "She and I were the only Obama signs in the
neighborhood. After we put up one yard sign each, our signs were
stolen. Then all these Romney signs went up. We each put up
another sign, and they were stolen again. I've lived in Grapevine
for years. I've had signs in our yard; they were never stolen before."

Kathleen doesn't know the politics of all her neighbors, but she
does know that there were many Romney signs throughout the
neighborhood.

For all that, she loves her town and it's a good place to raise her
boys. So far, she finds it to be a well-performing school system,

though she knows that Texas, as a whole, gets a bad rap because of the right-wing influence on its schools. "I know people running for the state board of education. Some of the worst of what has happened is over," she says with relief. "We're electing people who believe in science, who know that it's important to teach what happened in history. If my kids were older and were being taught creationism, or abstinence-only education, I would be angry. I haven't dealt with it yet."

Her fellow Democratic friend down the street has. "They're Jewish. Her eldest of two little girls has come home multiple times crying because someone at school has said something about Judaism and Christianity." Kathleen's own children have never heard such comments, "but I know it happens. It's totally appalling. You definitely get a sense this is a conservative town. You get that sense: don't be different."

This isn't just a feature of Grapevine. "In Keller, two communities over, this guy I know ran for school board. It's supposed to be nonpartisan. This guy is a Democrat. The same people who came after me went after him. My state representative and four other Tea Party state representatives came after him hard. They came out for his opponent. . . . She won because the Tea Party campaigned for her." Once she was elected, Kathleen continues, this new school board member made national news by complaining of a newly elected official in another town—"What a shame that South Lake now has a Muslim on city council"—and claiming that the Muslim woman didn't count as a representative because of her religion. The worst part, Kathleen adds, is that this Tea Partier is probably "saying what a lot of people think but know better than to yell in all caps on social media."

Texas is its own phenomenon, contends Kathleen. "We're close enough to Louisiana, Mississippi, Alabama, to be part of the South. But if you were in Louisiana or Mississippi, you'd see Confederate flags. That's not considered normal around here."

Yet Texas's conservative influence looms large in the country—from the impact of Texas's school board on the content of textbooks used across America to the current crop of presidential aspirants . . . and, of course, the last Texan to occupy the White House. With all the talk of today's Republicans becoming more extreme due to the Tea Party's sway, Kathleen doesn't forget that the Bush governorship and presidency were just as conservative.

"A lot of people are and were embarrassed by President Bush. When President Bush was still in office, we had pretty thriving local activist groups. While I wouldn't say any Republicans would violate Reagan's eleventh commandment," referring to President Reagan's famous caution that Republicans should not speak poorly of fellow Republicans, "I think some were embarrassed. I wouldn't say Bush was any better than Perry or Abbott. Karl Rove is the embodiment of dirty politics. Tom DeLay, with his redistricting plan, really set the stage for what we have now, ridiculous districts. They tried to redistrict Senator Davis out, because they had done it before. She took them to court, fought it all the way up—and won."

Will Texas continue to boast a favorite son in the upcoming presidential campaign? In the summer of 2014, there were several Texans weighing their options. "I hear clamoring for Ted Cruz in north Texas, but not here in Grapevine—except for our local Tea Party. I don't know who Rick Perry thinks he's kidding with another presidential run."

But Kathleen's real goal is to encourage people to give their attention to something other than national politics. "On the Democratic and progressive side, there are people who get fired up on the national ticket," she notes. "I will try to engage them in what's happening in local politics. No matter where they are on that spectrum, that's who I try to target."

She also thinks that her fellow liberals around the country should calm down a little about our current president. "I have friends who live in Texas, but they are from other states and may go back to other states. I'll hear them critiquing national progressives on a number of issues. When you do that, I can always tell you're not from Texas. You come from a state where you don't know how good you have it. You have politicians who believe in science, care about water quality, care about air quality, care about not causing earthquakes as is happening here through fracking.

"I have a friend from New York who complains about Obama over little issues. I say to him, you're from New York. You've had it so good, you don't know how lucky you are. I have gay friends who say Obama hasn't done enough. I say look at all he's done. Because of his leadership, we've come as far as we have. People outside Texas complain things aren't as good as they could be" in terms of their politicians, and the fight for progressive values in their states. "We don't even have the basics here."

Maybe change is coming to Texas, but not yet—Wendy Davis wasn't elected governor. Maybe next cycle, or maybe in a decade. Either way, Kathleen won't wait. She'll help it come fast, and will speak up in the meantime. "I know that comments will come," she says, of times when she voices her progressive views. "I've had Wendy Davis's state senate bumper sticker on my car. Every now and then a man in a big truck would flip me off on the highway. People will say disparaging comments around town if I wear a shirt they don't like. I am who I am. I'm not going to be silenced by a bully. I'm not going to be afraid."

Greg Leding

FAYETTEVILLE, ARKANSAS

It was a blue state, but not a liberal one.

Greg Leding has chosen to spend much of his time surrounded by conservatives. Although his home during and since college has been Fayetteville—one of the liberal oases in Arkansas—he passes many days in Little Rock. While that city itself is more cosmopolitan than much of Arkansas, where Greg hangs out leans far to the right: the Arkansas State Legislature.

"Most of our Democrats would not be recognized as Democrats in California," says Greg. On reproductive rights, LGBTQ equality, and the social issues that animate much of the party's base, Greg's fellow Arkansans—including the significant number of Democrats who continue to serve in the state legislature—are pretty conservative. Arkansas had a long Democratic legacy, yet as Greg cautions, "It was a blue state, but not a liberal one."

Arkansas is one of the many states where Democratic fortunes have waned, despite a long history of positive party affiliation. The white working-class Arkansas Democrats of past decades have increasingly moved into the Republican Party. In many cases, they are still registered Democratic but don't feel aligned with the national party—and the Democrats that do get elected land far to the right of the gentleman from Fayetteville.

In his midthirties, charming and unassuming, polite and intelligent, Greg doesn't have the good-old-boy pedigree you might imagine of someone who rises through the ranks of southern party politics. Growing up in the nearby conservative area of Springdale, it certainly wasn't his plan. He took almost no interest in politics during high school, and relatively little in college. "I thought it was cool the president was from our state but didn't have much more interest," he admits.

In a story one hears again and again, the 2000 election and the presidency of George W. Bush sparked Greg's political awakening. "I was a political late bloomer. The year 2000 was really the first time I was paying attention. I wasn't happy with how the election shook out, though it wasn't a strong feeling. Then President Bush's first term unfolded, and by 2004, I knew where I stood on the political spectrum."

He became engaged during that election cycle and remained active afterward. Among other pursuits, he started a chapter of Drinking Liberally—the national network of political social clubs—in Fayetteville. He was working as a graphic designer and this weekly gathering felt like an easy way to stay involved with his progressive community between elections. What he didn't count on was that it would actually draw him deeper into the political life.

In 2010, he was elected to the Arkansas State Legislature. Fayetteville is one of the few areas where the Democrat is still the likely victor in the general election, so his tougher battle was in the primary. It was an open-seat election, where proving one's progressive bona fides was key to clinching the support of the liberal electorate. Greg was elected by proving himself true left—and immediately began serving in a body that was headed due right.

So for part of the year, each week Greg leaves a town where, as he describes it, "If you talk politics at work or at a bar, it's a safe bet that people around you are Democrats and that their politics are similar to yours." And he heads to an office where he is in the minority flank of the minority party.

This conservative dominance of Arkansas politics spiked the year Greg was elected. It was 2010, just as the Tea Party brand of conservatism was sweeping the nation. It was going to be hard enough for Democrats to beat back some of the harshest Republican proposals. It was even more far-fetched for a lefty from Fayetteville to promote any liberal agenda of his own.

From the start, Greg had a tough choice. "I had to find the balance between being effective as a legislator and representing the views of my district," many of which were so liberal they would never get passed. For the sake of getting things done and effectively governing, Greg found himself forging compromises in ways his constituents didn't want. "On a daily basis." He sighs.

This challenge was clear as soon as he took office. His predecessor had established her reputation as being someone conservatives couldn't work with. Her view was that a conservative body needed someone championing liberal views—and that was her mandate. She aggressively pursued ratification of the Equal Rights Amendment, an issue that was so little known in Arkansas by the time she took it up that she found herself educating her fellow Democrats on it. The first time she proposed it, she faced a fierce backlash, but that didn't stop her from introducing the bill annually. She had endorsed Greg's candidacy, and many of her supporters expected him to pick up the torch.

"I intended to," he admits. "Then it was a really bad year for Democrats. If she couldn't get it done with the majority we had at the time, I wasn't going to get it done with even fewer

Democrats. I had to spend the first term establishing my own reputation. When it came out that I wasn't going to file the ERA in my first term, it was as though I had joined the Republican Party." His own constituents, including enthusiastic supporters of his campaign, were "miffed."

Greg set out to make his mark. If it couldn't be by passing the most liberal legislation, he decided to find another way. As he explains it, "When it comes to serving in a conservative house and you want to be effective, there is a certain amount of surrender. David Pryor [a former governor, senator, and congressman from Arkansas and father of then senator Mark Pryor] said he wished people would stop looking down on the word 'compromise.' It used to mean you were someone people can work with. Now it's negative."

Greg has given this question of compromise a lot of attention. "Do I want to be effective and compromise? Former congressman Robert Wexler wrote an autobiography called *Fire-Breathing Liberal*. He was a rhetorical warrior. He knew his reputation was going to prohibit him from getting legislation passed, so instead he saw his role as giving voice to important issues—being the tip of the spear on issues that gave room for more moderate, effective Democrats. I decided I was going to be as effective as I could be. I wanted to do what I could for my state and my district. It's been a learning experience ever since—learning how to represent the views of a liberal district while being effective in the house chamber."

Greg is proud of what he did accomplish. In addition to helping repel right-wing legislation, he worked with Republicans to pass "the private option," the route Arkansas took to expanding Medicaid after the passage of Obamacare. Greg speaks precisely and comfortably as he dives into the nuance of the legislation. "The Court said to leave Medicaid expansion to the states, and many states turned away. We knew it would be hard in Arkansas.

We lost the majority, so many options were off the table. Fortunately, our governor refused to take no for an answer." The governor found Republican leadership that would help achieve this goal and agreed to do it their way. The state took federal Medicaid dollars and spent them through private exchanges so the rolls of private insurers, not the state's public rolls, expanded.

"It's not the path we would have gone had we enough votes," Greg argues, "but in a state with a Republican-controlled legislature, it was the only chance to expand health care, which is in line with our liberal priorities. It was a conservative approach to a Democratic goal." And ultimately a Republican bill that Democrats rallied around.

Another achievement Greg points to is purely political. After the 2012 election banished Democrats into the minority, he and other Democrats actively found a more reasonable Republican they believed they could work with. They told him that if he could bring one other Republican along, they would whip the forty-nine Democratic members to elect him house speaker. In the end, this representative brought five fellow Republicans, who, along with the Democratic caucus, handed him the speaker's gavel. "We helped elect a Republican speaker as a matter of survival," Greg declares, with a hint of pride. It was that speaker who worked with the governor and Democrats on the Medicaid expansion.

In addition to these achievements inside the chamber, he has also accomplished something outside the chamber: a functional, even amicable, relationship with colleagues who are far more conservative than he is.

Greg counts two fellow legislators among his best friends. They are both Democrats but represent very different constituencies than he does. They are from far more rural, conservative areas, which doesn't hinder their friendships. He also has good relationships across the aisle.

Overall, there's a civility among his colleagues. "Generally, you don't see D.C.-style nastiness at the statehouse." There are occasions when Greg is reminded that he's working side by side with people who embrace a diametrically opposed perspective to his own. "Every now and then a Tea Partier will say something offensive or will call to impeach the president," Greg says. He recalls that during the Boston manhunt for the marathon bombers, one house member tweeted, "I wonder how many Boston liberals are cowering in their basements, wishing they had an AR-15."

"It was just incredibly insensitive," Greg observes in his matter-of-fact tone. It's his even temper, in part, that has earned him the respect of other legislators. His fellow Democrats, though more conservative, elected him minority leader. And he believes that the Republicans, with a few exceptions, know he is someone they can disagree with without his becoming a villain to them.

Ironically, Greg can count more conservatives with whom he has friendly relationships in the legislature than in his everyday life back in Fayetteville. Growing up, his high school friends were more conservative, even though he hadn't given it much thought at the time. Through college, he fell in with friends who turned out to be more liberal. By the time he graduated, most of the people he counted as his closest friends were Democrats.

Over time, he just saw his conservative friends less, often for reasons that had nothing to do with politics. He has had one close friend from home for whom politics has been a distancing factor. "In the last year or two, it's become more difficult. He doesn't accept that we just think differently. He can't help but get angry." Greg sounds a little wistful as he reflects upon this friendship that has slipped further away. "Conversation becomes all but impossible."

He has kept one good friend who is a moderate Republican. "We never raise our tempers . . . but then, I've known this guy since the first grade. He's my longest friend. He is who he is. I am who I am. While we disagree with each other, we both approach the bigger things in life with common sense."

And daily life back home does involve some political navigation. He and his wife, Emily, moved from the heart of Fayetteville to a neighborhood that he actually lost in the 2012 election. As soon as they moved, he noticed he had a neighbor with a Romney bumper sticker on his SUV. "It might take a little longer to get to know some neighbors," he jokes.

For the most part, though, it's easy being liberal in Fayetteville. "Our general reputation, fair or unfair, is that Fayetteville is a hippie enclave," Greg explains. "We're the tree-hugging environmentalists who love gay marriage." He laughs—because, more or less, it's true. "Recently it was announced that Fayetteville is going to get the state's second Whole Foods. Lots of people were very excited, my wife and I included. That made us the stereotype."

Greg knows that his home life makes him and Emily outliers among Arkansans. He notes that you don't have to travel far to see the occasional Confederate flag, and that across the state there will be anti-Obama bumper stickers that range from mildly offensive to shocking. "Some of them are nothing worse than we had when Bush was president," Greg describes in his characteristic evenhandedness. "Others you can't believe people would have on their vehicles."

Yet Greg is also quick to remind friends from other states that there is a progressive history in his state—more so than most people, including Arkansans, tend to think. He points to Senators Pryor and Bumpers as progressive for their time, and Senator Fulbright, despite a few glaring faults, as he puts it. "There is a progressive streak that people don't realize," and it could return.

The distance between Springdale—the conservative town where Greg grew up, and where his parents still live—and Fayetteville is only ten miles, a twenty-minute drive along U.S.

Route 71. But the divide between Greg's childhood home and the city he's lived in since college is as wide as the political spectrum. Even for conservative northwest Arkansas, explains Greg, "Springdale is pretty puke red."

He's learned more about his parents' politics since he took office. His father is a registered Republican, though Greg is quick to note he would not classify him as far right. For most of Greg's life, his mom didn't speak up, but now he realizes that while she and his father are aligned on a number of social issues, she is closer to Greg politically.

"With Dad, I keep conversations about politics short," Greg recounts. "Mom wants us to keep them short. We spar a little bit, but it doesn't get disrespectful."

Greg's parents are Catholic and as a result there are a number of issues they just don't agree on. Greg's father has a regular Wednesday breakfast group with other members of the church, but when Greg stops by, none of their friends lecture or criticize him. "They respect the fact that I represent a liberal area, and they think I have a good head on my shoulders."

Most important, even if they don't see eye to eye on politics, his parents admire him for what he has achieved. "My father is proud to introduce me to people. He tells them that I was the house minority leader . . . then he also makes a point of saying what party I am."

Chris Sonne

YANKTON, SOUTH DAKOTA

It turns into a tribal thing. When you grow up in a small town, that's your identity; that's what you are. If you suddenly switched sides and became a fan of the rival school—well, that wouldn't happen. The same with party brands.

Chris, a forty-five-year-old technical writer, is a lifelong South Dakotan. He was born in a small town and lived on a farm— "a hobby farm," he explains. Both his parents were teachers. He comes from Scandinavian stock, a heritage he mentions periodically, sometimes as a point of pride, sometimes simply as a matter of fact. Other than a few years scattered among Washington State, Iowa, and Nebraska—around his and his wife's college and graduate studies—his home state has remained his home.

He knows that most Americans don't see South Dakota quite the way he does. "Visitors come here, they want to ride a horse, see buffalo, stereotypical cowboy stuff." He laughs, noting that there aren't as many cowboys left as there used to be. He doesn't mind those expectations—after all, beyond Mount Rushmore and the Black Hills, there isn't much that his state is known for nationally, other than conservative politics.

South Dakota has had its fair share of right-wing ballot initiatives and a few notable Tea Party politicians who have made headlines. As Chris notes, though, it's not the whole story. It's also the state of Tom Daschle, Tim Johnson, and Stephanie Herseth, Democrats who have managed to be elected in statewide elections as recently as 2008.

"I'm more of a liberal than a Democrat, and I'm not afraid to say that," states Chris. His state may sometimes elect Democrats, but those politicians aren't as progressive as he'd like to see. "If all Democrats were like Bernie Sanders, Elizabeth Warren—and I know they're not the same, but like them—I would identify as a Democrat first," he explains, identifying two icons of American liberals. "But I was not a Stephanie Herseth Democrat, even though I voted for her," referring to the more centrist Democrat who recently represented South Dakota in the House of Representatives.

"I'm a liberal just like Jesus is a liberal," he jokes, then quickly attributes the quote to a favorite comedian and commentator, John Fugelsang, a performer who has amassed a niche national following with a show on the now defunct Current TV and frequent appearances on MSNBC.

Fugelsang, a onetime host of *America's Funniest Home Videos* who veered more deeply into political comedy and now hosts a left-leaning show on SiriusXM radio, often explains to his audience that Jesus—the brown-skinned Middle Eastern Jew born to an unmarried mother, who loved the poor, hated the banks, and had no opinion about gays—is the ultimate liberal. Chris lives in an area where many conservatives lay claim to Christian teachings, so he sounds relieved that someone with a national microphone echoes what he is thinking. He just wishes more of his fellow Yankton residents believed the same lessons he does.

Chris himself is Lutheran and active in his congregation. He serves on the board of deacons, which is responsible for making sure the worship space is prepared properly for special occasions, ushers are coordinated, and communion is set up. He served as president of the board ten years ago, a position he achieved through acclamation more than election. "They always need a warm body and nobody else wanted to do it."

He wouldn't call his church liberal or conservative. "Those labels don't apply. If I had to bet, I'd guess our pastors are both Democrats. But as a church, you shouldn't do politics. Ours doesn't do politics." He knows that it is more open and inclusive than some other congregations and is aware of other liberals who attend, but there are plenty of fellow parishioners whose politics he does not know at all. "Within these congregations, you're going to have really conservative people and really liberal people."

He pauses, thinking through the familiar faces he sees at service or stands near in the choir. "There are a lot of people at our church who I'm sure are Republican, who are very conservative. We would never talk politics with them; we wouldn't want a falling-out. There are conservatives, I'm sure, even in our choir—but then you'd be surprised. There's a local football coach—he's in the choir; he's a good guy—and it turns out he's a Democrat." Chris had known him for years but only recently learned his party loyalty when saw him at the South Dakota Democratic Convention. "I thought, 'I didn't know that!'" He chuckles to himself. "Who knew?"

Chris's church has the word "evangelical" in its name, but he is quick to note that it is "going for the old-school meaning of evangelical"—he wants to make sure to distinguish it from modern-day evangelicals who are plentiful in conservative politics, including in Yankton. And the conservative churches, Chris notes, are not as restrained in their political engagement as the Lutherans are.

In Yankton, "there are plenty of congregations that are more conservative. There is another Lutheran church, which broke off from the main church body—members didn't think it was conservative enough. The Baptists are more conservative. The Catholic priests, actually, are more liberal—but the bishop is more conservative." Chris pauses again, reflecting on the congregations that dot his city. Then, with his customary temperate tone, he adds about the more conservative churches, "Within them, who knows? There may be very good people who just feel like they have to line up with the conservatives."

There are other more liberal religious groups too. The local United Church of Christ is liberal—"they are known for the music; so are we," Chris boasts—and a humanist society recently renovated an old car dealership into a new meeting place. Overall, though, "it's easier for churches that are conservative to attract members. They attract people who are looking for easy answers, looking to be told what to do. Same with conservatism. But, if you're going to tell me to do this and do that, most liberals wouldn't put up with it."

That said, Chris does credit his own church with being a partner in his own liberal development. "The Lutheran Church probably taught me liberal values." They never said to be liberal, he explains, but "if you're listening to what they're teaching, you know which party matches up with what's the right thing to do. You see values modeled and talked about, and you know which side matches up better."

Chris learned those values at home as well . . . but he did not learn politics in his childhood. His parents were a mixed marriage: "My dad's side of the family is all Republican; my mom's side is all Democratic. So we never talked politics as a kid."

They did talk values, though—specifically civic values. "My dad is from the '50s. You wouldn't find a more fair-minded, civic-minded person. He taught us to do the right thing, that you should have pride in your community, you should fix the roads. He should have been a Democrat, honestly."

Chris thinks his father—and many people—relate to party affiliation the way you might feel loyalty to a sports team. "It turns into a tribal thing. When you grow up in a small town, that's your identity; that's what you are. If you suddenly switched sides and became a fan of the rival school—well, that wouldn't happen. The same with party brands."

As a result, Chris rarely tries to convince his father to reconsider being a Republican. "If I pushed, it would turn into my team versus your team. He'd feel attacked for picking the wrong team," he explains with genuine sympathy. "I don't want people to feel bad."

Also, Chris doesn't need his father to identify with the Democrats—secretly, he suspects his father already votes that way. "He talks about fixing the roads, and he's no dummy; he knows how that happens. I'm certain he voted for the last three Democrats" to run in high-profile statewide races for federal seats, Chris says—a mixture of confidence and hope. "I'd be shocked if he did not vote Daschle, Johnson, Herseth—if he voted for their opponents, I'd be shocked—but I never asked."

He recognizes that his connection to the Democrats is just as much a sense of team loyalty, even if it's a team that often disappoints him. He wants to believe he could be open-minded. "I'd like to think that if the Republicans were suddenly more liberal than Howard Dean and Bernie Sanders that I'd make the switch," he claims. Then he adds, "We'll never see that."

Chris suspects that one reason he knows more folks who identify as "independent" voters is that it provides a way for someone to evolve politically without fully changing their loyalties. "You can't break that label and go for the other team—you see people become independent." He also knows that people can surprise you around different issues.

He gives the example of his Republican grandmother, who is

now ninety-four years old. The right wing has put a series of referenda on the ballot over recent years. On one antiabortion issue, Chris had given his grandmother the information for his pro-choice point of view. He sat with her and they discussed in detail what the initiative would do, more specifically than being pro- or antichoice.

Recalling how his grandmother had absorbed what he said in a way that surprised him, Chris recounts, "People were going door-to-door on this issue. Real conservatives, ankle-length skirts." After Chris's grandmother listened to those people for a while, she informed them that she had looked up the issue and what they were saying wasn't true. "She told me that she put up with their lies, then said: 'Well, I didn't ask their opinions, but they gave them to me. So now they're going to hear mine.' She followed them down the sidewalk to tell them her side!" Amid laughter and pride, Chris announces, "Shows you never know on any given issue."

This is the same grandmother who teased Chris's Democratic mother, "How'd you raise kids to be Democrats in South Dakota?" Chris just claims it happened during the 1980s. He remembers watching the news. "I didn't like Reagan then. Nobody talked to me about it; nobody told me what to think. I don't know where I picked up stuff. But Iran-Contra . . . cutting food stamps . . . being racist . . . even kids can pick up what's going on."

Chris also fondly recalls his childhood enjoyment of the comic strip *Bloom County*, one of the few popular comics run in newspapers nationwide that had more political sensibilities. "I don't think it made me liberal. I think I liked it because I agreed with it." Then he adds, mischievously, about a national conservative-leaning comic strip of the same era, "I like to think nobody finds *Mallard Fillmore* funny, even Republicans."

His hometown now has two hundred people. There were sixteen in his graduating class. By comparison, Yankton—where he has lived for thirteen years—is quite large, though it has a population of only about 23,000. Sioux Falls, South Dakota's biggest city, is about a hundred miles away, so Yankton serves as a regional hub. "We're not a big city by any stretch, but we are a population center for South Dakota—take that for what it's worth."

Yankton isn't considered a liberal hub or a conservative stronghold by South Dakota standards. Those standards, though, lean to the right. "The default is that you assume people are Republican," says Chris. "At least I do. It's safer—whether it's always true or just because all of the active Republicans are the loudest ones."

The political tone of a place can be set by those who make the most noise. In many places—especially recently—the right wing seems to play that role. Chris tries to be balanced in his assessment but sees that happening in Yankton. "It may be unfair, but you think about the Tea Party types. Anyone who is complaining tends to be a Republican, and they are not afraid to shoot their mouth off."

Chris doesn't feel inundated by conservative rhetoric constantly, but it's not unusual to hear views he opposes or language he finds offensive. "There's always a loudmouth wherever you go. Sometimes it's with an older set—older people use certain terms they don't think of as racist, but it comes out that way. You're not going to change an eighty-year-old."

He recalls a particular time he was hearing a nun speak about her social justice work. "Someone in the lecture hall was spouting off—right behind me. I mean, what? Do you think you're in your car talking to Glenn Beck? Eventually I turned around—'We're trying to listen!' By my nature I'm not confrontational. In general you're not going to change anyone's mind that way."

Most days Chris doesn't have to be confrontational. It's not his personality. "I'm Scandinavian passive-aggressive," he teases. "I'll just mumble something." He's not the only one—in general, he thinks the Scandinavian influence makes people more reserved. There is also the effect of living in a small community. "In a smaller state, where everybody knows everybody, you tend to be prudent."

Again, that's especially true for liberals. Chris works from a home office, so he doesn't hear conservative opinions in the workplace. His wife is a lawyer, and more of her colleagues are conservative. "Even with people our age who we would like to go for a drink with, we wouldn't want to talk politics," Chris states. "You could alienate someone you have to do business with."

He avoids talking politics with his conservative friends as well. It's not worth the aggravation. He isn't afraid to be known as a liberal, but he picks and chooses when and how he advertises it.

One area he tries to avoid is lawn signs. He and his wife live on a prominent street in town, but he rarely puts signs up in his yard. "I worry what one unhinged person could do," he explains. On occasions he has put up signs, the signs have sometimes been stolen off his lawn.

Of course, even the conservative feel of Yankton may be overstated. After all, they do have a Democrat representing them in state government. "Our Democrat is Mr. Positive Thinking, which is very refreshing."

This politician—Bernie Hunhoff—was elected in part on name recognition, something that holds significant weight in smaller communities where families have lived for generations.

According to Chris, Hunhoff has an approach that works in a divided area like Yankton. "You can never have everybody like you, but pretty much everybody likes him. He's Catholic and this is a big Catholic area. He's positive. He's skilled. If you have the personality, you can connect with people"—and retail politics, the art of person-to-person campaigning rather than relying on TV ads and major endorsements, holds sway in smaller cities. Chris thinks that Daschle had similar appeal before he became too distant from South Dakota and too connected to Washington.

Chris feels that Hunhoff is further evidence that you're not going to convince people by confronting them. "If you come head-on, you get into your camps. You have to convince people around issues."

There are Republicans, too, who can have that same appeal and can cross over to Democrats. "There is one—our lieutenant governor—a really good guy. He almost never votes the right way because he goes along with the party's marching orders. But he's better than that." Chris points out that his wife, an attorney, believes that the conservative governor has made good judicial appointments because of the influence of the lieutenant governor.

As for whether any Republicans ever convince Chris, he likes to think they could . . . if only they would make reasonable points. "I might think Obama is wrong on something. But I also think he's born in America. On Benghazi, they are like a blind squirrel trying to find a nut. On taxes, it's usually just grousing. But if they get detailed, say that it's not fair that this type of property is taxed at this kind of rate, I could see a point."

However, that is not the tenor of South Dakota politics these days. The state that Chris loves and has always called home is going further and further to the right in terms of its policy. "Slashed education budgets. Making the wrong budget priorities. A few weeks ago, the Republican Convention passed a resolution calling for impeaching Obama. Fighting Medicaid expansion . . . regressive taxation . . . underfunding schools . . . ," reads Chris's litany of concerns.

He gives an example related to immigration. A Lutheran social services agency has played a role in helping Sudanese immigrants who have come to South Dakota. "The Rush Limbaugh crowd says that the Lutheran social services are bringing immigrants here. No, they're not. They are just helping them get settled."

For all the conservative politics, though, Chris does not feel its negative impact in his daily life in Yankton. He chuckles that

South Dakota recently made it onto a list of top ten states by quality of life. Is life that good? "I want to say yes—or I wouldn't live here. But I have an inherent bias. I grew up here. We have the Black Hills; it's beautiful out there. We have good beer. We have good people. That helps.

"I love Sioux Falls, went to college there. It has grown a lot since then. The rural areas are emptying out, but Sioux Falls has jobs. They may not pay a lot, but there are jobs if you want to stay in the state. There are two Ethiopian restaurants, a Cambodian restaurant. More diversity than you might think."

He chuckles, acknowledging that it may not sound like a lot compared to the country's biggest cities. However, that's much more diverse than Yankton. "Swedes versus Danes is our racial diversity. Or the Czechs."

Chris has enjoyed his travels to bigger cities and does realize there are certain things that aren't as easy in Yankton: "riding the tube in London, going to a play, going to an Indian restaurant." On the other hand, he has it better than past generations of liberals, thanks to his access to media from around the globe.

South Dakota media is fairly conservative, but that doesn't matter as much as it did. "Twenty years ago, you could imagine what it was like for someone my mom's age—it was stultifying if you didn't agree, no other avenues for you, it would weigh on you. We're lucky in that respect; there is more cross-pollination." Chris reads a host of blogs daily; he listens to Stephanie Miller and records and watches Rachel Maddow. "I should record Chris Hayes, but there are only so many hours in the day."

As for the fear that he is hearing only one side, he contends he keeps an open mind. "Some argue you read what you want. No— but I don't go to Drudge because I know it's crap."

He reads the Yankton paper and thinks the editor is not too bad, but believes that "they always feel like they have to walk a fine line to not alienate the foaming-mouth" conservatives. An example: they carry columns by the conservative national commentator Michelle Malkin. "I tried to be a liberal and I proposed a solution: Why would your paper pay to have someone like her? I'm sure there is someone in the state happy to write a weekly column as a conservative—it would cost you less, or maybe nothing, and it would be local. Why not do that?"

His proposal didn't go anywhere, but he was happy to have suggested it.

One improvement in Yankton he will boast about: better beer. Access to microbrews has increased, and he keeps a separate refrigerator for craft beer. "My favorite bar downtown has twenty taps, with a minimal lens devoted to Coors Light," he boasts.

Every now and then, he enjoys escaping to Omaha, where he lived for two years. "It's a significant metro area. Not huge, but a neat urban vibe. Lots of nice restaurants, concerts, sporting events, lots to do." Ultimately, though, it's in just as conservative a firmament as Yankton. "Outside of Omaha, the whole state is ruby red, and that weighs on you after a while. Living in Omaha would be like living in Albany if New York State didn't have New York City."

For now, though, and maybe forever, he'll stay in Yankton. He and other liberals hold their ground. Again and again their predictions—about the impact of Republican budgets, climate change, and conservative hypocrisy—are proven right. Often too late, but it's a fight they need to keep fighting.

"You get to play Cassandra forever and ever and ever. But when things do change, you never get credit." He reflects for a moment, then proudly declares, "It's like living in a Greek tragedy, only you don't have to blind yourself."

Diane, Al, and Cass Chulick

SPARTANBURG, SOUTH CAROLINA

You have to understand that we live in the South.
The culture here is one of politeness.

Cass Chulick and her parents, Al and Diane, live in the part of
South Carolina where former senator Jim DeMint came from.
It's a county in which Democrats sometimes have trouble fielding
candidates. The elected officials are some of the furthest right in
the state.

And during election seasons and moments of national political debates, the local conservative community comes out in force,
making it uncomfortable to be liberal. The Chulicks recall attending a health care town hall in 2010.

Cass had an Obama bumper sticker on her car at the time and
she recalls being nervous to park it in the lot of the town hall. The
Chulicks were among the only proponents for health care reform
in the auditorium. They had gone hoping to speak up for their
views—but felt very different when they arrived.

"It was a very intimidating experience," Diane recalls with a chill.

"People were screaming," describes Al. "Everybody there was a Republican except for us three."

"And they have scripts," adds Diane.

Al continues, "The Tea Party folks were all scripted. One person would say something and everyone would say, 'Yeah, yeah, yeah!' and wouldn't let the representative talk or explain anything."

"No way in hell would we get up in the middle of that meeting," interjects Cass.

"We tried to be invisible," explains Diane, reiterating, "It was really intimidating."

Moments like those stand out as exceptions to the enjoyment of their Spartanburg life. "It's hard to reconcile in my head that I see so many wonderful things going on all around me," says Diane of the town she's come to call home, "except we don't have health care, a maintained infrastructure, a quality educational system. Why do all these people I love to socialize with keep voting for these radically right candidates? It's an enigma."

The fact is that Cass interacts with conservatives "every day, all day long." Sometimes she knows it; at other times, it's a surprise. "I have a co-worker, we have so much in common, we could be the best freaking friends, man. Except one day several years ago, she posted some shit on Facebook that was not OK with me. We just don't talk about it. I go to her music festival; she goes to mine. We're fine, except she's a nut and we just don't talk about it."

The Facebook comments were mostly connected to religion. One had been about not being certain the Earth was millions of years old. The co-worker supports candidates Cass finds objectionable. Her Facebook page also talks frequently about her love of guns.

"I was floored. It kind of broke my heart," admits Cass.

From time to time, Cass will challenge the co-worker on Facebook, pushing back in a comment here or there. But she would never bring it up at work, or anywhere in person. Just online.

Al and Diane, retirees in their sixties, have dear friends who are conservative. They avoid political arguments with these friends—and sometimes that means avoiding politics altogether.

"In many ways, this is a little village," describes Al. "There are folks that we go out to dinner with every now and again; they are conservative. We found common ground to share with them—it happens to be the Stone Soup Storytelling Festival. We invited them to it, had a wonderful evening, we had dinner together, heard stories from professional storytellers. So we are friends with these people. When we leave town, we tell them. When they leave town, they tell us. We take care of each other."

"We're good neighbors," interjects Diane.

"I can't just say that I can't talk to this guy because he's too conservative for me," continues Al, "too radical, too right-wing. I need to talk to these people. And maybe we can appreciate their views; maybe they can appreciate mine. We may not convince each other, but at least we're talking."

Their connection does have its limits. "The woman in this relationship exchanges books with me," continues Diane. "On one occasion I offered to loan her a book by Vincent Sheheen," a Democratic politician in South Carolina. "She explained to me that she was more conservative than I. She thanked me. I didn't push it. She declined the offer."

Diane concludes, "What keeps us on a friendship basis is that we each make an effort to be very respectful of each other. Good manners cannot be overestimated in relationships between conservatives and progressives."

Adds Cass, "We all kind of live here together."

Diane returns to the theme of mutual respect. It's not just her preferred approach but one she sees as part of South Carolina life. "You have to understand that we live in the South. The culture here is one of politeness."

As she speaks, Al periodically chimes in with "Good point, good point," delighted to defer to his wife to make the argument running through his head as well.

Diane speaks deliberately, words carefully chosen. "You can have an occasion when you think you're having a conversation with someone. They'll look at you, smile, nod . . . and never really respond verbally. They'll give you the opportunity to say what you like, but when the interaction is over, we go our separate ways. It's almost separate but equal on a political basis. We simply don't interact."

Al acknowledges it goes both ways a little: he rarely gets through to a conservative, and they rarely manage to convince him. "I have not yet convinced a conservative person to the liberal or progressive view of my thinking. But I think about what we do with our neighbors—we're opening the door to get to the conversation about politics. We go out with each other on social events, we support each other, we become more comfortable with them. We're already comfortable, that's no problem—but we're getting comfortable enough to sit around the dinner table and bring up the conversation of politics. I think we're almost there; I think it could happen."

The family considers another conservative they know, a man who used to join their regular happy hour for liberal conversation. Cass giggles when Al mentions him. "He was fun. An open listener. He was Southern Baptist, set in his religious ways. But he would listen and respond and he would discuss topics with us. Until he moved away. Then he started posting on our Facebook page and the comments got out of hand. We had to cut him off. We had to unfriend him."

Diane softly objects. "You said that he listened. I think he just

remained quiet while other people talked, waiting for an opportunity to voice his opinion. I don't think he listened."

"Good point."

In-person interactions are characterized by a politeness that
seems set on avoiding conflict. In the social media space, where
the rules of civility are more lax, the conversation often heats up.
Occasionally, though, a genuine interaction can offer a pleasant
surprise.

As Cass recounts, "I was hanging out in the daytime at the
Nu-Way," her regular bar. "Becky, the owner, was hanging out
with a friend. When she left, I kept talking with the friend. He
was very conservative, he heard I was liberal—and it was like,
'Ooh, let's talk.' We did. He had some really good points. I listened to him. We both said, 'Huh.'" In general, though, Cass is
cautious about where and when she talks politics. "I avoid political conversations at work. Mom and Dad are retired. They can
have those conversations."

Al understands that concern completely. "When I was working,
I was extremely guarded in my views. Northwest Arkansas" where
he was living and working at the time—"was very religious.
Though it was very blue in terms of politics back then, it was conservative. I was guarded; it was my career. I dealt with the public
and I needed them to have a whitewashed opinion of me."

He adds that the main views he had to balance were not his
politics—but the fact that he was an atheist. "I knew that we had
moved into the South, by choice. Where we were is just a beautiful part of the country. I realized that just about everyone was
Southern Baptist and darn proud of it. My career depended on
my getting along with these people. They had to trust me; I had
to trust them. I consider my career a successful one, but maybe
if I had joined a church, it might have been more successful. But
I wasn't going to do that. It was a small town, everyone knew
I didn't attend church, but no one knew my beliefs."

Al recalls another occasion when he did decide to speak his mind. "When I interviewed for a loan officer position in 1984, the bank CEO, knowing that I was from California, remarked that he thought it must be tough to make loan decisions with all the blacks in California. I thought about that statement for about three seconds, knowing that I was qualified for this position, and responded: 'There are only four things that make a good loan—the four Cs: credit, collateral, character, and capacity. Nothing else matters.' I think it took him aback for a few seconds, but I wasn't going to compromise my beliefs . . . even though I really wanted the position. He must have been impressed because he hired me. Maybe it was a test, as he turned out to be a great guy. I used to go to his house for Saturday afternoon cocktail hour after the bank closed. I miss him."

Al became more involved with politics and outspoken when he no longer had a career to balance. "After I retired, I cast it aside. I could talk to anybody, voice my views. It's not going to hurt me financially, career-wise."

Al thinks about the neighbors he is forming relationships with, and others in Spartanburg he is getting to know. "We're still in a very religiously conservative part of the country, but I've found that if I can explain my beliefs effectively, and others can do the same, we may not agree, but we all can get along and be friends. I love it!" In fact, he and his family seem to thrive in their conservative surroundings. "I am very interested in talking to conservative people. To find out what they're thinking. They have all these views . . . and what in the world are they thinking?"

These stories have been shared by the Chulicks many times before. They share anecdotes as completely as they share their politics. "Very seldom do we disagree on politics," admits Al of his relationship with Diane. "There are times. We've been together since we were twenty-one. That's a long voting career. We just celebrated our forty-fifth anniversary."

"I come from a staunch Republican family," confesses Diane. "When I was in junior college in Sacramento, I was a member of the Young Republicans." Her daughter laughs at this, a familiar tale she's heard before. "It seemed perfectly normal at the time."

"And I married her," declares Al, adding a punch line to the story.

"Obviously, I did some thinking and changed my mind," explains Diane. "To this day, my mother, in her mideighties, and I—we unfortunately continue to have political arguments."

"Well, you don't talk politics with her," Al corrects.

"I try not to," says Diane regretfully, "but she goads me."

"She is good at that," Al agrees.

"I truly believe she loves it. It's a source of enjoyment."

"Very true."

Diane doesn't enjoy the arguments with her octogenarian mother. She likes talking politics, but "it's the ranting and the elevated volume that I find unpleasant." Cass never had that kind of rift with her parents. She inherited their politics completely, rarely disagrees, and has never thought of their politics as being of the wrong generation. She doesn't remember being explicitly raised a liberal, but she was raised with Diane and Al's values. And her location and timing helped firm up her party loyalties.

"I was able to vote for the first time when Bill Clinton was running for president," she recalls. "As governor, he had given me a scholarship. I was riding high. He was known as an education governor and it seemed that he'd be a great president." While that was her first vote, it wasn't the definitive declaration of political allegiance. "I never really identified as a liberal . . . until I don't know when."

Al chimes in, "I don't know when I became a liberal. I know when I became an atheist. I was raised Catholic. I was in a small church in Jackson, California, and I saw my friends going to communion. I said I could do that, and followed them. My sister grabbed me and said, 'You have to go to confession first.' For three or four years, I went to confession—but I was six or seven. I didn't do anything wrong. So I made up stories. I'd say I had lied to my mom, this or that—I had nothing to confess—but now I could go to communion."

His voice holds a sense of nostalgia as he continues. "This went on for a while. Another rite—confirmation—happens in eighth grade or so. I tried to go into confirmation class, but it interfered with basketball practice. I went home and said to my mother that I didn't want to go anymore because of basketball. She said OK. I said, 'OK. I'm out. I don't have to prove to anybody that I believe in God.'"

He pauses and reflects. "I don't want to equate being atheist with being liberal. . . . I don't like to label people . . . but maybe . . ."

"It can be hard to be very religious and be liberal," agrees Cass.

"I think you can pull it off," asserts Diane. "I think the progressive movement would be nowhere without the churches of this country."

"Because we have grown up so much in the South, we equate churches with conservatism. That may not be true," suggests Cass.

Together, the three of them can name plenty of congregations with more liberal leanings: the Methodists, Presbyterians, and Unitarian Universalists. There's a bishop who joins pride events and leads rallies against hate. There is a coalition of ministers who are part of a network called the Progressive Alliance.

And one can be conservative without being a churchgoer as well. "I have conservative neighbors who don't attend churches," says Al, "that are not outright, forefront, God-fearing people. But I know they are conservative, just by being in their house, seeing what they are reading, talking to them from a friendly place. So I'm not sure you can equate conservatism with religion."

"But I do," confesses Cass.

As with many deeply religious communities, Spartanburg also has active atheist and humanist groups that meet on a regular basis. They are part of what Al refers to as "small, little sparks of freethinking" that he sees throughout the county. "There are lots of things going on in this area. I don't like to label everybody conservative versus liberal, but for lack of a better word, there are sparks of liberalism in this area."

"Maybe this area is more liberal than we perceive it to be," assents Diane. As an example, she and Cass mention the pride parade, which has grown in size and acceptance each year. "However, our elected reps are extremely conservative."

There was one Republican representative whom Cass had voted for. "I believe he was running against a Democrat. But Democrats in South Carolina sometimes aren't really Democrats. They are very conservative. I'm not a Democrat. You don't have to register. If you did, I would not register. I vote for whoever would do the better job." In the case of this Republican representative, "He was the better choice." However, since that election, he proved too liberal for the Republicans because, as Cass puts it, he was willing to talk about compromise—and as a result he lost his seat.

When a Democrat has inspired them, Diane and Al have been willing to be public with their support. They worked for one candidate in particular and even put up a yard sign. "We felt very strongly about her candidacy," Diane recollects. But regarding the sign they proudly mounted in front of their home, "not a single one of our neighbors ever mentioned it. Like I hadn't even done it."

"Out of respect, I think," suggests Al.

"I don't think anyone was paying attention," counters Cass.

Despite sometimes feeling like the odd ducks, the Chulicks don't have any designs on moving. For one, they like their life in Spartanburg.

"On a day-to-day basis, living in this area is quite nice. Obviously some of the people we associate with are voting for Tea Party candidates," Diane adds with regret. But overall, she's happy.

There is room for improvement. But there is a walkable downtown. There are more artists and comedians and musicians coming through each year. And their neighbors—conservative and liberal—look out for one another.

Could the life be improved? When Cass drove to Wisconsin and saw windmills along the road, she dreamed of more wind energy in South Carolina, but knows it won't happen. She also worries that the local comedy club, one source of entertainment, might close down. And of course, one of the biggest obstacles to quality of life: "If you want to drink on Sunday," Cass explains, "you've got to think about it on Saturday."

"Before seven p.m.," specifies Diane.

Liquor laws are still strict . . . but they're used to it.

When Cass first bought a house in the area thirteen years ago, her boyfriend told her not to wear tie-dyed shirts on the porch— "that people would judge me, I wouldn't make good impressions on my neighbors." Now she wonders if that was just his perception, the sensibility of someone who grew up in the South. But even the South, notes Cass, is changing.

"I thought I'd come to South Carolina for a couple years, then move on. Been here fifteen years. I'm not bored. I'm having a fantastic, fun life; I've found all types of people. I don't want to go anywhere else. I'm in love with the people of Vermont, their thought processes, their election results. But I don't want to do winter in the North."

Besides, she adds, "I feel like I might be bored in Vermont. What are you going to fight for, man?"

Al feels the same way. "If you're going to be a liberal in California or New York City, you have an easy life. You've got friends who agree with you, most things political are on the liberal slant. Move to Arkansas. Move to South Carolina. You want a challenge, you've got it."

And in spite of the challenges, they feel like they can move the needle.

"Perhaps things are slow to change because people think they never will," suggests Diane.

"It takes newcomers to come in and change it," elaborates Cass. "Things are changing, and I believe things are changing for the better."

Diane offers the coda: "We're always hopeful."

Al begins to offer a theory on how climate may impact political thinking, and it's clear Diane is ready for this train of thought to come to an end. "Al's been espousing this theory for years," she explains.

"One of these days," replies Al, in what is clearly a frequent rejoinder, "I'll prove it."

Cass, who had let her attention wander, turns back. "Sorry, I missed part of it."

Diane reassures her, "You've heard it a hundred times."

Lenzi Sheible

*Have you ever seen a human embodiment of "Keep
Austin Weird"? To me the embodiment is a white
guy with dreads on a skateboard. Keep Austin Weird
is a white-person thing—it's also a commodity. . . .
But I feel out of place because I'm not the typical
"Keep Austin Weird."*

"Hey, guys, there's a new organization in town called Fund Texas
Women that provides transportation for women to get abortions," read the Facebook post. "Why don't we pose as volunteers,
pick up the women, drive them around for three hours, talk to
them about God, and then park them in front of a church?"

That was the greeting Lenzi Sheible, in her midtwenties, and
her colleagues received when they launched their new nonprofit in
the late summer of 2013—and it quickly guided them to change
tactics. Their goal was to make sure women had access to the
health care they needed, especially in the aftermath of a draco-
nian set of laws that would result in the closure of most abortion

clinics in the state of Texas. Many women who wanted to end a pregnancy would have to travel five or six hours—at great hassle and expense—to get the care they needed. Fund Texas Women, which soon became Fund Texas Choice, intended to help solve this problem by providing bus and train tickets for women who couldn't afford them.

It was never Lenzi's intention to get volunteers to provide the transportation. "We're talking long distance," Lenzi explains. "You won't find many volunteers to drive six hours to pick women up, then six hours to bring them to a clinic, then back and forth again." And as soon as right-wingers broadcast their interest in kidnapping vulnerable women for antichoice harangues, it confirmed for Lenzi that purchasing tickets for public transportation made a lot more sense.

"We definitely don't drive people around," she says with a laugh. And in any case, "I don't think the pro-life people could effectively pose as volunteers. I doubt it—we'd be able to tell. But as soon as that happened, we decided we didn't need any volunteers at all. We got nervous at the idea of entrusting someone to people we don't know. So we just provide travel we can buy. I doubt Greyhound would drive you somewhere else," other than your ticketed destination.

The Facebook harassment was a reminder of the culture that Fund Texas Choice was up against, and an important learning opportunity on how to handle attacks. "We didn't respond. We didn't know who they were. But we did get this around in the media: 'Texas Abortion Kidnapping'—Google it and you'll find it." Sharing this actually helped make the antagonists look ridiculous and gave her own supporters something to rally around.

Soon after the initial provocation, they started seeing online messages that called them "an abortion travel agency." Anonymous posts would hatefully claim that "Fund Texas Choice will offer you the luxurious vacation of an abortion trip," Lenzi recalls. "We were told that we are the trains sending the Jews to Auschwitz."

She sighs at the venom and the absurdity, but also points out the opportunity. "The best thing to do" when there are offensive attacks, Lenzi believes, "is to point them out and laugh at them. This can invigorate our supporters. If I show other people an awful article that calls us Nazis, it creates a bond among all of us. Nobody likes being called a Nazi, but we're together in this; we are a group being attacked."

While Lenzi is a founder and board president of the organization, it's not a paid job. It's a labor of love that began while she was still an undergrad at University of Texas at Austin and has continued through her first year of law school there.

The organization's origin story is in the 2013 fight over anti-choice legislation that commanded national attention and galvanized Texas liberals. "These bills had a lot of drama—they were a package of abortion restrictions that should not have come up at all," Lenzi explains. Since Texas has a part-time legislature that meets only every two years, there is a limited period of time to get much work done. "In 2013, there had been a truce" among legislators: "let's not talk about abortion, it's divisive, takes time, and then you don't pass bills about transportation."

Yet that summer, Governor Rick Perry called a special session, something the governor has the prerogative to do, pushing the abortion restrictions onto the calendar. The main result of these bills, critics argued, would be to reduce the number of abortion providers in Texas from around forty to as few as eight.

Lenzi had spent part of the previous semester volunteering for an organization that had supported women in the southern half of Texas who couldn't afford abortions on their own. So though she was in Houston that summer, she commuted every chance she could for the committee meetings on these bills that would make it more expensive and prohibitive for many women to receive medical care. She also then commuted back for the dramatic fili-buster by state senator Wendy Davis, whose actions grabbed the national spotlight and successfully postponed the bill.

Then the governor called another special session—and Texas passed these new laws. "There were ninety days before the laws went into effect. It was like saying, 'Hello, activists, you have ninety days to figure something out.' There were groups that al-ready paid for procedures but were not ready to deal with travel. I envisioned buying plane tickets for people. A lot of people don't have the Internet."

Since then the fund has made arrangements for nearly two hundred women. Lenzi's count includes all the women they make reservations and buy tickets for, though, she acknowledges, "they may not go in the end."

Lenzi is not new to travel. She was born on a road trip between Houston and Dallas. "I was born in a nursing home because there was no hospital nearby," she says. She was raised first in San An-tonio; then at seven she moved to Houston. In college, she moved to Austin, where she lives now.

Her political evolution started in junior high school. At age fourteen, "I was radicalized because my mom found out I had a girlfriend and lashed back. I was confused—'How can she be so mad?' " Lenzi remembers thinking. "In my Googling, I found it was a cultural thing."

Lenzi is half-white, half-Asian by birth, and Mexican by up-bringing by her adoptive parents. "My mom is very conservative. I'm not sure why. I grew up broke, but Mom always had the idea that she'd have money one day. At the time I thought it was silly that she complained about taxes. I couldn't really talk to her about anything. She was conservative politically and culturally."

Her father didn't share her mother's views. "He's really an apa-thetic atheist. He doesn't talk to Mom about anything political or cultural, but he is really a libertarian and always has some new libertarian theory."

The websites Lenzi found when she was searching to understand her mother's reaction to her girlfriend were radical ones. As a result, Lenzi explains, "I got a little theory in my wanderings. I'd go to the half-price bookstore and buy books on gender, which gave me words. I went to summer camp at UT Austin as part of the debate team. One of the sessions was about feminism. I found more words there."

This continued through Lenzi's high school experience. "By then, I had acquired words about race. I went to the half-price bookstore and bought books about race—bell hooks was one of the first. I started hanging out at a bookstore in Houston called Sedition Books."

When it was time to head to college, "I went to Austin. I thought, 'That's where communes are.' But it's not as radical as I thought."

Most people would think that Lenzi has found herself in the most liberal spot in this famously conservative state, a city with the unofficial motto, "Keep Austin Weird." Lenzi sees it differently. "Have you ever seen a human embodiment of 'Keep Austin Weird'? To me the embodiment is a white guy with dreads on a skateboard. 'Keep Austin Weird' is a white-person thing—it's also a commodity. Maybe a bar on Sixth Street can say, 'We're weird, we sell drinks for fifty cents, look at us!' But I feel out of place because I'm not the typical 'Keep Austin Weird.' "

Part of what distresses Lenzi on a daily basis is the segregation of the city. "I like Austin, but I also don't like it. I imagined it as a utopia of liberalism. It's a place where people were gay in public. Now that I live here, Austin is more full of itself than Houston, whiter, more segregated, and more segregated by class."

She gives the geography of the city as an example. "The

highway divides the city east and west. And it divides the city white and black. It's weird. I used to live on the east side," which, she explains, is where the black population lives, "but I had to move, because the buses stopped running. There used to be a series of shuttles to the university. Then the university decided to cancel them."

So, now Lenzi feels like a fish out of water. "I don't identify as a white person; I identify as a Hispanic person. To have to live on the west side feels like having to give something up."

She continues, "I look racially ambiguous. People don't always know what to make of me. People can err on the white side or nonwhite side depending on the day. If people decide to read me as white, I feel it. That doesn't happen very often in Austin. White people in Austin are really, really white."

The university itself also embodied more of a white culture than Lenzi, at the height of her radicalism, was expecting. "But it would be illogical, impractical, to say 'screw this full scholarship.' That's not something I'd ever do. I knew I had to come. Even though it's an institution."

So she did what she could: "I chose the most radical studies I could—gender studies and black studies. Black studies is an amazing department, one of the biggest black studies departments in the country. And I surrounded myself with radical people."

The transition to the law school, though, was harder. It was more difficult to surround herself with radicals. "The law school is also really white. The culture of it is very white. I stick out. I have a shaved head, tattoos. I don't look like them." As a result, there is a distance between her and her classmates. "I can't buy into that culture. It's not a good fit. And [not fitting] doesn't have much currency at the law school."

It's not that she's alone in her politics, so much as the sense of the entire experience. "There are liberal people there. I'd say liberals are the underserved, under-attack minority. Not because politics comes up a lot. But if you want to be a successful lawyer, it's defined by getting a good corporate job. So regardless of politics, everyone still talks about how much they love oil and gas," two of the big regional industries into which the law school sends graduates.

There are some fellow liberals and radicals—"but if that's your politics, all you do is have a sad face," she says wryly. There are "the traditional conservative Texas types," whom she tries not to spend much time with. And then there are "classical libertarians that culturally love it here. It's OK—I find it less disturbing to be around someone who is culturally liberal but fiscally conservative."

Unlike the tribalism of her undergrad experience, "in law school, it's a completely different world. There's no way I can avoid the people I hate," she says with a laugh. "It's designed like a high school. You have lockers because your books are so heavy. You stay there nine to five. So you're surrounded all the time."

As a result, "I do have relationships with people who are conservative because I have to. I tend not to bring politics up. It's usually not relevant." She recalls that early in law school, she felt it was more important to promote her views. "In my introductions in my constitutional law class, we went around and said who are you, what do you do. I talked about Fund Texas Choice—and then there was minimal discussion about it ever again. I felt like I staked my claim; I had chosen to be out [as a pro-choice activist], and it was nerve-racking . . . but I did it. Now looking back, it was probably not necessary. When people look at me they assume I'm that kind of person."

It was telling that so few of her classmates ever talked with her about her work again, although there was one notable exception. "When Fund Texas Choice was in the *New York Times*—lots of classmates read the news to seem informed for job interviews. A few said, 'I saw you in the *New York Times*. Good job.' I did not expect that at all."

As the semesters passed, Lenzi became less vocal because "slowly law school wore away at my spirit." In particular, there was one "really bad experience being out as a radical. It made it not worth it."

The occasion took place in her criminal law class. Lenzi knew they were going to be discussing a case about a person who had a mental disability. As she recalls, "The way the opinion was written, it treated the person like crap. I could see it coming. The class discussion was going to be awful."

Lenzi stopped the professor as they were walking in and asked to speak to her quickly. "Can we not say the *r*-word?" she requested, meaning "retarded." "If she doesn't say it, other people won't either. The professor looked at me. 'No,' she said, and she kept walking. She was very not down, which was unfortunate. I thought for sure she was more liberal than most."

The class began. "I sit down, and I wait for this thing to happen—and at first she doesn't say it. Everyone is being polite, talking gently about the person in the case. Then, all of a sudden, the professor says it"—the *r*-word—and "the tone of the room shifts. People start making fun of the person, using the *r*-word a lot, talking about him like he's nothing. I can promise you that if he were in the room, no one would talk to him like that."

That night, Lenzi wrote an e-mail to the class using a group listserv the professor had set up. "I wrote why the *r*-word is bad, that if you want to be compassionate you wouldn't use this word. I got a horrific response from one classmate. 'Free speech, you can't control what I say, I'm going to say it all the time now.' It was so disheartening. And that's all I got. Everyone else did not respond at all."

But there was one other reaction. "The next day, the professor closed the forum. She shut down the ability for students to e-mail other classmates. She said, 'Students shouldn't be correcting fellow classmates.' "

This shocked Lenzi. "I was mad at her. She missed an opportunity for dialogue by shutting the list down. And she demonized me as the kid always stirring up trouble."

Lenzi took the issue to an assistant dean, who was understanding but didn't think it was his place to take any action. Then Lenzi spoke to the dean himself. "He just doesn't understand. At least the assistant dean had some framework to analyze why I was upset. The actual dean, a white man with power, was trying to be compassionate toward me. He was trying to make me feel better. But he could not understand why I felt attacked."

She recalls their inability to communicate around this issue. "He was confused. 'We have lots of women here, lots of people who are nonwhite,' he said. He had never analyzed whiteness. All he could imagine was that it was his job to make me happy, but he didn't understand there was a larger system happening. It was almost worse—he was trying to fix it but could not see the system happening at all."

Lenzi doesn't conform to many expectations, and that conversation with her dean was illustrative of so many of the interactions she has at school, in Austin, and as she pursues her work with Fund Texas Choice. Even politically, she doesn't see herself conforming to the term "liberal." "I'm more radical, even anarchist," she admits, "but I can stand being grouped into liberals for the sake of conversation."

Her intention is to stay in Texas, where she has always lived and where there is plenty of work to do. She expects to move on from Fund Texas Choice. "I have a feeling Texas is not going to change its mind anytime soon on abortion policy. So the organization will not shift, but I will. I want it to survive without me, but I want to do something else. Doing abortion work is hard. I don't want to be running it after I finish law school. My vision is that it lasts as long as there are poor people who can't afford to travel. And when I'm gone, I want it to be just as radical."

She daydreams that maybe she'll move to a small town or a rural area that needs a lawyer. Her current intention after law school is to provide criminal defense for poor people. Though that may not constitute a break from the harshness of abortion work. "Yeah," she admits, "that might be equally emotionally draining."

As exhausting as it is to feel always in the minority, Lenzi does have her moments of pride. Though her mother is conservative, she's also pro-choice. And she approves of Lenzi's line of work—in part because of what Lenzi has achieved. "She likes what I'm doing because she likes to see me successful. I'm doing something other people in the world are recognizing."

Joe Litton

BRANDON, FLORIDA

There was the big bombing in Nigeria by Boko Haram. It made me think of Timothy McVeigh. I haven't read all of the Koran, but I've read a number of scriptural texts. It doesn't teach you that all non-Muslims must be killed. I did some research: you don't find many Quaker terrorists, but for any other major religion you can find that fringe element.

Sometimes, Joe Litton has found the conservative politics that permeate Brandon, Florida, popping up in odd places. "I usually change my own oil, but I went to a Jiffy Lube once, and the guy doing the oil change—I'm paying him—and he starts bad-mouthing Kerry. It's just not appropriate in the workplace."

At Jiffy Lube, Joe, white and in his fifties, could at least talk back—that's not always the case. "I've had people try to remove stickers from my car. When I first moved down, I had a John Kerry bumper sticker. I was parked on the street, a guy slowed down and shouted 'Fuck John Kerry!'" This is not an everyday occurrence for Joe. But it wasn't isolated either.

In some ways, this conservative strain was more frightening when Joe and his wife, Shirley, attended a health care town hall in Tampa in 2010. "We left because it looked like it was going to turn violent. The riot squad was showing up." When a Democratic leader tried to speak, "the conservative element would scream. The agenda was not to let the event take place." It's an extreme example, he admits, but not the only time he's felt silenced by the area's conservative community.

This is something he has wrestled with since he and Shirley moved to Florida from the Pacific Northwest. The transition involved serious culture shock. One change affected him on a daily basis: the lack of public transportation.

"Tampa in general is spread out. There is not a livable downtown core. The area grew up with the idea of cars. . . . I wish we had mass transit here. When I worked in Portland, I took the train every day," recalls Joe fondly. "I had worked for Enron. I was laid off before the big implosion. Shirley"—his wife of thirty-five years, with whom he has one adult son—"had grown up in Vancouver, and she said, let's go to the sunshine. One of the first things I did, I went online to check out the mass transit, and it's crap."

They made the move nonetheless, and Joe sought ways to avoid buying into the car culture. It wasn't easy. "There is a bus system. If I wanted to take a bus to work, there's a quote-unquote express bus—it runs once an hour. If you miss it, you wait an hour. There's nowhere to park at the bus stop. In the Northwest, there were park-and-rides all over the place, a bus every fifteen minutes, train every five. We don't have that kind of thing. Here the bus stop is at Walmart. I'd have to park there. So I called Walmart and asked, 'Can I park in your lot to take the bus?' 'No.' So you can cheat and park there, or find other means."

One alternative would be bicycling. However, "it's rugged when it's ninety-five degrees, one hundred percent humidity, in business attire, carrying a laptop." So Joe became one of the many Americans who drive for their daily commute.

"Where I work, the building has LEED certification. There are parking spots for carpoolers and fuel-efficient. There is slow growth in that," he points out, hopefully.

There was another big concession Joe and Shirley made when they moved. "We swore we'd never do this, but we live in a gated community. It's insane. When we were shopping around for houses, turned out we liked this one."

Liberals in Brandon—a city twenty minutes east of Tampa—may have to work a little harder to create a comfortable life that also reflects their values, but it's far from impossible. Joe's house has a solar attic fan. Recycling used to be more difficult, but now they have curbside pickup. Joe and Shirley are vegan—"one of the single main things people can do to support the planet"—and even that isn't as hard as it once was.

"People are starting to understand what vegan is. Square 1 Burgers has a vegan burger. It comes with a side of broccoli—that normally has butter on it," Joe jokes. "A vegan friend turned us on to an idea: look at the entire menu, see what food they serve that could be vegan, and ask the server if they can take certain ingredients from different meals to put together in a way that's vegan. You can't do that with a giant corporate monster like the Olive Garden, but who wants to eat there anyway?"

Joe knows this is a limited solution. "I have friends in New York. Oh my gosh, it's so easy to eat well there. There is a vegan place an hour away at the beach in St. Pete. There was another place an hour east in Orlando—it moved and it's now an hour and a half." Still, Joe sees change coming to all of Florida, even to Brandon.

To some extent, change is inevitable in Florida, a state that is continually refreshed with waves of newcomers, as corporations import younger workers from around the country to commingle with retirees from colder—and sometimes, more liberal—regions. In some ways, the state of Jeb Bush, Marco Rubio, and Rick Scott ("the bastard," Joe says, chuckling), of stand-your-ground and hanging chads, is a poster child for the right wing, but this critical swing state twice chose to give its electoral votes to Barack Obama. As even a casual political observer would note, Florida is a puzzle.

"In Florida, down the sides it's more liberal; as you go inland, it's more the South," explains Joe. "Tampa and Miami are not the South. When you get inland, you hear southern accents, and you hear conservative views."

Joe's workplace reflects the mixed population of Florida. "There are a lot of transplants in the metro areas. I don't even notice it anymore, but where I work, it used to strike me that I'd hear accents from Boston, from New York, from Chicago, along with the Deep South. If they are from one of those places, it's a higher chance they are liberal. If someone is from the Bible Belt, he tends to be more conservative."

Perception, though, is not always the reality—both at work and in the neighborhood where Joe lives. "We moved down ten years ago from Washington State. There, we assumed everyone was liberal. In our group of ten or twelve, my boss was the only conservative—even that was odd. Down here, it's the opposite. You assume everyone is hard-core conservative." And yet, he notes, "It's not really the case."

He recounts campaigning in his neighborhood for a Democratic candidate. "Turned out in our neighborhood, fewer than half of the people are registered Republicans," he says with surprise.

By and large, his co-workers stay out of politics. He's a software engineer—"I can't say where," he quickly adds—and "geeks don't care. There are a lot of liberal geeks. There are some conservative geeks." There is a libertarian streak among elements of the tech community, but mostly they don't talk politics.

There are some exceptions. "My former Enron boss, he was definitely conservative. I worked in a tight space, with folks on both sides. The guy to my left was a liberal, the guy to my right conservative. My first day there, the guy on the right said something about the ACLU; the other guy and I both pulled out ACLU cards."

Joe doesn't always leap into the rare workplace political conversations. "I do hear comments. Trash-talking climate change, *Inconvenient Truth*, Al Gore inventing the Internet. I was about to jump into it and decided it's not worth it." When he does, though, "It's usually civil at work. If we start talking at lunch, and differing views come up, it's not so bad."

Plus, the politics of his employers does not negatively affect their workplace. "It's a conservative organization, but the office is very supportive of gay rights, of people all across the political spectrum. We also have people with piercings, tattoos. It's not like years back when if I wasn't wearing a tie, the CEO got on my case."

Joe feels passionately about his political views but also finds it important to get along in the more conservative environments around him. He also says he would rather "talk facts than simply argue feelings"—and attributes that preference to both his background in tech, a field in which he believes rational arguments prevail, and a healthy sense of skepticism he says he developed in college. He explains that even when he's feeling passionate, "I don't typically fight. . . . When someone quotes the news channel that we don't think of as news—Faux News—I say, you need to give me more information—a link, a study, something other than 'some people say.' "

He holds his side to the same standard. "Too often, liberals will forward an Internet meme without checking sources," he points out. "I credit that skepticism to the Evergreen State College in Olympia. It forced critical thinking. We'd have lectures from professors with different perspectives in the same course."

This may be the same reason that Joe doesn't watch MSNBC. "I used to. In my mind, it skewed too much. Not as crazy as Fox, but it's trying to emulate the Fox model to improve ratings. I get my news from our independent local paper, the *Tampa Bay Times*. And a number of Internet sources."

The ability to exchange ideas is part of what makes his friendships work with people who don't share his politics. "Our neighbors across the street are conservative. He is career military. We have vacationed with them." The friend, though, is not the kind of hard-core right-wing Republican Joe sees across the state. "He's more libertarian. We can have conversations."

Through these conversations, Joe notes, he has learned that "my conservative military buddy considers himself liberal—in the laissez-faire sense. He believes you should have free rein, that everyone has the right to do whatever as long as they are not hurting somebody."

This conservative couple actually joined Joe and Shirley several times at the liberal social club they host. The conservative newcomers came open to the experience, but the liberals who regularly attended the gathering were not so thrilled. "A couple of the other folks in the group didn't like that," Joe admits. "They felt like we live in a bastion of conservatism. This is our sanctuary. Our moment of sanity. Our chance to chill. The members of our group, we refer to it as 'Church.' And there are two feelings. Several of us like the opportunity to engage in civil discourse with folks who don't share the same opinion. Others just don't want the argument."

Maybe Joe's own background makes him particularly comfortable—and interested in—blending liberals and conservatives. He was born in New Jersey, where he attended Catholic school through ninth grade, before moving to Washington State. "My mother and father were registered Republican. Her dad was a very active Democrat. He died when I was pretty young. Mom's mom moved with us to Washington." When Joe became involved in the Mo Udall presidential campaign, "I remember sitting at our dining room table, petitions spread out, and Grandma said Grandpa would have been proud to see me active."

His own generation is a political mixed bag. "There are five siblings. My oldest brother is a Catholic deacon and a liberal Democrat. My sister is an ordained minister; she works as a counselor in a Christian church, and she is much more conservative. My other brother is a hard-core fundamentalist Christian, and he had been a Republican. He worked for the post office and has started reading a range of online views and has completely switched.

"Another brother thinks Rush Limbaugh is fantastic," Joe continues. "We've had shouting conversations on the phone. So we avoid politics. Neither of us is going to see the other side. His only issue is abortion. All of his voting, all of his campaign work, is about which candidate is the strongest antiabortion person. What about all the deaths from gun violence, from wars? Doesn't that matter? Is it all secondary?"

While he engages with his siblings to different extents, he never found it worth it with his parents. "I didn't talk politics ever with my mom. With my dad, he was just too crazy. My dad's side had always been Republican. My mother, being a hard-core Catholic—I think she took literally the wedding vow to love, honor, and obey," he says, emphasizing the last of the vows. "If she had any other leanings, if her husband had said you will be this, that's what she would have been. It gives me a bad taste."

Religion has influenced the values of everyone in Joe's family, but he finds it frustrating when religion leads to conservatism. "If you look at teachings of any organized religions, none of them say put the burden on the little guy, send them off to your wars," he claims.

"I was raised Catholic. I'm a recovering Catholic. I used to be on the boards of churches. Now—organized religion is against my religion. With religion, people too often shut down their own critical thinking rather than thinking for themselves."

Joe sees a serious problem when religion is used to justify extremism. "There was the big bombing in Nigeria by Boko Haram. It made me think of Timothy McVeigh. I haven't read all of the Koran, but I've read a number of scriptural texts. It doesn't teach you that all non-Muslims must be killed. I did some research: you don't find many Quaker terrorists, but for any other major religion you can find that fringe element."

The influence of more conservative congregations is felt in Brandon. Joe references the Dixie Chicks lyrics to describe the "crucifix skyline" of the region. "This isn't a heavily populated area. There are strawberry fields. There are cows. Yet, I can walk five minutes and hit two or three churches. I've never seen so many Baptist churches."

Joe thinks about this and sighs. "The Republicans couch everything in religion and patriotism." And, he believes, this helps them appeal to many folks whose core interests aren't served by right-wing politicians at all. Yet conservative tendencies run throughout the state. Even Joe's one Democratic elected official is further to the right than Joe would like: "Senator Bill Nelson—and I don't consider him a liberal."

Nelson isn't the only Democrat Joe finds subpar. "The two main parties are different—I argue against folks who say there is no difference," he is quick to note. "But there is too much corporate support of both parties. That's part of why I'm Green Party. I've read the platform of various parties. I don't think it's valid to say Republicans are bad, Democrats are good. But it's been many, many years since I voted for a Republican at any level of office. The days of rational discourse have been obliterated."

Joe has also been frustrated with local Democrats for the way the party operates. "We had a Democratic candidate who would have been perfect; another Democrat, who was very active in the party, came along. I don't know what went on, but the earlier person bowed out. That was a case where the party organization was completely wrong. That goes on in both parties. My wife and I would love to see instant-runoff voting" as a solution that would allow voters to cast more votes on principle rather than along party lines—a technical fix, suitable for a professional geek.

Then again, there are times when there isn't even a mediocre Democrat to support. "We have races where there is no challenge to a GOP incumbent. I understand, I wouldn't want to run. I understand why there aren't candidates . . . but it's depressing."

Thus, there are real dangers resulting from the role Floridians do—or don't—see for their government, and from the culture that reflects those views.

"Auto inspections—that was nixed by voters. You'll see cars spewing crap. There used to be a motorcycle helmet law. Not anymore. . . . There's a high rate of pedestrian injury and bicycle injury. It's just too dangerous. Even where there are bike paths, drivers don't care or are blind or both."

Joe believes there can be a more connected, compassionate, and sustainable community—and government can play a part in creating that. "My ideal would hew far closer to the Scandinavian model of government—that is, tax-funded education, health care, mass transit. Regulations on working environments, et cetera. Maybe progressive is a better term, I don't know."

He smiles to recall one anecdote. "I have a T-shirt: it says 'Proud Liberal.' It's always interesting when I wear it. Walking into Lowe's, all eyes on me. To me, liberal is like any other label—all kinds of meanings to different people. All labels are just an easy form of categorization to start figuring out where somebody's belief lies. But there are people on either side of the spectrum I'd agree with."

That agreement goes only so far. Joe knows one liberal friend whose wife is a conservative Republican. "I don't know how that works. I wouldn't want to be in that type of relationship, when you don't agree on core values."

Joe is technically in a mixed marriage. His wife is a Democrat while he "registered Green as a statement." That said, they pretty much agree on politics. And they have passed that along—they have one son who is married and lives not far away. "Oh yeah, he's liberal. Thank God."

Glenn and Christina Wiech

MILFORD, MASSACHUSETTS

I would say there are some Democrats who are dis-affected. They believe Obama is a socialist; they go back to the Republican Party to see what it has to offer.

Christina Wiech is willing to go door-to-door to campaign for progressive candidates, but there are lines she feels she has to respect. "I had a Don Berwick sign in my car" during the 2014 Democratic gubernatorial primary, when Berwick was a progressive candidate, she recalls. "I would put it up when I left work. At home, I would leave it up. When I drove back to work, I left it up. Then at work, I'd take my briefcase out of the car and take down the sign because I need the job. I just don't know what to expect."

Even though Christina's employer isn't political and explicitly allows political involvement by the staff, Christina also knows she has Republican colleagues who might look unfavorably on her signage. "They may even have given to Scott Brown's campaign," she confesses, referring to a conservative candidate. She doesn't want to cause a stir.

Christina's husband, Glenn, has work that gives him a different sort of freedom. "I'm an IT consultant—I fix people's computers. I go into a lot of homes and easily half the time Fox News is on in the background. I know what I'm in for."

Unlike Christina, Glenn doesn't worry about compromising his job over politics. "One fellow I see once a month—he's superconservative—I've let him know on multiple occasions where I stand on things. We actually agree on a lot of things, which is kind of funny." With other clients, Glenn will take "whatever issue of the day, the deficit or some other thing that happens to be a hot issue, and I'll just ask them how they feel about it. I won't necessarily give the party line, but I give them a different perspective they won't necessarily get."

"It's different for me," says Christina. "I go into the same job every day with the same people. I know for a fact certain people are very conservative. While the company has a policy, you're allowed to be involved politically any way you want to, I don't want to push this issue."

There are some occasions when Glenn doesn't want to push the issue either. "I belong to a small business networking group. After Scott Brown won, a good group of the guys gave a cheer. I found that demoralizing, but I couldn't say much—I did have to edit myself. There were people who'd seen some things I was up to—I had been quoted in a paper at a rally—and one of the guys pulled me aside: 'I saw the quote; we agree with you.' He was quiet too."

The need to be quiet about one's liberalism is a common refrain heard in South Carolina, Idaho, and Oklahoma. But it might seem odd for a couple of folks living in Massachusetts.

You can't get a more liberal state than Massachusetts—at least that's the Bay State's reputation. It's the land of the Kennedy dynasty, a leader in marriage equality and universal health care, and home to Elizabeth Warren. "Massachusetts liberal" was the type of epithet that became a slur, dogging two Democratic presidential nominees in the past thirty years.

Yet it's a state that elected Elizabeth Warren only after a tough race against Republican Scott Brown, who had won his campaign to succeed Ted Kennedy. It's the state that gave Mitt Romney the title "governor." It's a place that in living memory has been the center of racial tensions and class struggles. As with most places, the closer you look, the more mixed it is.

That's what Glenn and Christina Wiech have discovered in their two decades in Milford, a town of less than thirty thousand about forty miles southwest of Boston.

If you were to stumble upon Milford, "I think you'd feel like you were in a liberal place," states Christina. Scratch beneath the surface and that's not their experience. They interact with conservatives on a regular basis and believe that there's an overall conservative ethos to the area. One measure, the polling numbers, back up this claim.

"Elizabeth Warren lost our town by seven points," Glenn offers as way of illustration. "Scott Brown lived fifteen, twenty minutes south of here. We'd go campaigning and hear, 'Scott Brown is practically our neighbor—where's Elizabeth Warren from? Cambridge?'" He adds a sneer with the last word, clearly an inflection often used by fellow Milfordians.

Even though he was sponsored by hedge funds, Scott Brown was an everyman, Glenn observes with disbelief. And that kind of approach works for Republicans in this region. "If you consider the four towns that make up our district, they are much more conservative of late. Our town is kind of a mix, leans conservative, not so heavy. Look at some of the other towns: Hopedale, seventy percent conservative; Mendon, also very, very conservative; part of a town called Medway—it's pretty fifty-fifty. In this district, our rep has a pretty liberal voting record, but with redistricting it's gotten more conservative."

Both Christina and Glenn, white and in their late forties, are natives of Connecticut. Christina is from Greenwich—and is very familiar with conservatives close to home. "I have four siblings—one is very conservative. I really, at this late age—almost fifty—struggle a bit to relate to them politically. Really, my brother—we're a year apart—he's really conservative. I can't understand—we were brought up a year apart. I can't believe he has such different beliefs. I can't even talk politics with him."

Her brother may eye her with the same surprise: after all, she grew up in a Republican household. "My father was a farrier—he put shoes on horses for wealthy people. They voted Republican. We were raised that way," she recalls.

"I didn't really pay attention to politics until recently," Christina admits. One exception: "My grandmother marched for the women's right to vote. The minute I was eighteen, she made sure I was registered to vote."

Now she chuckles at what she did with that voter registration. "My first vote may have been for Reagan," she acknowledges with a touch of hesitation. "I'm pretty sure if I voted, I voted for Reagan."

"Greenwich is Bush's hometown," Glenn interjects.

"And my dad is George H.W. Bush's age," adds Christina. "My dad knew who he was."

That era, though, "was a very different time. When I was a kid, the wealthy saw the poorer people differently than they do today. In no way would I ever hear from one of my father's clients that we were sucking on society. You now hear that out of Fox News."

While Christina's other siblings tend to be more Democratic, she still finds it difficult to talk politics with them. "One of them said Chris Christie is great," she recounts, a reference to the New Jersey governor. "My head almost popped off my neck. 'He's a bully! What makes you think he's good, let alone fabulous?' I was stunned by it. I didn't push the issue." Even after "Bridgegate"—a scandal in which top Christie aides, perhaps with the knowledge of the governor (though he has denied this) closed traffic lanes around the George Washington Bridge and created massive gridlock as political retribution against a local elected official— Christina didn't force the subject, though she wanted to ask, "Do you really think this guy is good enough to be governor, let alone president?"

Glenn leaned Democratic from an earlier age. "I remember not particularly liking Nixon when I was young. I saw that guy and didn't like him. It was a visceral dislike of Nixon, for whatever reason."

He grew up in the town of Seymour, in the Connecticut valley. "See less in Seymour" is the town motto, he says, laughing. "One movie theater, a pizza parlor, not much else."

His family leaned differently than Christina's but was largely apolitical. "My parents are fairly unconventional. They didn't really raise me with any religion or structure per se. I had a somewhat—in comparison to what other kids had— unconventional childhood. I always sensed politically that my parents were somewhat leftish, but it's not something we talked about in the house."

During his youth, and for a while after, "I never really got involved," Glenn confesses. Yet there was always a spark of interest. "I kept abreast of things; I was always interested in politics, even when most of my peers were more interested in sports."

When Christina and Glenn met, politics did not play a large role in either of their lives. Their fortunes rose and fell, but not enough to politicize them. "We were very lucky," Christina says.

"We did well in the Clinton years. Not so much in the Bush years. I was laid off twice. Glenn had to work to death." Christina is a technical writer and Glenn a software engineer.

It wasn't Bush's economy or his foreign policy that pushed them off the sidelines, but something that happened after the Bush presidency—a decision influenced by a series of Bush appointees on the Supreme Court.

"Glenn and I both started to get involved after *Citizens United*," the Supreme Court decision that struck down a number of campaign finance regulations and opened new floodgates for corporate money to dominate the democratic process. "That really poked me and made me pay a lot more attention," Christina recalls with energy in her retelling. "I mean I voted—we were pretty good about voting—but *Citizens United* really frightened me. That's when I started to look at things in a different way, really analyze things more."

There was also a personal hook for her. "This would be something we did together as we grew old together. As we started to get involved, it felt really important."

"*Citizens United* was part of it," agrees Glenn. "There were two other things that also caused me to get involved. The Scott Brown election—it was a real shocker, but you also saw it coming a mile away. The other is that I started, after the financial crash, listening to and seeking out what would be considered 'liberal media.' Ultimately, I found a fellow named Thom Hartmann," the progressive radio and television host and author. Glenn recalls that he regularly ended his radio program with " 'Get out. Get active. Tag, you're it.' I heard that for six months or nine months before I took it to heart to do something. . . . It always left an impression on me."

This period of time politicized them both. They became involved in local campaigns. They found themselves watching *The Ed Show* on MSNBC with their dinner most nights. They even started finding some friendships strengthening while others slipped away. They began to think of their political views as a core part of their identity.

While Christina came to think of herself as a political person, there were certain labels she has been slower to embrace fully. "I don't like to say to someone I'm a liberal. They think 'hippie.' Not that there's anything wrong with that, in my opinion—but to them, it's a pile of dung. Liberal has a negative connotation on the other side—it's not fair, but I prefer 'progressive.' We've seen other countries that are progressive and successful. I look to people like Bernie Sanders and Elizabeth Warren. Those are people who really represent me. I don't have to watch their votes. There are other people who are Democrats who concern me, even people I have canvassed for, that I have to keep an eye on."

Glenn embraces the label "liberal." "I'm not afraid of the negative connotation. The word has been viciously attacked for decades. If there's any way of planting a flag, drawing a line, staking a claim, that 'liberal' is fine, I'll do that."

He also sees it as a word that helps differentiate types of Democrats. To Glenn, liberal means "being more open and accepting, making sure things are good for everybody, not just myself. And what Chris said about Elizabeth Warren and Bernie Sanders is true. The Democratic Party has split over the last twenty-five to thirty years. There's a struggle going on even though we don't like to talk about it. Which side is going to be the standard-bearer—Republican-lite or actual Democrats again? Will we believe in championing the working class and middle class again?"

As a sign of where they fall on the Democratic spectrum—and a reminder that the party is far from a unified monolith—they share their views on the potential Hillary Clinton candidacy. "I know there are a lot of people excited about Hillary," observes Glenn. "I'm not one of those."

"I'm not either," agrees Christina with no hesitation.

"I hope there are other choices. If not ones that can win, then ones that can move her to the left," Glenn offers, perhaps an allusion to his own senator, whom many liberals in the summer of 2014 had hoped would consider a challenge. "We're uncomfortable with Hillary Clinton's friends, uncomfortable with her policies."

Glenn sees primary campaigns as the place where liberals can push back against conservative Democrats. "I was hoping this election would help us make that choice and move the party left, when for so many years we've been moving right because Democrats have decided not to push back on Republican talking points, and because people have not been that engaged to build the movement."

The election Glenn was referencing was the 2014 gubernatorial primary in Massachusetts. Glenn and Christina poured their volunteer hours into a candidate many considered the long shot: Don Berwick. "We were very enthusiastic about Don," he explains, painting the political landscape. The other candidates were Martha Coakley, "who famously lost to Scott Brown" for a Senate seat a few years before (and who went on to win the gubernatorial primary, then lose the election). And Steve Grossman— "good credentials, not particularly inspiring. Don was the right guy for the right time—much like Elizabeth Warren was the right woman for the Senate seat. He wasn't your run-of-the-mill politician, trying to evade any stance."

Christina and Glenn were in the field on a regular basis— knocking on doors, talking to neighbors, and often getting an earful. These experiences have helped demonstrate to them just how conservative their surroundings are.

If you arrived in Milford for the first time, "I don't think you would be able to tell" how conservative it is by walking down its main street, explains Christina. "I think if you were to canvass with us, in ten minutes, you'd know."

Christina continues that many voters in Milford "call themselves unaffiliated," but that's not the whole story.

"A lot of them tend to be Republican voters, sick of the party not winning, who broke away but tend to be more conservative," explains Glenn. "For whatever reason, we see a bunch of those people."

Additionally, in a state like Massachusetts, where the Democratic primary is often the main event, many more conservative residents, who might be Republicans elsewhere, could be registered as Democrats in order to participate. All told, it means that even when working for a primary candidate, Glenn and Christina are not just talking to liberals.

"Some will engage in conversation, which is fine," recounts Glenn. "Others—we've been ordered off a porch more than once. No discussion, just angry gesticulation. It can be a real trip depending on what door you knock on."

Glenn is no longer surprised by some of what he'll hear from registered Democrats. "I would say there are some Democrats who are disaffected. They believe Obama is a socialist; they go back to the Republican Party to see what it has to offer. Three weeks ago, I talked to a Democrat and tried to engage with them about single-payer health care," one of Berwick's signature issues. "Totally not having any of it—'Obamacare has gone too far' " is what Glenn heard at the door.

"There was the sewing machine . . . ," prompts Christina.

"We came to the door; this fellow was in the process of sewing something," recounts Glenn. "He was leaning Republican, felt we needed more balance. Although we have a lot of Democrats in our statehouse, a lot of them would be registered Republican if they felt they could win as Republicans. Balance wasn't the right way to look at our situation—we have many conservative Democrats in the legislature." They spent a while chatting as the man sewed. He didn't chase them away; they didn't give up. In the end, "he came around a bit more to investigating Don," Glenn says with a touch of pride and a dose of hope.

As Glen explains, Milford may be more conservative than Boston—but the situation gets bleaker for liberals just down the road. Because of all the campaigning they do, they know the numbers. Glenn maps out the area: "If you were to go further west, ten minutes west, it's beet red—eighty percent Republican. It's very sad. Every town has its own Democratic town committee. In many of the towns further west, the Democratic town committees no longer meet—they don't exist—there's not enough Democratic activity. It's very sad that in a state most people consider very blue, there are towns that can't get up enough liberal mass."

Milford is more mixed than that. And thanks to their campaign involvement, they don't have to guess at who is on which side of the aisle. "Because we canvass," Christina asserts, "we actually know."

"It's about fifty-fifty in our neighborhood," Glenn chimes in. "We know about the neighbors on either side; we don't know about the new neighbors. Directly around us, our neighbors lean liberal. We know people further up the street are much more conservative." Despite the fact that he enjoys engaging people in political conversation, Glenn is a little more circumspect in talks with his neighbors. "We haven't had conversations necessarily about some things," he says of the conservatives up the block.

A social shift happened as Christina and Glenn became more politically active. Due to a confluence of factors, not one particular reason, "We drifted to more liberal people," Christina acknowledges. "There's a couple who is very conservative—I really love them; I worked with them. We all got laid off and we have that camaraderie. But we find it very difficult to talk about politics."

Christina doesn't say whether it's due to her own increased political engagement or because people are becoming more divided generally, but she finds "that everything somehow seems to be political in a way it wasn't in the past." When you talk about almost anything, you find yourself taking a stand on something.

She goes on to illustrate her point. "A good example in Milford—we have undocumented workers who live in town. We had one undocumented worker who got drunk, got in his truck, hit and dragged and killed a young man on a motorcycle. The victim was named Matthew Denice," she recounts sadly.

"This is a big thing we deal with every time we canvass. 'What does this person think about illegal immigration, because I'm a friend of the Denice family?' " is a question she hears frequently. "For me it's about drinking and driving. For conservatives, it's about illegal immigration."

They admit that they now see their conservative friends less frequently, though point to other factors too. "Glenn and I chose not to have children. The conservative couple has children"—and that lifestyle difference can make it harder to remain close.

While their friendships with conservatives may have drifted apart, Glenn and Christina do find occasional conservative allies—especially in debates about local development in the area. "Last year, a casino wanted to build in town," Glenn begins. "There was a ballot initiative to determine whether to have one or not. Interestingly, it was a cross-partisan effort. We ended up defeating the measure sixty-five, thirty-five. We were really happy about that. We didn't want to see a casino in town. Whatever good it offers is outweighed by the many ills."

Glenn used the anti-casino campaign as a way to suss out other political views. "We'd stand out at events, hold signs, and chat amongst the group. I'm a little bit of an instigator. I'd chat about how they feel about certain issues. You can tell right away who leans conservative and who doesn't, in their answers and in how they approach issues."

It was an informative experience. "We met a lot of people we didn't know in town. Working on that issue was an eye-opener. We got to meet people from the other side of town. Interesting to see who the other people were and where they stand on other issues. They had their own reasons for opposing casinos. We had our own reasons. For whatever reason, we were able to cobble a coalition together."

The coalition, though, has had trouble expanding beyond that one fight. "There is another group now, formed out of the anti-casino group, but the viewpoints are so very different on how to proceed in town, what's important and what's not," observes Glenn. "I'm part of a group called Move to Amend, trying to roll back *Citizens United*, to go around the Supreme Court to get Congress to regulate campaign finance. We were holding a workshop at the local library." Glenn approached the former members of the anti-casino organization about promoting the event. "Not only did they not really engage me when I asked them to consider it and to consider publicizing it, but they were almost hostile in their response. I haven't attended any of the meetings for the new group because of that. I don't know there's much to go on to continue any participation."

In general, though, Glenn believes there is the opportunity to find common ground and help people rethink positions "if you actually engage people on issues." He sees this with client after client. "After having a discussion, we are surprised how many things we agree on. Policy solutions we may not agree on entirely, but what's wrong most people agree on. If we can get to the bottom of what solutions are, to some degree an educational process on both sides, we could come out going in a better direction. It will take a lot of effort; a lot of people like us are trying to engage more people."

Through these political and advocacy efforts, they feel a greater familiarity with Milford and more invested in the town. "Not having kids, we didn't really know anybody in town, and we didn't know much about politics in town. We could've been living anywhere, to be honest," Glenn explains. Activism, he adds, "has given us the feel for what's on people's minds. This helps us appreciate the town more."

"We went to elderly housing and talked to this woman," recalls Christina. The woman watched C-SPAN daily, had a more detailed knowledge of Milford than Christina, but she chose to vote only in presidential elections. "We spoke for an hour and finally she said, 'What are you really looking for from me?' 'I want you to vote in every election, every local election, every state election, every presidential election.'"

Christina pauses, then concludes. "I don't know if we got through to her, but if taking the day off to get her to vote would have worked, I would have."

Byron Stuart

POMEROY, IOWA

I love The Daily Show *and* The Colbert
Report. . . . *There are a few people in town that if
they're in here, I won't even turn it on, because I will
not listen to the crap they're saying during it. But
there was one night I was watching it, and this one
guy who's a regular, his wife was there and she said,
"This is really funny—I've never seen this before."
I bet you haven't!*

"I'm a firm believer in don't discuss politics or religion in a bar,"
declares Byron Stuart. "Alcohol frees you up so that you think
you can say anything you want."

In Pomeroy, Iowa, where he owns and runs Byron's, the local watering hole, talking politics or religion would be more a
hazard to Byron than to his customers—because his conservative
and Christian regulars would be forced to recognize that Byron
is neither.

"I also dislike arm wrestling," the sixty-two-year-old throws in as a matter-of-fact addendum. "It brings out too much testosterone. It leads to a fight. If I see someone start, I say, 'Not in here.' "

Both arm wrestling and political argument would wreck the mood of his establishment, adorned with band photos, Grateful Dead memorabilia, and tie-dye accoutrements. It would also wreck the mood of the proprietor, who clearly walks to the beat of a different drummer than most of the residents of his hometown.

Fortunately, Byron doesn't have to break up too many tense moments at his venue. "I notice if two people aren't getting along—that I better get over there, get them separated, get them laughing or something. I've always done that. It's more instinctual. I don't like fights. My bar is Grateful Dead themed—peace and love. I don't have much trouble."

There are rarely political fights because there aren't often that many customers interested in politics, and very few willing to argue from the left. "It never really comes up to shut them up" about politics, he explains. However, occasionally, someone will make a comment that Byron can't tune out.

"We were watching the news the other night and something came up about Obamacare. Someone said, 'Niggercare.' That takes you back to reality."

That time he didn't say anything—he let the comment slide. That's not always the case. "One time a guy came in, we were watching a golf game. He said, 'Is the nigger winning?'" I turned to him and said, "Excuse me?!" He stopped and said, "Is the black guy winning?" I just stared at him. Finally, he said, 'Is Tiger Woods winning?' 'No,' I said, 'he isn't winning.' "

There are many days that remind Byron he's a little different from his fellow Pomeronians. "I love *The Daily Show* and *The Colbert Report*," he declares. "There are a few people in town that if they're in here, I won't even turn it on, because I will not listen to the crap they're saying during it. But there was one night I was watching it, and this one guy who's a regular, his wife was there and she said, 'This is really funny—I've never seen this before.' I bet you haven't!"

Byron keeps comments to himself. "I've got to live with these people every day. The clientele is the same every day." It's part of why he doesn't put political signs or stickers in his bar windows. "I gotta be careful who I get pissed at. They'll take their friends and not come back to the bar. I gotta rely on the weekday crowd, to have fun with my Sunday crowd," he says, referring to the unique and more diverse clientele who come to his live music nights.

It's not just business. Keeping up civil relations is also part of living in a small town. One regular—the husband of the woman who was delighted to discover *The Colbert Report*—is one of the most aggressive in terms of spouting right-wing rhetoric. "It doesn't bother him at all. He's right; everyone else is wrong. He's a blowhard. When he talks, everyone has to hear him. He has no indoor voice. Thank God he's a trucker, so he's gone most of the time." But this objectionable character is someone Byron has known his whole life. "He's a year younger than I am. His sister was married to my brother until he passed away. We used to be at family events together. I would stay away as much as possible."

While his regulars have pull with Byron, he also has an important bit of leverage. "I'm the only bar in town. I got a monopoly," he brags with a chuckle. "I've owned it for eighteen years."

One bar serves a town of 650 people—"at least fifty percent are fifty or older," Byron adds, many of whom he knows, because it's the town where he was raised.

"I grew up here. Went to Ames for school for a few years, then came back," Byron explains. He's a native Pomeronian and still has family around. It's not only a conservative and Christian area, but also pretty racially uniform. "It's pretty white. Growing up, I never saw a black man at all. One, I guess, in the '40s, was living in Pomeroy and they ran him out of town. They almost ran a German preacher out of town too. That was before I was born. Now, there's one couple: he's white, she's black. They've only been to the bar a couple times. There are also beginning to be a few Mexicans."

It's a small town but rich in one asset: religion. "There's one bar but five churches," described Byron. "I'm agnostic. I grew up in the Methodist Church. They tried to teach me to hate Jews, blacks, homosexuals." Byron sighs at the memory. "They've torn the church down. I was happy to see it go. I mean, I wasn't happy to see the building torn down—it was a nice building."

Byron stopped attending church in college, though he would sometimes pick up the habit when he returned home. "I have a twin brother, just as liberal as I am, and a little more outgoing. We'd be home and our mother would say we were going to church. My brother said he'd go to church but not take communion. My mother says, 'Then stay home.' She didn't want people asking her why he wasn't taking it. When she said we didn't have to, I wouldn't. When she wanted us to go, I would. And I would take communion. In the Methodist Church it's just grape juice anyway."

That was one of many transformations that college facilitated. "In high school, I didn't even have FM radio," Byron recalls. "When I was in college, I hung around pot smokers. Someone said they were going to see the Allman Brothers. 'Come along, think you'll like it.' So I went. Jesus Christ! Where were they hiding music like that?!"

The cultural awakening was one part of a radical expansion of Byron's perspective. "The main thing was hearing different points of view. Someone was a chemical engineer. What the hell is chemical engineering?! Never heard of such a thing. I'd never been around even the word. That was really great to see so many different people."

It was different from what he'd experienced in Pomeroy. "If

you just see the same thing every day, you think that's normal. Then you get out and see other people that are different than that."

He was also exposed to new political thinking. "I went and protested, marched down the streets of Des Moines. 'One-two-three-four, we don't want your fucking war.' My group was peaceful. And I think we got it to change," he remembers fondly.

"That's when I first realized I'm no longer a Republican. No longer that kind of Republican," he declares—though he has kept the party affiliation. "I'm actually a registered Republican, but very forward-thinking Republican. Also, I'm gay. I think most of the town knows it, but I'm not out. I'm out to my friends, but that's it."

Even before college, Byron's knowledge of his own sexual orientation made him know that he wasn't the run-of-the-mill hometown boy. "Politically, I knew I was different. And I knew I was gay, attracted to men, not women. I had to keep it a secret. Other than that, I was a normal Pomeronian. Until I went to college, and it was so different. We'd drink and talk and drink and talk, just hear different things. I was still deep in the closet even in college."

Byron may not be deep in the closet any longer, but he's not quite out either. It's just one of those things—like politics and religion—that he and his neighbors don't talk about. "I think most of them know, but nothing's said," he admits. "I live with a guy. For younger people, it just doesn't matter to them anymore. My clientele—hard to tell. But I've never had anybody write shit on the walls or paint something on my garage. I'm sure people know it—but they're more accepting now." He adds with a flourish, "Now, if I was living with a black guy, that'd be a whole different story."

The example of younger Pomeronians shows Byron how much the town has changed. Iowa's status as a leader in same-sex unions meant that one younger local man married his partner. "It's a young man from Pomeroy who lives in Des Moines. His family is pretty accepting. Two uncles wouldn't go to the wedding. They said it's not because he's gay but because he's making such a big deal about it," Byron explains in an exaggerated tone. "That doesn't make sense to me. Shit, hetero weddings are huge fucking things. And people go to them."

But the rest of the family showed how Iowans have evolved. "The father of the guy, I thought was über-conservative. Now he welcomes his son-in-law with open arms. I was shocked and pleased."

That young man hadn't come out in Pomeroy. "I don't think it was spoken about until he moved to Des Moines. He's so much younger than me that I wasn't familiar with the details. But another young kid—he took his boyfriend to the prom." Byron recounts this with a touch of awe, then acknowledges, "I was deep in the closet when I was in high school."

While Byron sees that the younger generation can be open about their orientation, he remains guarded. He's been with Roger for eleven years, they live together, and it's still not expressly discussed, even with Byron's sister. "My sister is über-Republican. We love each other, so we don't talk politics. She lives a couple blocks away." They also don't talk homosexuality. "I assume she knows too." He shrugs. "She invites Roger over for supper. She's gotta know. But I've never come out and said, 'Hey, I'm gay.' I never did that to anybody until my fifties."

In contrast, Roger, who grew up in a military family, came out when he was seventeen. "Wow, that takes balls," marvels Byron. "He'll stand up if someone makes a disparaging remark. He'll throw them against a wall, say, 'What the hell did you just say?' " Roger's example encouraged Byron to come out to more friends and members of his community. "He gave me the courage to do that."

When he did come out, his biggest worry proved unfounded. "I haven't lost any friends because of it. That's the main fear—that you'll lose friends."

Though they live together in a long-term committed relationship, they are not married. "We never really discussed it. I don't need to be married." However, the politics of marriage has been on the forefront of political conversation in the state for years. After the Iowa Supreme Court ruled that same-sex couples could marry, a backlash movement sought to defeat several of the judges in their subsequent judicial election—and it was successful.

"I didn't really think they'd get judges out of office," Byron says with regret. "The Constitution says all people are created equal. This issue is black-and-white for me. If you're equal, you can get married. They brought in all sorts of outside money, scared older people in the state, and voted [the judges] out."

While the population as a whole is more tolerant each year, the opponents are as vocal as ever. "We've still got a big guy, Bob Vander Plaats, head of the Family Leader. He organizes a big conference in Des Moines, a bunch of candidates spoke at it, presidential hopefuls. But they are nothing more than a homophobic organization," Byron laments. "It wouldn't surprise me if Vander Plaats is a closeted homosexual. He's so much against it that it doesn't make any sense." He laughs and adds, "Me doth think he protests too much. I have a friend who has initials on his guitar—F-Y-B-V-P—Fuck You, Bob Vander Plaats."

In addition to Vander Plaats, Byron saves a special dislike for Congressman Steve King. "What an idiot!" he cries. "He's about an hour away. He covers almost all of northwest Iowa. I thought we could get him voted out, but we didn't do it. There's just way too many conservatives around here who really don't think when they vote."

Byron considers these voters. "It just means they're thinking from back in the '50s. They haven't grown." He says it with some sympathy, knowing he was a Republican voter once himself. "I'm a Republican because that's how I grew up. That's how I signed up originally, and I've always kept it."

As with many Iowans, Byron sees the election system up close. Iowa's first caucus puts it in the spotlight every four years, and as a swing state, it often stays in play until Election Day. Thus, there is no shortage of political aspirants and entourages coming through the state. However, Byron reports, none of the major candidates come near Pomeroy. "I've never gone out of my way to meet them. My friend Roger has met quite a few. He likes to go see them. But as far as I know he's never gone to a protest. I went to Occupy Iowa. They were camped out for sixty days. I didn't do that, just showed up to show support."

That small act of activism once more put Byron at odds with his fellow Pomeronians. "I get back, the same idiot whose wife had never seen *Colbert Report*"—his bar regular and brother's widow's brother—"says in a loud voice, 'Anyone who participates in Occupy Iowa is a stupid motherfucker.' I just said, 'Thanks a lot,' and walked away."

Byron has plenty of conservative friends—but with them, "politics is not the main topic." He also has "one friend who calls himself a libertarian, doesn't want to be called a liberal or anything else. I kind of like his attitude." But especially in an election year, when you get "phone calls every five minutes," people are sick of talking about the race. "There's much more talking about farming around here."

If he has a complaint about Pomeroy, it's that he wishes there were "more art, more culture." He uses his bar to try to address that issue, hosting Sunday live music events. "The crowd comes from all over—fifty to sixty miles away—because there are no other venues like this in the area, not even in northwest Iowa. The Sunday crowd is much more liberal and open-minded. And it's all about the music." Byron admits that this is a passion project. "I'm losing money on this. But I love it so much, I'm going to do it until I can't possibly do it again."

The closest movie theater to Pomeroy is twelve miles away, and Byron suspects you'd have to go as far as Des Moines for a political film or documentary. "I would imagine movie theaters around here are hurting. Netflix. You'd just as soon sit home as go out."

Which is also a problem for Byron's line of work. "A lot more people drink at home. It used to be that the bar was open until two in the morning. The last customers would buy a few bottles, pull up their car, sit out front. We'd have gutter parties." Those occasions recede into nostalgia. "Now we usually close at midnight. There's nobody in there anymore."

But Byron has no plans to leave his hometown—and finds joy in Iowa life. Occasionally, he will go to Des Moines for events but treasures the return journey home. "I went into Des Moines with my nephew" for a concert. "Coming back at four in the morning, I could stop and take a piss on the side of the road. And I thought, this is why I like Iowa."

Byron has a twin brother who lives in Seattle. Byron knows that Seattle has plenty to offer, but it would never suit him. After all, as he says, "too damn many people. . . . And too many people are going to be trouble. When there's nothing to do, they get crazy."

Byron now lives back in his childhood home. "I moved in thirty-three years ago for three weeks. I'm still here. My parents passed away, and I got the house." He values the familiarity of Pomeroy, even if it's not perfect. "I'm very happy where I am. I think you're going to have both sides of the coin any place you live. "

Acknowledgments

Thank you to Lisa, Spike, Rebecca, Chris, Diane, Dan, John, Susannah, Rita, Dean, Desmond, Kathleen, Greg, Diane, Al, Cass, Chris, Lenzi, Joe, Glenn, Christina, Byron, Gary, Ed, and Heather for sharing their stories.

Thank you to Katrina, Matt, David, Jeremiah, Amie, Linda, Mark, Steve, John, Bill, Saad, Matt, Stephanie, Nicole, and Rachel for creating the space for those stories to be shared.

Thank you to Diane, Jed, and The New Press family for wanting to share these stories more widely.

Thank you to Casey for asking me to tell all the best stories I can.

About the Author

Justin Krebs is the founding director of Living Liberally, a national network of more than two hundred local, progressive social clubs, including Drinking Liberally happy hours and Laughing Liberally comedy shows, giving liberals everywhere the opportunity to find their political communities. He is also the lead campaign director at MoveOn.org Civic Action, the nation's largest independent, progressive grassroots membership organization.

Justin was a founder, and serves as board president, of the Tank, a Manhattan-based nonprofit home for performing arts and public affairs. He has managed a citywide parks advocacy campaign, produced an award-winning PBS documentary on civic engagement, and served in the office of the then U.S. senator Hillary Rodham Clinton.

Justin is a former senior fellow at the New Organizing Institute in Washington, D.C., and a former activist fellow with CREDO Action in San Francisco. He serves on the boards of the New York Civil Liberties Union, Humanity in Action, Get in the Game, and the Cobble Hill Playschool.

Justin is the author of *538 Ways to Live, Work and Play Like a Liberal* and *Grounds for Play,* a history of New York City's playgrounds. His work has been featured in *Mother Jones,* targeted by the *Weekly Standard,* and lovingly lampooned on *The Daily Show.*

He is a graduate of Harvard University; native of Highland Park, New Jersey; and resident of Park Slope, Brooklyn.

Publishing in the Public Interest

Thank you for reading this book published by The New Press. The New Press is a nonprofit, public interest publisher. New Press books and authors play a crucial role in sparking conversations about the key political and social issues of our day.

We hope you enjoyed this book and that you will stay in touch with The New Press. Here are a few ways to stay up to date with our books, events, and the issues we cover:

- Sign up at www.thenewpress.com/subscribe to receive updates on New Press authors and issues and to be notified about local events
- Like us on Facebook: www.facebook.com/newpressbooks
- Follow us on Twitter: www.twitter.com/thenewpress
- Please consider buying New Press books for yourself; for friends and family; or to donate to schools, libraries, community centers, prison libraries, and other organizations involved with the issues our authors write about.

The New Press is a 501(c)(3) nonprofit organization. You can also support our work with a tax-deductible gift by visiting www.thenewpress.com/donate.

Neo-Nazis

A Growing Threat

Kathlyn Gay

—Issues in Focus—

Enslow Publishers, Inc.

40 Industrial Road   PO Box 38
Box 398   Aldershot
Berkeley Heights, NJ 07922   Hants GU12 6BP
USA   UK

http://www.enslow.com

Library of Congress Cataloging-in Publication Data

Gay, Kathlyn.
   Neo-Nazis : a growing threat / Kathlyn Gay.
      p. cm. — (Issues in focus)
   Includes bibliographical references and index.
   Summary: Discusses the history of neo-Nazism, examples of
organizations and activities spawned by this ideology, and evidence
of the spread of anti-Semitism, racism, and hate crimes.
   ISBN 0-89490-901-0
      1. Neo-Nazis—Juvenile literature. 2. United States—
Race relations—Juvenile literature. 3. Racism—United States—
Juvenile literature. 4. White supremacy movements—
United States—Juvenile literature. [1. Neo-Nazis.
2. White supremacy movements. 3. Racism. 4. Prejudices.]
I. Title. II. Series: Issues in focus (Hillside, N.J.)
E184.A1G36 1997
320.53'3—dc21   96-40872
                                                        CIP
                                                        AC

Printed in the United States of America

10 9 8 7 6 5 4

Illustration Credits: Anti-Defamation League of B'nai B'rith, pp. 10, 20, 49,
68, 80, 87, 100; AP/Wide World Photos, p. 92; © Corbis Digital Stock,
p. 27; © Corel Corporation, p. 61; Reproduced by Enslow Publishers,Inc.,
pp., 15, 34, 43, 46, 82; National Archives, p. 77.

Cover Illustration: AP/Wide World Photos

Contents

1

Neo-Nazi Victims

*In January 1996, two neo-Nazis, Daniel Bean and Ronald
Gauthier of Columbia Falls, Montana, were visiting their
mother in Houston, Texas. The two are half brothers and
belong to a group known as the German Peace Corps. They
boasted they were "going to get a fag" and then trapped a
homosexual in his van and stabbed him thirty-five times.
Police say the killers showed no remorse for the murder.*

■ ■ ■

*In December 1995, two white soldiers, Privates Malcolm
Wright and James Norman Burmeister II, while stationed
at Fort Bragg in Fayetteville, North Carolina, shot and
killed an African-American couple. The soldiers had first
harassed the couple while they were walking down the street.
As self-styled skinheads, Wright and Burmeister were bent on
acting out their white supremacist beliefs. "Police reportedly
found a Nazi flag, hate literature and a bomb-making*

manual in an off-post mobile home rented by Burmeister," *according to* Newsweek.[1]

■ ■ ■

In October 1995, Roy Ray Martin, a skinhead, along with two Hispanic friends, attacked three African-American men in Lubbock, Texas, killing one of them. The three apparently had "discussed their mutual hatred of blacks" and were eager to "start a revolution or race war" to destroy African Americans, according to an indictment against the three. A photograph of Hitler, a Nazi flag, and a swastika were found in Martin's home.[2]

■ ■ ■

In July 1995, an estimated two hundred members of white supremacist organizations in the United States and Canada met for a world congress at the neo-Nazi Aryan Nations compound in rural Idaho. Participants were urged to gather information about government facilities, civil rights organizations, and media personnel—all considered enemies of the Aryan Nations' cause. Speakers also told the primarily neo-Nazi audience to stockpile weapons and prepare for what the group believes is an impending race war.

■ ■ ■

In May 1995, the Montreal Gazette *in Quebec, Canada, reported that at least six skinheads belonging to the neo-Nazi organizations Northern Hammerskins and Heritage Front tried to infiltrate the Canadian armed forces.*

■ ■ ■

In April 1995, the Alfred P. Murrah Federal Building in Oklahoma City, Oklahoma, was bombed. Many were killed and injured. The prime suspect in the case, Gulf War veteran

Timothy McVeigh, has been described by some of his fellow soldiers as an avowed racist. McVeigh also reportedly read and sold copies of The Turner Diaries, *a novel published in 1978 by William Pierce. Pierce is the notorious founder of the National Alliance, and many neo-Nazis call his book a bible. The novel is like a manual describing a guerrilla war, or rebellion, against the United States government, people of color, and Jews. It includes a precise description of how to make a bomb with fertilizer and fuel oil, which is then placed in a truck to blow up the headquarters of the Federal Bureau of Investigation (FBI). The description matches the Oklahoma blast in eerie detail .*

■ ■ ■

In March 1995, newspapers in major cities across the United States and Canada reported the arrest of Gary Lauck from Lincoln, Nebraska. Lauck was arrested in Denmark on an international warrant issued by Germany. Lauck had thwarted German police for at least twenty years. Head of the National Socialist German Workers' Party Overseas Organization, Lauck's base of operations was in Lincoln, where he printed and supplied hate materials to fascists in Germany. Since the 1970s, he has spread neo-Nazi literature across Europe. He even declared that Jews were treated too well in Nazi concentration camps, claiming they were the instigators of World War II. After his arrest in Denmark, German police raided homes of eighty of his supporters (most of them teenagers) and seized weapons and Nazi propaganda.[3]

■ ■ ■

In February 1995, two Pennsylvania brothers, Bryan and David Freemen, were shown in TV clips and newspaper photographs with neo-Nazi symbols tattooed on their arms and shaved heads. They had murdered their parents and their eleven-year-old brother. Although they were apparently motivated by family tension, they were also influenced by skinhead philosophy and by neo-Nazi Mark Thomas, an Aryan Nations leader, self-proclaimed minister of Christian Identity, and once a "pastor" to the virulently anti-Semitic Christian Posse Comitatus of Pennsylvania. In December 1995, the Freemen brothers pleaded guilty to the murder and were sentenced to life in prison without parole. Their cousin, Nelson "Ben" Birdwell, III, who claimed to be a neo-Nazi and helped the brothers beat their parents to death with a pickax handle, was also convicted of one of the murders in April 1996.

■ ■ ■

These incidents of neo-Nazi violence represent just a small portion of those that have been reported on a regular basis in the United States throughout the 1990s. The Anti-Defamation League (ADL) of B'nai B'rith, a civil rights group, tracks incidents of assaults on and harassment of Jews. They state that more than two thousand anti-Semitic (anti-Jewish) acts were reported in 1994, a rise of 10.6 percent over the year before and the highest in the organization's history. The United States Federal Bureau of Investigation (FBI) recorded 5,852 hate crimes in 1995, which included attacks against Jews, people of color, and homosexuals. However, the ADL reported that in 1995 anti-Semitic incidents went down by 11 percent.

Racist skinheads, known for their shaved heads and membership in hate groups, have been responsible for some of the violent acts. However, it is difficult to pin down just which extremist groups in North America—and around the world—subscribe to Nazi beliefs, as outlined in the 1920s by the German dictator Adolf Hitler, considered one of the most evil men in history.

The new Nazis (or neo-Nazis) have formed groups or alliances with other radical far-right groups. In this book, the "radical far right" generally refers to those who favor a society with one language, religion, and way of life. They are often antigovernment or want as little government control as possible. People of the far right usually oppose—often violently—a pluralistic society, that is, a society with people from many different language backgrounds, religions, and lifestyles.

On the other hand, the "liberal left" is a term used to describe those who want government to play a role in programs and policies to benefit society. They usually favor a way of life that includes people of many different cultures. But radicals on the left can sometimes be as violent as extremists on the right.

There is little doubt that neo-Nazi groups are made up of people who despise those different from themselves. However, they often claim that those who oppose them are the ones full of hate. They also say their critics will not listen to reasonable arguments about Nazi views. Yet their so-called reasonable arguments are usually based on partial truths or outright falsehoods.

To many Americans, neo-Nazi and militant white supremacist groups seem strange but harmless. But "the movement is not [harmless] and does not mean to be," according to Raphael S. Ezekiel of the Harvard School of

Graffiti, such as the swastika painted on this synagogue, is just one of the forms neo-Nazi hate acts can take.

Public Health and formerly on the psychology faculty at the University of Michigan. In his book *The Racist Mind: Portraits of American Neo-Nazis and Klansmen,* Ezekiel declared that the goal of the movement is:

> . . . power and domination; its history, rhetoric, and analysis direct it into violence; its language draws to it people who will be capable of violence. . . . Violence is a key to understanding the multiple meanings of the movement.[4]

Another key to understanding the movement is awareness of the many paths it takes. There is no central neo-Nazi or white supremacist organization. Rather, the far-right movement spreads out in web-like fashion with members of various groups drifting away for awhile, becoming active again, and networking through a variety of communication systems.

White supremacist activities are global in scope and are described briefly in some of the following chapters. But the primary focus of this book is on how neo-Nazis have found a place in the radical far-right movement in the United States and Canada and have invaded some mainstream organizations and media. Fortunately, there are individuals and groups who alert the general public to the ways and means of their hatemongering (spreading hate messages). This book describes the activities and reports of these watchdogs who are dedicated to justice, tolerance, and the preservation of a pluralistic society.

11

2

Roots of Neo-Nazism

Most neo-Nazis today worship Adolf Hitler. In the 1930s and 1940s, Hitler led the Nationalsozialistische Deutsche Arbeiterpartei (National Socialist German Workers' party), or Nazi party, which had been founded in 1919.

Early in his life, Hitler developed a hatred of Jews and was obsessed with a false notion that Jews around the world were involved in a conspiracy to destroy what he called the Aryan race. In his view, Aryans were born to rule because they were superior to all other people. His political views were spelled out in his book *Mein Kampf*, which called for a nationalist Germany. In other words, he believed German citizens should be utterly devoted to their nation. His Nazi party supported fascism—a government headed by a dictator. Hitler set up a private army called the Schutzstaffel, known as the SS, and established a state police called the gestapo.

Once Hitler gained control of Germany in 1933, he set out to conquer eastern Europe and brought about World War II in 1939. He attempted to establish and engineer his superior society, an Aryan nation of white northern Europeans, free of Jews, Gypsies, the physically and mentally handicapped, and others he considered unfit and undesirable. He also set out to destroy those who resisted his hate-filled actions. As Germany conquered most of Europe during World War II, Nazis systematically persecuted and killed millions of Jews and others in a massive slaughter called the Holocaust. Hitler and Germany were finally defeated in 1945.

The Nazi movement has never included large numbers in the United States, but during the 1920s and early 1930s, some German immigrants formed small Nazi cells, or organizations. At the same time, other white supremacist forces were at work, among them the Knights of the Ku Klux Klan (KKK).

The Klan and Conspiracy Connections

One of the first terrorist groups in the United States, the Ku Klux Klan, began in Pulaski, Tennessee, after the Civil War. At first it was more like a social club, a secret society made up of Confederate veterans. To amuse themselves, they often dressed in sheets to conceal their identity and to play practical jokes on new recruits.

At the same time, newly freed slaves in the South began to vote. These new voters helped put Republicans, who often supported voting rights for African Americans, into office in southern states. The Klan gained membership and was led by Nathan B. Forrest, a former Confederate general who preached white supremacy. Klan members continued to disguise themselves in white robes as well as masks and made the burning cross their symbol. But their activities were no longer jokes—they set out to brutally attack newly enfranchised African Americans or anyone who sympathized with Republicans in power. In her book *Women of the Klan*, Kathleen Blee wrote:

> During the late 1860s the Klan spread its reign of terror throughout Southern and border states. Gangs of Klansmen threatened, flogged, and murdered countless black and white women and men. . . . Schoolteachers, revenue collectors, election officials, and Republican officeholders—those most involved with dismantling parts of the racial state—as well as all black persons, were the most common targets of Klan terror.[1]

By the 1870s, the Klan was so violent that national troops had to be sent to restore order in some southern states, and the organization faded from the scene in 1872.

The Klan did not disappear, however. Over the next few decades, the organization revived for a time, died out, then revived again several times, with leaders loudly proclaiming their views on white—meaning white Anglo-Saxon Protestant (WASP)—supremacy. The KKK continued to attack not only African Americans but also Jews, Catholics, and immigrants. During the 1920s, women who fought for voting and other civil rights and job opportunities were also targeted for Klan assaults.

The popularity of the Klan was at one of its high

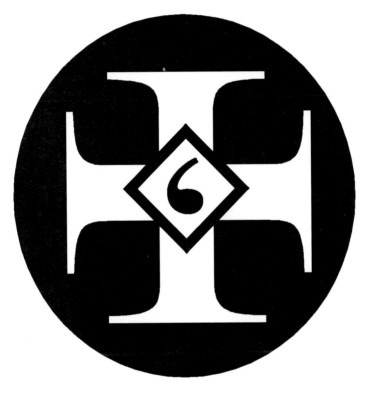

This is the symbol of the Ku Klux Klan, a violent and racist group that began its "reign of terror" in the South after the Civil War.

points in the 1920s, in part because of fundamentalist Protestant groups who believe in the literal truth of the Bible and rigidly follow biblical commands. They were convinced that values were decaying in the country and that Armageddon, the biblical final battle between good and evil, was fast approaching. The groups were rather like the far-right movement today in which numerous religious and political leaders decry the loss of American values and point fingers at scapegoats—others they can blame, usually immigrants and minorities.

The 1920s was also a time when the idea of a Jewish conspiracy to control the world took root and spread. This plan was supposedly revealed in a manuscript called *The Protocols of the Elders of Zion.* Though the myth itself is centuries old, the *Protocols* apparently stemmed from an essay written by members of the Russian secret police in the 1890s. These police claimed that a Jewish council planned to destroy Christianity and control the world. The *Protocols* was actually a forgery of a French satire on Napoleon III, but as James Ridgeway explained in his book on racists and neo-Nazis:

> In brief, the *Protocols* argue that people are incapable of governing themselves, and only a despot using armed force can rule effectively. For years, the *Protocols* say, the Jews have plotted this course, and now they must rise to power by pitting the gentiles against one another until, eventually, the Jews will be able to enlist the masses in overthrowing their indolent gentile leaders. Thereafter the masses will be kept under firm control through an efficient government that will banish unemployment, apply taxation in proportion to wealth, encourage small

16

business, and promote education . . . the Jewish masters will shrewdly promise, but never deliver, liberty.[2]

Because the *Protocols* could be used to justify hatred and fear of Jews, the work was widely distributed in Europe and the United States during the 1920s and 1930s. This fabricated account became the classic way to defend anti-Semitism and to support Nazism. Some prominent Americans, such as pilot Charles Lindbergh, known for making the first solo flight across the Atlantic Ocean, and Henry Ford, the automobile manufacturer, embraced the ideas in the *Protocols*. Ford financed a newspaper, the *Dearborn Independent,* that published a series of articles he wrote or helped write, perpetuating the myth about a worldwide Jewish conspiracy.

The myth was also spread through such organizations as the Silver Legion (or Silver Shirts) in the United States. Established in 1933 by William Dudley Pelley, the Silver Legion was patterned after Hitler's storm troopers, called Brown Shirts.

Another pro-Nazi group called the German-American Bund embraced conspiracy theories. Founded in the 1930s and led by Fritz Kuhn, a German who became an American citizen in 1934, the Bund recruited those who called themselves Germans in America rather than German-Americans. They looked forward to the day Nazism would triumph in the United States. Budesfuhrer Kuhn, as he called himself, organized paramilitary camps in New York, Pennsylvania, New Jersey, Michigan, and Wisconsin. Following Hitler's example, Kuhn encouraged parades of uniformed men who saluted in Nazi fashion with their arms outstretched and palms down. In an article for *American Heritage,* Gene Smith noted that in numerous cities the Bund:

> Held beer evenings, coffee hours, comradeship meetings; showed movies made in Berlin; sponsored soccer, tennis, hockey, swimming, and ski teams; went to the mountains for martial drill and hiking; and paraded in honor of Hitler's birthday. There were lectures on Nazi art and music. "PATRONIZE ARYAN STORES" handouts were distributed in front of Jewish-owned establishments.[3]

In spite of his organizing abilities, Kuhn was known to be a "liar, thief, forger, adulterous womanizer, braggart, lout, and boor—even Hitler didn't like him."[4] Eventually Kuhn was arrested for grand larceny and other felonies and went to prison. After World War II, he was deported to Germany, where he died in 1951.

American Nazi Party

A later Nazi organization, the American Nazi Party (ANP), was founded by George Lincoln Rockwell in 1959. Rockwell was a former United States Navy pilot who fought against the Nazis during World War II. He became involved with anticommunist movements in the 1950s and read Hitler's rhetoric against communists in *Mein Kampf.* This led Rockwell to believe that he was fulfilling Hitler's legacy by working for far-right groups such as the United White Party and the National Committee to Free America from Jewish Domination. Later, he organized the ANP, and he and the party published numerous racist and anti-Semitic materials.

One tract published by the party in Arlington, Virginia, and handed out in Washington, D.C., during the early 1960s declared that Rockwell was no more a bigot or racist than President Abraham Lincoln. The tract declared that Lincoln "preached EXACTLY the same doctrines now preached by Lincoln Rockwell—that Negroes are inferior as a BREED of human beings and must be SEPARATED from the superior White people of America."

The Nazi tract went on to claim that the "record of performance of the White Race compared to the performance of the Negro race is scientific PROOF that the Negro is a less advanced branch of the evolution of the species, homo sapiens." But Rockwell included no scientific proof. Indeed, no reputable studies to this day offer scientific evidence of this spurious notion of white superiority. Certainly Rockwell did not take into account that his and other white racist views hindered most African Americans. In addition, laws and customs denying equal rights and opportunities were responsible for the lack of performance or economic, educational, and social advancement for many minorities, whether Asians, African Americans, Hispanics, or Native Americans.

Other parts of the tract tried to link groups such as the National Association for the Advancement of Colored People (NAACP) to what was described as Jewish influence and Jews who supported "race mixing." Using the Jewish conspiracy theory, Rockwell stated—again without any evidence—that "Jewish businessmen have gained control of America's means of communication—our newspapers, radio, TV, movies, etc." and that

19

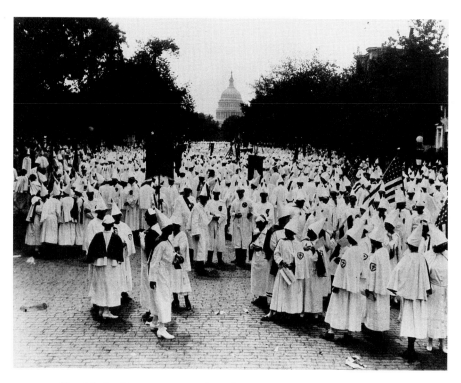

Neo-Nazis often recruit members from the Ku Klux Klan, like those shown here at the nation's capital.

"too many American Jews are fanatically engaged in destroying the WHITE, CHRISTIAN AMERICAN REPUBLIC as established by our Founding Fathers."[5]

In spite of hate appeals, membership in the American Nazi Party never reached more than two thousand members before Rockwell was shot to death by one of his own party in 1967.[6] A Rockwell associate, Matt Koehl, became the next party leader, changing the party's name to the National Socialist White People's Party. Although some remnants of the original American Nazi Party still exist, many members have drifted away to form their own splinter groups.

Still, more than twenty-five years after Rockwell's murder, one worshiper, A. V. Schaerffenber, praised Rockwell as a Nordic hero. In a nasty, anti-Semitic essay posted on the Internet's World Wide Web, he declared that Rockwell exhibited "Herculean bravery" in the 1960s for speaking at an outdoor forum in New York City's Central Park. Rockwell had taunted Jews, "deriding them to their camel-faces as cowards and fugitives from lunatic asylums." The essayist goes on gleefully with more and more insults and derogatory remarks about Jews, implying that they began a riot and police "crashed into the howling throng swinging night sticks. Kosher casualties mounted rapidly, as the cops obviously relished their sport. They blazed a path of splattering gore to the ever-battling Rockwell, and escorted him over the blubbering bodies of fallen Jews." The essayist finally proclaims that:

> The enemies of the White race would like to pretend that George Lincoln Rockwell never existed.

Certainly, they have done everything possible to expunge his name from American history. But their efforts continue to fail. His image and deeds are forever engraved in the hearts and memories of millions. . . . His writings and recorded spoken words continue to educate and inspire new generations of racial patriots.[7]

Whether Rockwell was the inspiration for the new generation of Nazis is debatable, although neo-Nazi groups try to keep his ideas and others like them in the public forum. After World War II, some Nazi groups in Europe remained active, and they too attempted to keep alive Hitler's anti-Semitism and his plan for an all-white nation. These neo-Nazi groups exported their extremist views to North America. Like their European counterparts, North American neo-Nazis saturated themselves with Nazi doctrine, reading books about Nazi beliefs and watching videotapes of Hitler.

Today, neo-Nazis still follow the Hitler doctrine, espouse white power and white supremacy, wear military garb, practice guerrilla and terrorist maneuvers, and usually tattoo themselves with swastikas that represent the Nazi party and other symbols to demonstrate their allegiance to their racist cause. They also spread lies about a so-called worldwide Jewish conspiracy and about the Zionist Occupation Government (meaning that the United States government has been taken over by Jews), often referred to as ZOG.

The white supremacist views of the Nazis are intertwined with and support the activities of today's Ku Klux Klan. However, the KKK is now in disarray because of internal strife and lawsuits brought against its leaders by groups such as the Southern Poverty Law Center (SPLC) and its Klanwatch Project. The SPLC files lawsuits on behalf of those who suffer from attacks by white supremacist groups, and Klanwatch was set up in 1979 to monitor KKK terrorist tactics and to provide help for victims.

By 1994, KKK members and other white supremacists had become closely linked with "the exploding ranks of the Aryan Nations, militias, states rights groups and a growing Identity movement," Klanwatch reported.[8] Yet these are just a few of the groups with neo-Nazi ties that are part of the radical far-right movement.

3

The Swastika
and Uzi Crowd

Among the approximately three hundred different white supremacist or Hitler-like groups that have formed since the 1960s and 1970s, many are local and do not achieve wide publicity. Although no two groups are exactly alike, all are openly or covertly against Jews, people of color, and homosexuals, according to Klanwatch and the Center for Democratic Renewal (CDR). The CDR, headquartered in Atlanta, Georgia, was founded in 1979 as a civil rights organization "that monitors the influence and spread of hate groups and teaches communities how to respond."[1]

As part of its ongoing efforts, the CDR keeps track of extremist groups that range from small religious sects to militant neo-Nazis. "The basic underpinnings of these organizations may be rooted in religion, they may be paramilitary, or survivalists, or anarchists," the CDR reports. Like other civil rights organizations that monitor hate groups, the CDR has found that Klan groups are declining, but:

> More Hitler-inspired groups, like the National Alliance and the Church of the Creator, are growing in numbers and influence. Swastikas and Uzis are replacing hoods and crosses.
>
> Each group is working to create a society totally dominated by whites by excluding and denying the rights of non-whites, Jews, gays and lesbians, and by subjugating women. The movement's links are global, from the pro-apartheid movement in South Africa and the neo-fascists in Germany to robed Klansmen in the deep South.[2]

Many of the swastika and uzi crowd in the United States and Canada are part of the KKK or Klan offshoots and may be recognized by names that include KKK or Knights. Flaming Sword Knights of the KKK in South Vineland, New Jersey, is one example. But the local and state organizations that are avowed neo-Nazis include names that are unfamiliar to some: Aryan Revolutionary Army in St. Louis, Missouri; Das Eisern Korps in Holland, Michigan; Euro American Alliance in Milwaukee, Wisconsin, and San Lorenzo, California; National Socialist White American Party in East Peoria, Illinois, and Middletown, Wisconsin; National Socialist White People's Party in Chapel Hill, North Carolina; and the White American Freedom Fighters in Overland, Missouri. Among the groups most often in the news are the Hitler-loving Aryan Nations, neo-Nazi skinheads, and groups based on the Christian Identity philosophy, such as the Christian Posse Comitatus, Church of Jesus Christ Christian, and Church of the Creator.

Christian Identity

Christian Identity (or simply Identity) ideas were being spread in the United States several decades before many of the current Nazi groups organized. During the 1940s, one of the main Identity spokespeople was Californian Wesley Swift, a racist originally from Louisiana. Swift preached a doctrine that stemmed from a hate movement known as Anglo-Israelism developed in Great Britain in the late 1800s, according to an ADL report.[3] Swift died in 1970, but the movement he led is based on a thinly disguised white supremacy doctrine and on Identity teachings that have become part of the basic concepts of many neo-Nazi and KKK groups.

Using pseudo-Christian teachings as a cover, the Identity movement is based on a "two-seed" theory of humankind's origins. The accepted story of Adam and Eve, as described in the Bible, states that the couple had two sons, Cain and Abel, and that out of jealousy Cain killed Abel. But according to Identity theory, Adam and Eve produced two sons, Abel and Seth. Then Eve also had sexual intercourse with Satan (who was in the form of a snake) and produced another son, Cain, who murdered Abel.

Seth's offspring (descendants of Adam) supposedly make up the white race, or what are called the Lost Tribes of the House of Israel or the true Israelites. Cain's descendants are called pre-Adamic people: Jews and blacks who are considered not fully human and have no souls. It is the mission of the Christian Identity movement to get rid of people who are not true Israelites.

Identity believers say "their true lineage has been

The Klu Klux Klan may be recognized by names that include KKK or Knights.

hidden for the past 2,000 years, supposedly since white people migrated out of Biblical Israel," the CDR explained. "They believe that their racial identity [thus the name] is important because of the fate of various racial groups during the period they refer to as the End Times," or the Second Coming of Christ.[4]

Many Christians who believe Christ will appear for the Second Coming to save true believers expect to be transferred to heaven in what is called the Rapture. But Identity preachers say the Rapture is a hoax. Thus, the CDR points out:

> If there is no Rapture, Christians can expect to suffer through the Tribulations [a time of plagues and wars] in order to reach the Kingdom. Identity teaches that the "elect" people of the Anglo-Saxon nations have a special role to play throughout the period of the Tribulations and until the establishment of the Kingdom. In Identity Christianity, election is determined by race, not by the redemptive grace of God.
>
> Since many Identity believers think that humankind is now in the period of the Tribulations, current events are interpreted as the fulfillment of dire prophecies. Some believe that social security numbers and drivers licenses are the Mark of the Beast [Satan], and should not be used.
>
> The Tribulations, they believe, are divine retribution for their sins; they have sinned by allowing the stranger—Jews and others—to live amongst them. They have sinned because society allows interracial marriages. They have sinned by allowing the sodomites (homosexuals) to continue their "evil practices." Since Identity followers believe

that the Bible commands racial segregation, they interpret racial equality as a violation of God's Law. If Christian ministers advocate racial equality, they are advocating breaking God's Law.[5]

An Ex-Con and Former Identity Leader

One Identity leader was the late Robert Miles, a former Grand Dragon of the Michigan KKK and an ex-convict. Miles was imprisoned in 1973 for his role in the 1971 bombing of six school buses that were to be used in the desegregation of the public schools in Pontiac, Michigan. After serving six years of a nine-year sentence, Miles was released. He set up and became pastor of the Mountain Church of Jesus Christ the Savior on his farm in Cohactah, Michigan, near Flint. From there he preached his brand of "gospel" and published newsletters proclaiming his views. In one, he wrote:

> WE BELIEVE THAT WE WERE CREATED IN THE ASTRAL [Starry] KINGDOM BY OUR GOD, WHO WAS THE FIRST WHITE EVER. WE BELIEVE THAT WE WERE SENT TO THIS EARTH TO SUBDUE IT AND TO QUELL THE REBELLION RAGING UNDER THE LEADERSHIP OF SATANEL. . . . UNTIL WE COMPLETE THAT TASK, WE SHALL FIND NO PEACE NOR REST. WE ARE THE SOLDIERS OF THE KING WHO IS OUR GOD AND OUR ONLY GOVERNMENT. OUR ASTRAL RACE IS OUR ONLY NATION.[6]

Miles also praised such notorious Nazis as Rudolf Hess, Hitler's second in command. (Hess was convicted of

29

war crimes in 1946 and sentenced to life in prison at Spandau in Berlin, Germany, where at the age of ninety-three he committed suicide.) In addition, Miles's tirades consistently targeted the United States government, which he often claimed was the worst enemy of the white race.

Miles and several other right-wing extremists were tried in 1988 on charges that they had planned a campaign of murder and sabotage in order to instigate a racist revolution and overthrow the government. An FBI agent who headed the investigation of Miles and his cohorts said the men used *The Turner Diaries* by neo-Nazi William Pierce as their guide. (The book has also been implicated in other terrorist attacks, including the 1995 bombing of the federal building in Oklahoma.) Miles was acquitted of all charges and continued his racist activities, hosting Klan rallies and neo-Nazi gatherings, until his death in 1992.

Counteracting Identity

The Identity theology seems absurd to many Christians who base their beliefs on the life of Christ and the love and mercy of God. The National Council of Churches, representing many Protestant denominations, spoke out against the false claims of Christian Identity in 1987. But only a few Christian denominations have made concerted efforts to call attention to the Identity movement and its misuse of the Bible. One in the forefront is the Evangelical Lutheran Church in America (ELCA).

In 1995, the ELCA adopted a resolution to expose the Identity movement's falsehoods. The resolution was prepared by Jerry Walters, pastor of the Zion Lutheran Church in Roundup, Montana. His church is in an area of the Northwest where a number of extremists have gathered "in a kind of Noah's Ark to heed the urgent call to preserve the white race," as Walters described it.

Walters, who uses his pulpit and the media to expose the white supremacy agenda of the Christian Identity movement, explained that people can easily be caught up in some of the social and political issues that extremists espouse. These include concerns about high taxes, job losses, and government interference in private lives. But Walters points out that such issues "can be handled more responsibly when the life-shaping, white supremacy theology is exposed." He cautioned, however, that it was a hindrance "to argue the interpretation of particular [biblical] texts. Be forewarned, you may not even get a word in edgewise with folks from the racist extremist groups. If you are white and disagree with the theology of Christian Identity, you're considered deceived and apathetic to the cause of the white race."[7]

The Aryan Nations

During the 1970s, another self-proclaimed Identity minister, Richard Butler, formed the Aryan Nations, the military arm of his Church of Jesus Christ Christian. Butler had been a disciple of Wesley Swift, taking over Swift's church after he died, and then moving it to Hayden Lake, Idaho. The church and the Aryan Nations included neo-Nazis, Identity members, and Klansmen, who Butler claimed had the divine right to hate. The group set up a fenced compound and began efforts to establish a

31

whites-only homeland in the northwestern states of Idaho, Montana, Wyoming, Oregon, and Washington.

Although the movement began to draw and unify white supremacists and neo-Nazis during the late 1970s and early 1980s, member Robert Jay Mathews formed a splinter group with eight other men in 1983. He called this group the Silent Brotherhood, which also was known at various times as The Order, the White American Bastion, and the Aryan Resistance Movement. Each member of this brotherhood made a pledge, "as a free Aryan man," swearing:

> An unrelenting oath upon the green graves of our sires, upon the children in the wombs of our wives, upon the throne of God almighty, sacred is his name, to join together in holy union with those brothers in this circle and to declare forthright that from this moment on I have no fear of death, no fear of foe; that I have a sacred duty to do whatever is necessary to deliver our people from the Jew and bring total victory to the Aryan race.[8]

Among assignments that Mathews outlined for his group were assassinations and the formation of a guerrilla army capable of sabotage in urban areas. Mathews also planned a course of action if he and his men were attacked by authorities. Each man was given a target to kill, ranging "from Henry Kissinger and the banker David Rockefeller to the heads of the three television networks, all of whom were perceived as enemies because they were either Jewish or 'fronts for the Jews,'" according to a *Rocky Mountain News* editorial.[9]

To finance their activities, Mathews and his crew

32

committed a number of armed robberies in Washington state during 1983 and 1984, including hijacking armored cars. They also set up counterfeiting operations, producing phony fifty-dollar bills. In the meantime, they continued planning their strategies for killing their enemies.

Another target for assassination was Alan Berg, a Jewish talk-show host broadcasting on KOA from Denver, Colorado. He was murdered by Mathews's hit squad in 1984. The murder was one of numerous criminal acts during an eighteen-month period. Federal agents tracked and caught twenty-four members of Mathews's group, and they were convicted on various criminal charges and imprisoned. Robert Mathews was killed in 1984 during a shoot-out with authorities on Whidbey Island in Puget Sound in the state of Washington. Other members of the group were jailed for various crimes.

Community opposition to and legal actions against Mathews's hate group brought an end to their actions and affected the militant Aryan Nations, which almost died out. But during the 1990s, the Aryan Nations began to attract more members again and has become what Klanwatch calls "the most dangerous white-supremacist organization" today.

Each year the Aryan Nations holds a world congress that brings together neo-Nazi and Klan leaders from North America and Europe. The congress, which began in 1979, has become increasingly Nazi-like in its ceremonies and rhetoric. One news report noted that the July 1995 congress was guarded by a security force who gave the "Seig Heil" salute used by Hitler's Nazis and

The Aryan Nations, which uses this symbol, draws its membership from neo-Nazi, Ku Klux Klan, and white supremacist groups.

wore "pins with swastikas and Third Reich 'SS' insignia." A swastika banner provided a backdrop for speakers.[10]

According to news accounts, several hundred people attended the 1995 congress. Klanwatch estimated that only about two hundred attended, which was still the largest crowd in several years. More significant, however, is the fact that Aryan Nations members at the congress

> began an intelligence operation that calls for the surveillance of government buildings and the offices

of civil rights groups and the media. Aryan Nations state offices have been ordered to develop counter-intelligence teams to photograph and compile information on employees of these organizations.[11]

One of the speakers at the congress was Louis Beam, a former Texas Klan leader known for his hostile anti-Semitic and antigovernment views. He also advocates "leaderless resistance," a concept for developing small revolutionary cells to independently carry out violent acts. During his speech, he reportedly urged his audience to join state militias and insisted that civil rights groups, in particular the Southern Poverty Law Center, its Klanwatch staff, founder Morris Dees, and the Anti-Defamation League "had to be stopped."[12] Dees is a trial lawyer who has brought lawsuits against many Klan and neo-Nazi leaders. Indeed, several months after the congress, the law center and its staff narrowly missed a bombing of their building, and three members of an Oklahoma militia were indicted for the plot.

In order to expand its membership, the Aryan Nations has been recruiting former Klan members and has drawn from militant militias and also from skinhead groups, known for their shaved heads and shiny black, steel-toed boots. Although skinheads are loosely orga-nized and the definition for skinhead varies worldwide, violence is what most skinheads are about.

Neo-Nazi Skinheads

During the late 1960s, skinhead groups organized in Britain. Youth from working-class families broke away from a cult known as the "Mods" and dressed and acted

35

the part of street toughs, shaving their heads and instigating fights at football [soccer] games as a way to show support for their teams. They also liked to hang out at dance halls and listen to their favorite bands, which played Jamaican music, known by such names as ska, blue beat, and reggae.

By the 1970s, the British National Front (NF)—the National Socialist Party—began to infiltrate skinhead groups, and some young people became NF street soldiers, adopting the skinhead look. They espoused nationalism and often staged protests against nonwhite immigration. That trend spread to other countries, including the United States and Canada. Today, skinhead groups in North America are known by such names as Hammerskins, Fourth Reich Skins, League of Aryan Warriors, and American Front.

The neo-Nazi skinhead movement became well-entrenched in the United States during the 1980s, and 144 groups were counted in 1991. Membership dropped over the next two years. By 1995, civil rights groups estimated that the total number of skinheads in the United States was between thirty-five hundred and four thousand, with at least that many supporters, including "wannabes"—kids who would like to be full-fledged skinheads or dress like them. Worldwide the total number of skinheads and their supporters is about seventy thousand.

Some skinheads have tried to retain their traditional 1960s appearance and affiliation with punk music. They adamantly deny ties to neo-Nazis. In fact, several World

Wide Web homepages have appeared to show that not all skinheads are racist. One page begins with this disclaimer:

IF YOU ARE LOOKING FOR ANY KIND OF RACISM, FASCISM OR ANY OTHER NAZISTUFF THEN THIS IS THE WRONG PLACE FOR YOU. THIS IS A PAGE FOR NON-RACIST AND NON-FASCIST SKINS AND THOSE WHO ARE INTERESTED IN IT.

Since the early 1990s, neo-Nazi skinheads have attempted to lure new members through music. In 1994, former skinhead members George Burdi of Woodbridge, Ontario, Canada, and Mark Wilson of Detroit, Michigan—two leading neo-Nazis in North America—established a racist record company called Resistance Records. Burdi was convicted of assault charges in Canada, and after serving a jail term, moved to the United States because of its free speech laws.

Resistance Records sells high-decibel rock music by bands with such names as Aryan and Aggravated Assault. The bands perform songs with titles like "White People Awake," "Third Reich," and "The Eternal Jew." According to a report in the *Detroit Free Press,* the lyrics advocating white supremacy and violence against people of color and Jews cannot be printed in newspapers because "they are filled with obscenities and racial epithets."[13]

Using the name George Eric Hawthorne, Burdi actually performs with a band called RaHoWa, which stands for "racial holy war," and a *Detroit Free Press* reporter learned that Burdi "wants Resistance to help define the skinhead culture." In an article for the record company's magazine, Burdi wrote: "We must reach our people, concentrating on the youth, and convince them that we have the only plausible and real answer to the nightmare that multiracialism has brought." In Burdi's view, "the progeny [children] of slaves cannot live with the progeny of slave masters."[14]

Although the music and lyrics of Resistance Records are legal and could be written off as the work of extremists, Richard Lobenthal, Michigan regional director of the ADL, warns that the music:

> Provides the galvanizing, the inspiration, the take-the-next-step ideology. The neo-Nazi movement, without its social underpinnings, would not be a movement. They would be disenfranchised, scattered bigots sitting around griping at home and floating around loose out there. But you come in with a neo-Nazi skinhead magazine and a concert, and you bring them together.[15]

The violence of some skinheads has created fears among many Americans, as well as people in other nations. Skinheads have been responsible for at least thirty-five murders and hundreds of brutal attacks against nonwhites, non-Christians, and homosexuals. Just during the first half of the 1990s, accounts of attacks by skinheads (or others with neo-Nazi affiliations) have ranged from vandalizing and defacing property to attacking and murdering individuals. Skinhead violence reported in the 1990s includes the following incidents:

In 1994, Randall Scott Anderson, the son of a teacher and an accountant, pled guilty to a 1992 bombing of a roller rink in Zion, Illinois, and to spray-painting threats on Am Echod Synagogue in nearby Waukegan. The threats included "Skins are going to kill U" and "Seig Heil." Anderson threw a homemade pipe bomb at the roller rink because he wanted to "send a message to the owner" not to welcome African Americans to the rink. He also painted a long, barely legible message on the outside walls claiming that "Neo-Nazis . . . Will Do What is Necessary to Ensure the Race and Make a Better World for Our Children."[16]

■ ■ ■

In 1994, skinheads used baseball bats and dogs to attack five African-American teenagers who were eating at a Taco Bell restaurant in Orange County, California.

■ ■ ■

Another 1994 incident involved Kevin Lee Fulcher of Georgia and several other skinheads who claimed to be members of the Skinheads for White Power. They kidnapped a Korean man, Savage Ellis, drove him around, threatened him with torture and death, and kicked him repeatedly in what they called a "boot party." Fulcher, the instigator, was convicted of kidnapping, robbery, and terroristic threats and was sentenced to life in prison. His accomplices received lesser prison sentences.

■ ■ ■

In February 1995, three skinheads fired gunshots at students leaving Antelope Valley High School in Lancaster, California. Four African Americans, including a one-year-old child sitting in a car outside the school, were injured.

■ ■ ■

In June 1995, skinheads in Phoenix, Arizona, viciously attacked a Hispanic man and woman. The man was stabbed ten times and beaten. After the attackers were arrested, a neighbor of the skinheads told police the skinheads "played hate music all night, beat on drums, yelled, 'Seig Heil! Seig Heil!' at each other and generally scared the hell out of everybody. I hope they never get out of jail."[17]

■ ■ ■

With a reputation and disposition for violence, skinheads are recruited for other hate groups, some of which are paramilitary. (A paramilitary group is organized like a military unit but is not part of a federal or state military or law enforcement troop.) Recruiters come from groups with warrior-like names, such as the White Aryan Resistance (W.A.R.) and Christian Posse Comitatus. They also come from pseudo-religious groups, such as the Church of the Creator (COTC). These groups, and others like them, develop compounds where they illegally stockpile weapons, manufacture bombs, and practice guerrilla tactics, preparing for armed conflict against the United States government and citizens who do not share their ancestral background and racist beliefs.

4

Armed Resistance

The paramilitary subculture that includes neo-Nazis and white supremacists has been building in the United States since the 1970s, according to those tracking far-right movements. Groups that recruit neo-Nazis are not only orchestrating street violence but also are helping prepare a guerrilla strike force to "purify" America by ousting or killing people of color, homosexuals, Jews, and other non-Christians. Among those groups are the White Aryan Resistance (W.A.R.), a decentralized network that operates within a philosophy known as leaderless resistance, people with ties to the Patriots movement, Posse Comitatus followers, and some armed militias.

White Aryan Resistance

"W.A.R. is the most radical racist organization in the world!" boasts the creator of a World Wide Web homepage for the White Aryan Resistance. The hate

41

group is masterminded by Tom Metzger, an ex-Klan leader, and his son John, both of Fallbrook, California. Father and son were convicted in a 1990 civil case of inciting skinheads in Portland, Oregon, to use violence against Jews and African Americans.

In the fall of 1988, according to sworn testimony in court, the Metzgers asked Portland agents to recruit members of a skinhead group called East Side White Pride (ESWP) for the Metzgers' W.A.R. organization. Two of the agents, Michael Barrett and Dave Mazella, kept in daily contact with the Metzgers and held a meeting with ESWP members, getting them fired up on W.A.R. and the Metzgers' hate messages. Barrett testified under oath that he and Mazella "told these Skinheads that blacks and Jews were the enemy of the White Aryan Race." They urged the skinheads "to use violence if they got an opportunity and to be sure and beat the hell out of the enemy."[1]

Not long after the meeting with the Metzgers' agents, three skinheads—Kyle Brewster, Steven Strasser, and Ken Mieske—began handing out the Metzgers' literature. Then in November, armed with baseball bats, they went looking for someone to attack. They happened upon three Ethiopians and brutally beat and kicked them, killing Mulugeta Seraw, a community college student in Portland. The medical examiner at the trial testified that Seraw was struck from behind and head injuries were so severe that they reportedly "split the seams that joined the bone plates at the base of Seraw's skull."[2] The three skinheads pleaded guilty in the case and were convicted. Ken Mieske, who bludgeoned Seraw, received a life

On its Internet homepage or "hate page," W.A.R. boasts that it is the world's "most radical racist organization."

sentence for murder, and the other two were sentenced to up to twenty years for first-degree manslaughter.

Although the Metzgers were in California at the time of the murder and were not charged with criminal acts, they were sued by the SPLC on behalf of the Seraw family, seeking payment for pain and suffering and punitive damages. The Metzgers were tried in a Multnomah County, Oregon, circuit court in 1990 and found liable for the skinheads' actions. The jury awarded the murder victim's estate more than $12 million, and by court order Tom Metzger's home, TV repair business, and other property were seized and sold, with the proceeds—about a hundred thousand dollars—held in trust until the case was settled. The civil rights organization sought the large award in order to bankrupt W.A.R. and send a signal to other hate groups that they should get out of the business.

Over the next few years, the Metzgers appealed the court decision to the Oregon Court of Appeals, the Oregon Supreme Court, and finally, the last resort, the United States Supreme Court. All refused to hear the case, and in January 1995, the first installment of the funds were released to Seraw's family in Ethiopia, including to his teenage son who will now be able to continue his education.

Because of the Seraw case, Metzger has lost some clout with skinheads and other neo-Nazi groups, but he still carries on his campaign via a hate telephone number and a White Aryan Resistance newspaper. Most recently Tom Metzger has launched a World Wide Web site on the Internet titled the "White Aryan Resistance Hate Page," which includes the telephone number for his

"24-hour Hate Line," a link to the W.A.R. newspaper, and crude, derisive graphics of African Americans, Jews, and white "race traitors." Visitors to the site are told that the "artwork changes often, so click on the art you want to see and check back with us soon." Those who access the page are also encouraged to download and use the illustrations to spread hate messages.

One of the so-called art images shows a spiderlike figure with a hooked nose and star of David on its chest surrounded by a mist from an insecticide fogger used by a white Aryan type. Alongside are crude attempts at a rhyme warning whites to take up arms and defend themselves against "kikes" by spraying them with poison gas. Another shows a vile caricature of an apelike creature grabbing a blonde white woman. An Aryan is beating the creature over the head with a blunt instrument, and the copy says: "Let's Face it! Rampant Black Crime is bringing this nation to it's [sic] knees. If you care about the future of your home, your family, and your race . . . It's Time to Strike Back!"[3]

These examples of loathsome descriptions are enough to make the point that hatred is out there in cyberspace. The Metzgers and other racists and neo-Nazis not only use the Internet to spread their propaganda but also to call for whites (Aryans) to take up arms through such movements as leaderless resistance.

Leaderless Resistance

The leaderless resistance concept has been promoted for years by Louis Beam, an Aryan Nations zealot and a former grand dragon of the Texas Knights of the KKK.

In addition to spreading its hate propaganda on the Internet, W.A.R. recently launched a 24-hour "hateline."

During the early 1980s, Beam led the military arm of the Texas Klan, which trained twenty-five hundred paramilitary soldiers in secret camps. In 1987, after being charged with sedition for his part in a plot to overthrow the United States government, Beam fled to Mexico and was on the FBI's "Ten Most Wanted List." He eventually returned to the United States and was tried and acquitted in 1988 by an all-white jury.

A former helicopter gunner during the Vietnam War, Beam has based his ideas on those of Colonel Ulius Louis

Amoss, an anticommunist who died in the 1980s. Amoss first wrote about leaderless resistance in 1962, and Beam noted that Amoss's "theories of organization were primarily directed against the threat of eventual Communist takeover in the United States." In an electronic posting of an essay, Beam explained that Amoss feared communism, but he (Beam) feared the United States government, which he called "the foremost threat to the life and liberty of the folk." He called for opposition to "state repression" and declared it "the duty of every patriot to make the tyrant's [government's] life miserable."

To further the objectives of the resistance groups, Beam proposed a phantom cell system—small secret committees—based on an organization that "does not have any central control or direction." He contends that a pyramid organization with a top leader and supporters below would be "easy to kill" by "ZOG or ADL intelligence agents," whom he claims "gather information that can be used at the whim of a federal D.A. [district attorney] to prosecute."

According to Beam, "a single penetration of a pyramid style organization can lead to the destruction of the whole. Whereas, leaderless resistance presents no single opportunity for the Federals to destroy a significant portion of the resistance." In order for phantom cells to be effective, supporters of neo-Nazi and racist causes are supposed to "acquire the necessary skills and information as to what is to be done." This is accomplished through distribution of published materials and computer networks.[4]

Other Groups Linked to Neo-Nazis

Widespread distribution of information, including training manuals that are practically reprints of the cell structure that Louis Beam advocates, has certainly taken place among the 5 million Americans who consider themselves Patriots. Who are the Patriots? According to Chip Berlet, an analyst at Political Research Associates in Cambridge, Massachusetts, they are a diffuse group of loosely-linked individuals and organizations. They believe a small number of elite insiders are manipulating key political and economic events in the United States.[5]

Most Patriots would not be considered neo-Nazis, but many share their views. "On the far right flank of the Patriot movement are white supremacists and anti-Semites, who believe that the world is controlled by . . . Jewish bankers," investigative reporter Daniel Junas wrote in an article for the Covert Action Quarterly.[6]

Posse Comitatus, which is a Latin term for "power of the county," is another group that believes Americans should be armed and prepared for action against "enemies" in Washington, D.C. Initiated in Portland, Oregon, in 1969 by Henry L. Beach, who was a member of the Hitler-like Silver Shirts in the 1930s, Posse Comitatus followers say they have the right to organize local governments with the local sheriff as the top elected governmental figure. The sheriff, they believe, should not be controlled by state or federal laws. Posse members argue that "the U.S. Constitution prohibits the collection of federal income tax, that the Federal Reserve is part of an international banking plot [code words for the

Neo-Nazis often place anti-Semitic and racist graffiti on stores, synagogues, and homes.

Jewish conspiracy theory], and that the U.S. should adopt a strict isolationist policy in world affairs."[7]

Although many in the Posse subscribe to these views and Christian Identity beliefs, not all live by racist and anti-Semitic convictions. Some are disgruntled small farmers, businesspeople, and landowners who believe that they are being persecuted by the federal government. Others are people who believe United States policies are leaning toward a world government and that the power of the federal government is too great.

Nevertheless, Posse Comitatus gained a reputation (justifiable in many cases) for militant confrontations with federal officials. Such confrontations were depicted in *Bitter Harvest*, a book about Gordon Kahl published in 1990. In 1991, a movie based on the book was presented on TV. Kahl was a World War II hero decorated for his service as a gunner on a B-35 bomber and during the war was indoctrinated with "Jewish conspiracy" ideas. He is now a hero to such neo-Nazis as Louis R. Beam.

Kahl also became a tax protester during the mid-1970s when he joined the Posse in Texas. He urged others to refuse to pay their federal taxes, which soon led to his arrest and conviction on tax evasion. He was sent to federal prison for five years but was released on probation after serving a year. Provisions of the probation required that Kahl stay away from the Posse and pay his federal income taxes. However, he refused to abide by those conditions and became a parole violator, insisting that it was time to "engage in a struggle to the death between the people of the Kingdom of God and the Kingdom of Satan."[8]

Eventually federal officials set up a roadblock to stop and arrest Kahl, who had vowed never to return to jail. Kahl and his son, who was with him, shot and killed two United States marshals. Kahl then became a fugitive, finding refuge with supporters throughout the Midwest and finally at an Arkansas home in the Ozark Mountains. In June 1983, FBI officials, United States marshals, state police, and sheriffs surrounded Kahl's hideout, and during the siege, Kahl was shot and killed.

Other Posse Comitatus groups with Nazi-like leanings have established paramilitary settlements in various parts of the United States. Some settlements have faded from the scene, but they reemerge in different guises—most often as militia movements. "Many militia ideas and conspiracy theories are directly copied from the white supremacist movement," the Center for Democratic Renewal testified in a United States congressional hearing in mid-1995.[9] Klanwatch, Political Research Associates, the ADL, the CDR, and others following activities of militant racists and anti-Semitic groups warn that some militias are not only armed but extremely dangerous.

Militia Connections

Like some Patriots and Posse followers, members of militant militia groups "also believe that a secret elite conspiracy is controlling the government, the economy, the culture, or all three. Many of the militia movement's themes are rooted in historic white supremacist states' rights arguments and classic antisemitic conspiracy theories," the Political Research Associates of Massachusetts reported in 1995.[10]

Militias have been part of America ever since colonial days—long before the war for independence from Britain. During the American Revolution, colonies organized militias to be prepared to fight against the British if necessary. After independence and adoption of the Constitution, the states were given the authority to train and discipline militias. More than a century later, in 1903, the militias were organized into one unit as the National Guard, independent of the regular army. In 1916, the National Guard became a reserve unit of the army. The National Guard along with the Air National

51

Guard are equipped and funded by the federal government and are considered the organized militia of the states and territories. States and territories may also have their own defense forces or militias that are regulated by state laws.

Militant right-wing militias organized today are not the same as the National Guard or state defense forces. Rather, they are unofficial paramilitary organizations, and most states have passed laws to regulate or prohibit these groups. According to Chip Berlet of Political Research Associates, these new militias, as they are sometimes called, want to:

> . . . create a private army bent on accomplishing a series of authoritarian or theocratic goals that include rejecting federal laws and regulations, treating people of color as second-class citizens, stopping abortion by force, putting homosexuals to death, and targeting Jews by claiming they are conspiring for evil purposes. It is important to remember that one of the most famous militia movements in the U.S. is the Ku Klux Klan that arose as a militia during the turmoil of Reconstruction.[11]

Armed militias and terrorist groups have seldom disappeared for any length of time from the American scene, and they have come to public attention in recent years because of several highly publicized events during the 1980s and 1990s. Those events have convinced numerous armed militia members and white supremacists that their government is out to get them and/or is under the influence of the bogus Jewish conspiracy. The Kahl shootout with law enforcement officials described earlier is one example.

Another example is a 1992 federal agents' siege of the remote cabin home of avowed white separatist Randy Weaver and his family at Ruby Ridge in the Idaho mountains. The Weavers had attended neo-Nazi Aryan Nations meetings and held Christian Identity beliefs, but apparently they were of no threat to anyone. However, federal authorities arrested Weaver in 1991 for selling two illegal guns to an undercover agent. Weaver was released on his own recognizance but refused to appear in court on federal weapons charges. As a result, federal agents monitored the Weavers' place for a year and in August 1992 prepared to arrest Randy Weaver again. But federal agents used inappropriate tactics, surrounded the Weaver cabin, shot the Weavers' dog, and induced a gunfight that killed fourteen-year-old Sammy, one of Weaver's four children, and his wife, Vickie. In 1995, a United States Senate subcommittee found evidence of bungling and "simply no justification" for the deaths.

In 1993, more tragic deaths at a cult compound in Waco, Texas, also galvanized armed militia groups and other extremists. The cult, known as the Branch Davidians, was headed by David Koresh, who was wanted on weapons charges. Federal agents tried to force Koresh to surrender by surrounding the compound in a siege that lasted fifty-one days. The Davidian compound was set afire on April 19, apparently by cult members, and Koresh and eighty-five of his followers, including young children, died in the inferno.

To many Americans who watched the television reports of the long siege and terrible fire, the Davidians were primarily responsible for their own deaths, although federal agents also made mistakes, which some later acknowledged. But to radical right-wing believers, the federal government and its agents had committed one more in a series of "murders," such as the deaths of the Weavers and Kahl.

Those who monitor neo-Nazis and white suprema-cists say the Waco disaster helped set the stage for another catastrophe in 1995. On April 19, the second anniversary of the Waco disaster, the Alfred P. Murrah Federal Building in Oklahoma City, Oklahoma, was bombed. Timothy McVeigh and Terry Nichols were arrested in connection with the crime; both had contact with a militant militia group in Michigan. In addition, *The Turner Diaries,* which McVeigh avidly read, contains a description of a bombing that is strikingly similar to the Oklahoma bombing. These parallels are shown on a chart (see page 55) adapted from a Klanwatch report.

The contacts McVeigh and Nichols had with hard-core militia units in Michigan brought to public attention the fact that some armed militias are part of or closely connected to hate groups. The Militia of Montana (MOM), based in the northwestern part of the state, has often promoted the views of its leader, John Trochmann. Trochmann is known for his ties with the neo-Nazi Aryan Nations. In 1994, Trochmann report-edly predicted that a destructive event would take place on April 19, 1995 (the date of the Oklahoma bombing), according to Senator Max Baucus of Montana. Senator Baucus testified before a July 1995 Senate subcommittee investigating terrorism and the militia. Baucus also noted that since militias have formed in Montana "terrorist acts

Turner Diaries	Oklahoma City Bombing
Target: federal law enforcement building Ⅲ➤	Target: building housed federal ATF agents
Bomb described as "under 5,000 pounds" Ⅲ➤	Truck bomb was 4,400 pounds
Bomb mixture: fuel oil and ammonium nitrate fertilizer Ⅲ➤	Bomb mixture of fuel oil and ammonium nitrate fertilizer
Bomb went off at 9:15 A.M. Ⅲ➤	Bomb blast at 9:05 A.M.
Bomb designed to blow off front of building, causing upper floors to collapse Ⅲ➤	Bomb blew off front of building, causing upper floors to collapse
Bombing sparked by federal gun control act Ⅲ➤	Suspects violently opposed to federal gun control laws
Main character, Turner, called himself Patriot Ⅲ➤	Suspects call themselves "Patriots"
Turner member of antigovernment underground cell Ⅲ➤	Suspects possible members of antigovernment underground cell
Terrorists robbed banks to fund war Ⅲ➤	Suspects unemployed but had thousands of dollars, ski masks, and pipes similar to those used in bank robberies described in Pierce's book
Turner openly racist Ⅲ➤	Prime suspect openly racist

and anti-Semitic incidents have become noticeably more frequent." Among those incidents cited were the bombing of a women's clinic, the desecration of a Jewish cemetery, and anti-Semitic graffiti on a school wall.[12]

Militias in the neighboring state of Idaho have also been a focus of attention, primarily because some members have been a part of the Aryan Nations headquartered near Hayden Lake. In addition, some Idaho politicians have supported militias. One is Representative Helen Chenoweth, who has often expressed sympathy for the militia movement, insisting that it is one way people can protect themselves. After the Oklahoma bombing, Chenoweth said the tragedy indicated there were problems within the federal and state government. The *Idaho Statesman* roundly condemned her in an editorial, noting that "the nation may have its problems, but paramilitary groups setting off car bombs aren't the answer. . . . Whether she realized it or not, Chenoweth is quickly becoming the poster child for such groups."[13]

Certainly not all militia members have a Nazi-like agenda, and many may not even be aware that some of their colleagues have links to hate groups. For example, out of more than a dozen militia units that have reportedly organized in Alabama, only one or two are known to have racist ties. Still, watchdog organizations are constantly monitoring militia units, and Klanwatch reported in 1996 that out of the estimated 441 militias and their 368 Patriot support groups nationwide, 138 have ties to racist groups or leaders or have expressed racist and/or anti-Semitic beliefs.[14]

5

Spreading Propaganda, Lies, and Hate

Dispatching information is a prime component of leaderless resistance and the networking functions of neo-Nazi and other hate groups. Thus it is not surprising that every type of medium is used to spread misinformation, myths, propaganda, lies, and theories. Even though such messages are hateful and offensive, they are protected by the First Amendment to the Constitution. This well-known amendment prohibits Congress from making any laws that restrict or abridge the establishment or exercise of religion, "the freedom of speech or of the press; or the right of the people to peaceably assemble." There are limits, however: The Supreme Court has ruled that speech and assembly can be restricted if there is a danger to the welfare of citizens.

For neo-Nazis and white supremacists, the print medium is basic to spreading their ideas. Many racist and anti-Semitic pamphlets, newsletters, and books are sold by mail order, at gun shows, or at militia gatherings. Short-wave radio, cable television, videos, telephone, and electronic Internet connections are also common ways to distribute neo-Nazi propaganda.

Beyond hard-core members of hate groups, an estimated two hundred thousand people subscribe to racist publications, attend marches and rallies based on white supremacist beliefs, and contribute to such causes. The CDR reports that about a hundred hatelines are in operation, delivering not only speeches denigrating nonwhite and Jewish groups but also publicizing racist meetings and rallies.[1]

In addition, with access to new electronic technology, at least fifty neo-Nazi groups have launched home pages since the early 1990s. Many of these sites are available via the Internet's World Wide Web, athough their addresses change frequently and/or are accessible only to those with a password. No one can be sure whether most visitors to these electronic homepages are actually members of hate groups or are simply surfing by, but some of the sites are certainly designed for public consumption.

Hate in Print

One of the most widely circulated publications among neo-Nazis and former Klan members as well as other racists is a weekly tabloid called *The Spotlight.* More than a hundred thousand people subscribe to the magazine, and another fifty thousand buy copies at newsstands or other outlets. It is published by Liberty Lobby, a major force in keeping anti-Semitism alive in the United States. The magazine has supported racist groups and their propaganda, the cause of white supremacist Gordon Kahl, and the British National Front, a neo-Nazi organization in Great Britain. According to the CDR:

> *The Spotlight* promotes the denial of the Nazi genocide of European Jewry, often blaming World War II on Jews, President Roosevelt and other "internationalists."
>
> *The Spotlight,* however, does not contain the crude language of some Klan and neo-Nazi literature. Instead, it codes its bigotry with anti-big government rhetoric.[2]

Liberty Lobby and its magazine were founded in the late 1950s by Willis Carto, who has been described by the ADL as "perhaps the most influential anti-Semite in the United States."[3] A Californian, Carto has worked behind the scenes for a long time establishing a "network of extremist publications and organizations." One of the publishing entities to which Carto has been linked is Noontide Press, which reprinted a racist book, *Imperium,* written by Hitler admirer Francis Parker Yockey. Carto wrote a thirty-five-page introduction for the book.

Although Carto denies he is racist and anti-Semitic, the evidence clearly shows otherwise. Cecelia Müllermeder, who is a former follower of Carto and an "unwitting puppet," as she called herself, noted in a 1993 electronic conference article that Carto has:

> Severely anti-Black and severely anti-Jewish agendas. Although far more powerful than, say, David Duke [former Louisiana Klan leader who was a Republican candidate for Congress], Carto is not well-known because it has been his method of operation to

personally shun the limelights, preferring to shine "the spotlight" on others who are sometimes witting accomplices or sometimes unwitting puppets.[4]

Müllermeder noted that at the time of her electronic posting Carto headed the Institute for Historical Review (IHR), "designed to appear to be a normal historical research organization." For ten years, she thought "it was precisely that. In fact there really IS a normal historical organization called 'IHR'. It is the University of London's Institute of Historical Research, founded during the 1920's." But Carto's organization was, in Müllermeder's words:

> specifically designed to fool people of basically NON-racist organizations into contributing funds . . . and to be conduits of Carto's subtle and often very subliminal propaganda that is designed to . . . subtly "convert" these people to anti-Semitism and to other forms of bigotry.[5]

Because of a feud within IHR, Carto was ousted from the organization in 1993, although he tried to regain control through a variety of methods, including lawsuits. IHR is now operated by staff members who broke away from Carto.

The Institute for Historical Review

According to claims of the Institute for Historical Review, it is supposed to be a research and educational center, "devoted to truth and accuracy in history," and "continues the tradition of historical revisionism . . ."[6] As Müllermeder noted, there is a "tradition of historical revisionism" in which serious scholars analyze historical

The United States Supreme Court has ruled that speech and assembly can be restricted if there is danger to the welfare of citizens. The Supreme Court Building in Washington, D.C., is shown.

records for accuracy and then publish their theories in widely respected academic journals. But others, such as the IHR, use revisionism to cover their own bigotry and hatred. In other words, the IHR and its leaders, who are known for their neo-Nazi views, are dedicated to distributing materials that argue the Holocaust is a hoax, in spite of the fact that there is abundant evidence that millions of Jews and others were exterminated by Nazis in Germany during World War II.

To promote its view, the IHR publishes *The Journal of Historical Review,* a monthly magazine, and holds an annual conference, which the Center for Democratic Renewal describes as "nothing more than an international gathering of neo-Nazis." The CDR also warns that the IHR "attempts to put an academic facade on its anti-Semitic agenda. Eighteen of the 25 editorial advisory committee members listed in the IHR journal hold doctorates. Others hold advanced degrees or teach at universities."[7]

The IHR also publishes numerous pamphlets designed to misinform or to present outright lies about the Holocaust. One that is circulated widely is called *66 Questions and Answers about the Holocaust.* It is posted on Internet World Wide Web pages or Usenet groups. At least two notorious revisionists, Greg Raven, president of the IHR in California, and Ernst Zundel of Canada, a prolific publisher of hate material, posted the pamphlet on homepages.

Another major Holocaust-denial page is maintained by Bradley Smith of Visalia, California. Smith is director of the Committee for Open Debate on the Holocaust

(CODOH) and has concocted Holocaust-denial ads that he has placed in campus newspapers. According to Smith, between 1991 and 1995, his ads ran in student-run newspapers at Brandeis, Cornell, Duke, Notre Dame, Oberlin College, Rutgers, Tufts, Vanderbilt, University of Michigan, University of Arizona, Wheaton College, and numerous others.

Some university newspaper staff accept the ads because they believe rejecting them would be a form of censorship and denial of free speech. But other university journalists have refused to accept Smith's anti-Semitic material because of their inaccuracies and offensiveness. Some advertisers have threatened to pull their advertisements from campus newspapers if Smith's revisionist material is published.

Occasionally, revisionist propaganda has been rebutted in magazine and newspaper articles and in book form, although in the opinion of some rabbis and leaders of Jewish organizations, there is little to be gained by debating revisionists on their terms. Many say it is more important to expose the revisionists for what they are— anti-Semites and racists.

Yet an informal, international network of amateur and professional historians on the Internet is counteracting revisionists' propaganda by exposing the lies and misrepresentations in the Holocaust-denial material. The network was prompted in part by Kenneth McVay, a self-educated scholar on World War II and the Holocaust. McVay is a former computer consultant and now operates a gas station and convenience store but will not reveal his exact location because he fears an attack on his family or himself.

Ever since the early 1990s, when McVay began surfing the Internet and found neo-Nazi and anti-Semitic propaganda, he has been battling hatemongers. He has collected more than one thousand computerized documents, including testimony from survivors of Nazi death camps and evidence from the 1946 Nuremberg trials of World War II criminals. He continually posts facts that refute claims of people like Zundel, Raven, and Smith through a World Wide Web page and a project called Nizcor. McVay began the project with his own financing, but in recent years, he has received some much-needed help from supporters to buy new computer equipment. Nizcor provides links to nearly all the Holocaust-related resources on the Internet with the hope that reasonable people who are given access to information on the subject will reach reasonable conclusions.

Just a few rebuttals McVay has posted in regard to the *66 Questions and Answers* are included below, but all are available at the Nizcor World Wide Web site. For example, the IHR posed this question: "What evidence exists that six million Jews were not killed by the Nazis?" Then the IHR claims that "extensive forensic, demographic, analytical and comparative evidence demonstrates the impossibility of such a figure. The widely repeated 'six million' figure is an irresponsible exaggeration."

But Nizkor points out that the IHR often says it has extensive evidence "to prove that something did not happen. Yet Holocaust-deniers often claim that they do not have to prove anything because, as they say, 'it is impossible to prove a negative.'"

The IHR also claims in a question-and-answer format that in 1933 "world Jewry" carried out an "international boycott of German goods." But Nizkor shows that such a statement:

> Is intended to blame the victims. The truth is that Nazi-Jewish relations from the early 30s onward are complex, with Nazis repeatedly committing affronts against Jews.
>
> To take single instances out of context like this is grossly unfair and misleading. For example, one could also ask "what hostile action did Britain and France undertake against Germany in 1939?" The answer would be, of course: "they declared war on Germany." But without the context—the fact that Germany invaded Poland, a country tied to Britain and France by treaty, knowing that the result would be a war throughout Europe—the question and answer are meaningless.[8]

The IHR also distributes and widely quotes Fred Leuchter of Massachusetts, a notorious revisionist. Leuchter claims to have made studies of "alleged gas chambers" at Nazi death camps; he issued a report *(The Leuchter Report)* that declares no execution chambers existed. Because of the report, he was called as an "expert" witness in the 1988 Canadian trial of neo-Nazi revisionist Ernst Zundel, who was charged with distributing hate material. But Leuchter had no training or experience in engineering or related fields on which to base his claims, and he has been discredited by numerous experts. At the trial, the judge dismissed Leuchter's report and said Leuchter could not testify on the subject of gas chambers because he had no expertise. Yet *The Leuchter Report* has sold widely.

The National Alliance

Along with the IHR, the National Alliance (NA) is another loosely organized network distributing Holocaust revisionist material and other neo-Nazi and racist propaganda. It began as a spin-off of a political group that campaigned for the election of staunch segregationist George Wallace, who became governor of Alabama in 1962. William Pierce, author of *The Turner Diaries*, led the way in forming the National Alliance. Pierce was a former assistant professor of physics at Oregon State University and thus was considered an intellectual whose ideas would be respected by the public.

According to National Alliance statements, members recruit and disseminate the organization's message to the public through the World Wide Web, video materials, numerous printed publications, such as comic books aimed at teenagers, pamphlets, magazines, and a weekly radio program called "American Dissident Voices." Members also spread their hate material by writing letters, making telephone calls to radio talk shows, and recruiting "selected individuals" through a variety of means. For example:

> A member who is on the faculty of a university looks for other faculty persons or for exceptional students who are receptive to the National Alliance message; a member who is a businessman seeks opportunities to sound out and recruit other business people with

whom he comes in contact; a member who is serving in the armed forces or in a police agency uses his daily interactions with career personnel to select exceptional individuals who are receptive, and he then gives them the opportunity to serve their race while carrying out their military or police functions.[9]

The National Alliance message is also carried in *National Vanguard* magazine, edited by Pierce, who declares that the publication "provides the information and the insights that White America's future leaders will need to guide our nation through the dangerous, revolutionary times ahead." Recent features in the magazine have denigrated Black History Month, blasted law enforcement for the Waco disaster and legislators who support gun control, defended the ideas that the Holocaust was a hoax, and supported other Nazi-like concepts.

More Hate Messages on the Internet

The increasing use of the mass media, particularly the Internet, by hatemongers concerns many watchdogs of neo-Nazi and white supremacist groups. With the Internet, there is the possibility of reaching millions of computer users, and an impressionable child (or adult for that matter) can easily find and read disguised or straightforward racist materials and believe the propaganda.

One World Wide Web page was created by Don Black of West Palm Beach, Florida, who is married to the former wife of David Duke. An *Atlanta Constitution* reporter who interviewed Black described him:

[He was] soft spoken, intelligent, appearing the benign househusband in a white polo shirt, khakis

Along with Klan members, neo-Nazi groups distribute materials and demonstrate as a way to spread the lie that there was no Holocaust.

and knockabout walking shoes. But he succeeded David Duke, the failed Republican gubernatorial candidate in Louisiana, as Grand Dragon of the KKK. Black also spent two years in federal prison in the early 1980s for plotting the armed overthrow of the Caribbean nation of Dominica, hoping to establish a "white state."

While he's left the KKK since, it's only a change of tactics, he says, not of ideology.

The Confederate flag hangs on the wall behind his computers and modems, as does a portrait of KKK founder Nathan Bedford Forrest, of whom he dreams of producing a filmed biography.[10]

Black states that his homepage "is a resource for those courageous men and women fighting to preserve their White Western culture, ideals and freedom of speech and association—a forum for planning strategies and forming political and social groups to ensure victory."[11]

After accessing this homepage, a computer user can link to other neo-Nazi and white supremacist pages and documents. One link, for example, brings up *Thunderbolts*, a newsletter. Another may be an essay dealing with Waco or Ruby Ridge. Or there is a link to *Up Front*, called "Canada's premier White Nationalist magazine." Or, if so inclined, an Internet surfer can go to the Aryan Nations' official site, the National Alliance pages, Resistance Records, or many of the other white supremacist sites.

In some cases, subscription services that provide access to the Internet have cut off neo-Nazi groups from membership, an action that the groups call censorship.

But other white nationalist groups with homepages have quickly provided links to the dumped sites.

Some members of neo-Nazi groups advise those who e-mail messages on the Internet to use encryption (a special coding) to overcome surveillance by civil rights groups and the FBI. As one writer who posted on an Aryan Nations site pointed out:

> The movement has two wings—the "above-ground" political and social front, and the other front. Electronic mail is for the political front. . . . The goal of secrecy and evasion is simply to make "them" work hard to figure out what we're saying. Let them spy on us with all their manpower and money while the underground does its job. . . .
>
> The volume of email sent back and forth prevents the government from reading every single thing we write. They probably use search engines, like the ones America Online and Prodigy use, that scan for keywords of interest. Good ones to avoid are "kill", "bomb", "terrorism", "Jew", etc. In place, you might write "off", "nuuke", "struggle", and "libr'l-elite". Misspelling and slang is unfitting for intelligent Aryans, but we are first and foremost creatures of necessity.[12]

African-American Anti-Semitic Views

Even as neo-Nazi groups spew their hatred of African Americans, Jews, and other non-Aryans, militant African-American separatists have also joined the fray in recent years. Although they are not neo-Nazis, these separatists often spout similar hate philosophy prompted by their own views or urged on by some leaders of the Nation of Islam (NOI). Louis Farrakhan is an example of a NOI leader whose well-documented, anti-Semitic speeches have been publicized for more than a decade. In a 1980s speech, he called Judaism a "gutter religion," and during another speech, he referred to Hitler as a "great man." Farrakhan's NOI also has published a bogus history titled *The Secret Relationship Between Blacks and Jews*, which supposedly proves that Jews dominated the slave trade. In addition, the NOI has reprinted the anti-Semitic forgery *Protocols of the Elders of Zion.*

The NOI and Farrakhan's views drew even more attention when one of his aides, Khalid Abdul Muhammad, delivered a three-hour speech in 1993 at Kean College in New Jersey. Muhammad sounded the themes so dear to neo-Nazis, suggesting that Jews deserved their fate at the hands of Hitler's Nazis, that Jews were part of a conspiracy to gain world power, that Jews "want nothing but money," that Jews worship in a "synagogue of Satan," that Jews are "sucking our blood in the black community," and so on. He repeatedly used terms to disparage Jews, referring, for example, to "Jew York City" and "Jewnited Nations."[13]

After these and many other anti-Semitic remarks and ridicule were published in a full-page *New York Times* advertisement placed by the Anti-Defamation League, there was a clamor from many sources, including some mainstream African-American leaders. But a number of anti-Semitic speakers such as Muhammad have continued to make the university circuit. In 1994, at mainly African-American Howard University, for example, a crowd of more than two thousand people attended a night-long event called "Documenting the Black Holocaust." During the event, African-American leaders gave speeches blaming Jews and Jewish organizations for a variety of plots supposedly designed to destroy the black community. Although the conference gained media attention, Howard University officials as well as numerous students denounced the anti-Semitic harangues and announced that the speakers did not represent the views of the vast majority of the student body.

Nevertheless, some militant African Americans have found another means to advance their point of view—through the Black African Holocaust Council (BAHC) led by Eric Muhammad, another Nation of Islam member. Established in 1991 in Brooklyn, New York, BAHC holds a conference every fall that is restricted to African Americans and Native Americans and is meant to honor ancestors of slaves. But the BAHC has become a vehicle for "hateful rhetoric," with adherents following the pattern of Khalid Muhammad, according to the ADL. In a 1994 report on the BAHC, the ADL noted:

> It is offensive that fifty years after the liberation of Europe from the Nazis, Americans must still confront neo-Nazi propaganda, neo-Nazi beliefs, from fellow Americans. That some African-Americans—themselves the objects of so much mean prejudice and oppression—would now become the vehicle for expressions of ignorance that are racist, anti-democratic, and pernicious at their core exceeds offensiveness; it is an outrage.[14]

Mainstream Rhetoric

The high-pitched anti-Semitic messages come not only from fringe groups and extremists—black and white—but also from some politicians and mainstream media, especially talk show hosts and callers on radio and television. Some of the rhetoric could easily be classified as far-right or Nazi-like hate speech. Notorious examples have been broadcast on Bob Grant's afternoon radio show on WABC in New York as well as on two black stations, WWRL and WLIB.

But the hate talk also erupts from many other broadcasts across the United States. According to the Center for Democratic Renewal:

> There are 150 independent racist radio and television shows that air weekly and reach millions of sympathizers. This estimate does not include commercially-backed broadcasters like Rush Limbaugh who also spew racist vitriol, or the countless mainstream talk shows that regularly feature racists during ratings week sensationalism.[15]

Of course, most talk show hosts deny that their views or those of their listeners are harmful. They also cite the First Amendment right of people to express their opinions even though they may be repugnant and offensive to others—a right that has been upheld by the Supreme Court. On the other hand, those organizations and individuals concerned about the effect of hate speech, including neo-Nazi rhetoric, say it should be answered. They believe hate speech should be countered by the reasonable speech of fair and decent Americans presenting information that exposes the agenda of white supremacists and anti-Semites.

6

European Neo-Nazi Links

Language—spoken and written—is one of the most powerful forces in keeping neo-Nazi ideas alive. Methods of communication today, such as the Internet, faxes, and broadcasts, make it easy to distribute neo-Nazi and far-right propaganda worldwide at a fast pace. Rapid communication also provides opportunities for groups to internationally recruit members, prompting young Germans, for example, to join skinhead groups in Canada or vice versa.

From their beginnings, neo-Nazi skinheads have had global connections. Although there is no centralized organization, "Neo-Nazi Skinheads are bigotry's shock troops in much of today's world." As the ADL reported:

> In Germany, they have mobilized against the Turks; in Hungary, Slovakia and the Czech Republic, the Gypsies; in Britain, the Asians; in France, the North Africans; in Brazil, the Northeasterners; in the United States, racial minorities and immigrants; and in all

countries, homosexuals and those perennial "others," the Jews. In many places the targets include the homeless, drug addicts and others who are the down-and-out of society.[1]

According to the ADL, the neo-Nazi skinhead movement is active in no fewer than thirty-three countries on six continents. Of its total seventy thousand youths worldwide, half are hard-core activists and the rest supporters.

The countries where skinheads are found in the greatest numbers are Germany (5,000), Hungary and the Czech Republic (more than 4,000 each), the United States (3,500), Poland (2,000), the United Kingdom and Brazil (1,500 each), Italy (1,000 to 1,500), and Sweden (over 1,000). France, Spain, Canada, and the Netherlands each have at least 500 skins. Some skinheads are also in South Africa, Japan, Australia, and New Zealand.[2]

Recruitment to a particular group is just one goal of international purveyors of hate. Like American neo-Nazis and white supremacists, their counterparts in other parts of the world have planned and carried out attacks on non-Aryans, particularly nonwhite immigrants and Jews or people thought to be Jewish. Many of the publicized incidents have taken place in European countries, including Great Britain, Germany, Italy, Austria, France, and Poland. "While the number of neo-Nazis and neo-fascists in Western Europe remains minuscule, ugly pictures of straight-arm salutes, street hooligans and racial hatred are haunting reminders that the old ideologies are not dead," *Time* magazine reported recently.[3]

German Neo-Nazi Groups

Neo-Nazism has been part of the German scene ever since the end of World War II, but the Nazi dogma appeared more widespread after the fall of the Berlin Wall and the 1990 unification of East and West Germany. Reunification was accompanied by an economic depression blamed partly on the high costs of rebuilding East Germany and the "takeover of one system by another." East German monetary, legal, educational, and other bureaucratic systems were replaced by those of West Germany, which in effect destroyed "every remnant of East German life," wrote Stephen Kinzer in *The Atlantic Monthly.*[4]

Economic and social problems were intensified when German Chancellor Helmet Kohl failed to address growing neo-Nazi violence and the familiar racist tactic of blaming scapegoats for unrest and unemployment. One notorious incident occurred in 1993 when three young men with professed Nazi-like sentiments firebombed an apartment building in Solingen where Turkish immigrants lived, killing five people. The three suspects were arrested, tried, and convicted of arson.

In 1994, neo-Nazis in Luebeck, Germany, firebombed a synagogue. Then in 1996, a fire was set in a Luebeck building housing numerous immigrants, killing ten and injuring dozens. The three men arrested for the crimes were known extremists, one a skinhead.

Other victims of neo-Nazi assaults have included Africans seeking political asylum; descendants of Middle Eastern, African, and Asian immigrants who are German citizens; and Jews, who have been scapegoats for centuries.

76

Neo-Nazism has been part of the German scene ever since the end of World War II. Neo-Nazis subscribe to Nazi beliefs, as outlined in the 1920s by German dictator Adolf Hitler, considered one of the most evil men in history.

Racist violence rose steadily from 1990 until 1992—that year twenty-six hundred assaults were reported. The number of incidents dropped in 1993 to twenty-two hundred, and reportedly attacks have been diminishing steadily ever since.[5]

Nevertheless, the declining figures are not much comfort to victims. In January 1995, for example, Adolpho Washington, an African-American boxer, went to Frankfurt, Germany, to help German boxer Henry Maske train for a championship bout. While walking down the street, Washington was stoned by skinheads.

Another victim was Hans Dade, who was forced out of business by neo-Nazi skinheads. In 1993, Dade opened an Irish pub in Schwedt on the Polish border. Business was brisk for a time—until skinheads decided the pub was too "foreign" for their tastes and began to threaten Irish employees. One was beaten in the parking lot, another was the victim of a carjacking, and some who waited tables received bullets as tips. As one after another of his employees quit and customers refused to come to the pub, Dade was forced to close his business at the end of 1994.

Since that time, violence has decreased in Schwedt, but a news report noted that:

> Skinheads have moved into extortion and protection rackets. . . . Gangs of skinheads hang out for a few days at a new restaurant, cafe or club, scaring away customers until the owner agrees to pay a monthly fee to guarantee the thugs will take their patronage elsewhere.[6]

In the opinion of German psychoanalyst Werner

Bohleber, the violence in the Federal Republic of Germany since 1991 has been "motivated by ultraright ideas." He believes the violence has flourished not only because of serious economic and social problems but also because of xenophobia (fear or contempt of strangers). In Bohleber's view:

> A xenophobic mentality is always a strong sounding board for right-wing [political] parties and provides for young people especially a consensual focus for a shift to the right. Hatred of strangers is also the unifying motive for most violence among youth. Eighty percent of them belong either to extreme right-wing organizations or the skinheads. Violence has its origins within the mainstream of society. Anti-Semitism has also flared up again. It has all the characteristics of a defense mechanism against guilt. Ultra-right youths who defile Jewish cemeteries and attempt to destroy monuments and memorial places are trying to erase the memory of Nazi crimes. They want to remove this blemish from Germany.[7]

Whatever the motivations for skinhead and other neo-Nazi violence, it is not condoned by hundreds of thousands of German citizens who have marched in the streets to demonstrate their disgust. In addition, German lawmakers began to deal with neo-Nazi violence by outlawing paramilitary organizations like the German Alternative, National Front, National Offensive, and Viking Youth. The latter group, which was banned in 1994, had a membership of about four hundred. They were led by a "federal fuehrer" and were dedicated to restoring a fascist state in Germany. Although the group

Anti-Semitism, like this act of vandalism, is not limited to white supremacists. Some African Americans, like Louis Farrakhan, have been known to spread messages of hate toward Jews.

had not committed any violent acts, it was a link between members of former neo-Nazi organizations.[8]

By 1995, the German government had shut down eleven neo-Nazi groups, and some state and local governments had banned neo-Nazi marches and concerts. Germany has also passed laws prohibiting distribution of neo-Nazi propaganda and symbols. For years, Gary Lauck, the neo-Nazi publisher based in Lincoln, Nebraska, was a major distributor of such materials, particularly the newspaper *The New Order*. It was published in twelve languages and was distributed along with Nazi arm bands and other paraphernalia in European countries where free speech is protected. His main target was skinheads who, Lauck hoped, would use his materials against the "enemy"—Jews. Lauck smuggled his wares into Germany, where authorities issued an international warrant for his arrest, and in March 1995, he was apprehended while visiting neo-Nazis in Denmark. Months later he was extradited to Germany for trial. On August 22, 1996, Lauck was convicted by a Hamburg court of inciting racial hatred. He was sentenced to a four-year jail term.

Nazism in Other European Countries

In Italy (and other Mediterranean countries) where Nazism was well entrenched during World War II, fascist groups continued to form after the war and into the present decade. Neo-Nazi skinheads (or Nazi-skins as they are called in Italy) have been responsible for attacks in many European countries. The Associated Press reported in June 1995 from Lisbon, Portugal, that:

> a group of 50 skinheads with iron knuckles attacked every black they could . . . injuring 12 people. . . . A 27-year-old man was reported to be in a coma. Seven men and two women in the group of skinheads were arrested. Racist incidents in Portugal have become more frequent with worsening economic and employment conditions.[9]

That same month in Denmark, three skinheads were on their way to a neo-Nazi rally and attacked a group of immigrants, using their favorite tools—their metal-tipped

As this symbol shows, the activities of white supremacist groups are not confined to the United States.

black boots. After their convictions for the kicking assaults, the judge sentenced the skinheads to eighteen months in jail. When released, they will not be allowed to wear their boots on the street.

In the summer of 1995, skinheads in Bratislava, Slovakia, torched a bar and apartment used by Gypsies. They also poured gasoline over a seventeen-year-old Gypsy and set the boy afire; he died from the second- and third-degree burns.

Soccer games in Europe appear to be stages for skinhead violence. Since the 1980s, drunken rowdiness by British soccer fans has been a major problem, and these fans instigated a riot in Belgium that resulted in the death of thirty-nine people. After that, British teams were barred from international competition for five years. This hooliganism, as it is sometimes called, appeared to subside for awhile. Then in 1994 and 1995, news services reported that some European soccer fans were giving "Seig Heil" salutes at games and that neo-Nazi groups were behind some disturbances at soccer games in Spain, Italy, France, Ireland, and Great Britain.

United Action

Since the early 1990s, a number of groups have formed in Europe to protest and counteract neo-Nazi and other radical-right violence. In 1994, for example, 142 representatives of antiracist and antifascist organizations from thirty-five countries gathered for a week-long conference—UNITED for Intercultural Action—in Strasbourg, France. Called the largest such gathering ever, the conference issued a manifesto designed to influence European politicians and encourage the electorate not to vote for party candidates who have racist and fascist tendencies.

As a result of the conference, there have been numerous activities in various countries across Europe to inform the general public about racism and fascism. Groups have held silent candlelight demonstrations, produced and distributed posters, and held festivals to raise awareness of neo-Nazism and white supremacy.

7

Combating Hate Crimes

For the past two decades at least, numerous watchdog groups and experts on hate crimes—whether in Europe, North America, or another part of the world—have been attempting to find ways to combat radical far-right violence. Part of this process is analyzing the dynamics of hatred and what prompts some people to join neo-Nazi or other racist groups that target victims solely for their skin color or religious affiliation.

Along with understanding the motivations of hate-mongers, individuals and organizations have taken steps to inform themselves about groups who undermine democracy and encourage terrorism and white supremacy. Some groups have taken action in the form of political campaigns, supporting government officials or candidates for office who are committed to developing model legislation to stop hate crimes. Others are dedicated to educating the public, working with law enforcement, educators, parents, and the media. In short, they are trying to find solutions to problems rather than looking for scapegoats upon whom to place blame.

The Dynamics of Hatred

Experts on extremism say that historically people have always used hate as a means to ease the personal pain and anger they feel toward themselves. They can also make themselves feel right and good if they make others appear wrong and bad. People seem to need enemies. "We hate our enemies so we don't despise ourselves," was a brief explanation given by Howard Stein, editor of the *Journal of Psychoanalytic Anthropology.*[1]

Still other factors motivate people who commit hate crimes. Sociologist Jack Levin and criminologist Jack McDevitt of Northeastern University in Boston studied hate crime in the Boston area and categorized three types of motivations: "thrill, defensive, and mission." Explaining their findings in their 1993 book *Hate Crimes: The Rising Tide of Bigotry and Bloodshed,* they wrote:

> Thrill hate crimes are committed by offenders who are looking for excitement and attack the victims for the "fun of it." Defensive hate crimes involve offenders who perceive themselves as protecting their neighborhood, their workplace, or their college campus from "outsiders." The third type, mission hate crimes, involve offenders who have committed their lives to bigotry. Their crimes reflect dedication to this cause.[2]

Mission hate crimes are the least common—about one percent of the total hate crimes—but they are the most violent. Someone committing such a crime is in

85

many cases a member of a racist or neo-Nazi group and usually "has failed to fit into society. He blames his personal failures on the members of any group he believes to be different. . . . He seeks to rid the world of all members of the 'inferior' group as well as its symbols," the authors noted.[3]

Dan Korem, an investigative journalist, author, and nationally known expert on gangs and cults, began scrutinizing Texas skinheads in 1989 to learn what motivations and characteristics prompted their hatemongering. Korem found that "in most cases, the desire to belong to a Skinhead gang (or any other type of gang for that matter) is the result of trouble at home." The skinheads he has interviewed over the years across North America and in Europe come from families with similar characteristics:

> divorce, separation, physical and/or sexual abuse, and dysfunctional parents. These conditions are further compounded by joblessness, poverty, lack of education, language barriers, academic deficiencies, and destructive elements from pop culture, such as violent themes in music, television, and films.

In an article for *Klanwatch Intelligence Report,* Korem observed:

> Many people believe that Skinheads come only from poor families. But my interviews in Germany, Austria, Hungary, Poland, and the U.S. confirm that Skinhead activity in most cities is now more common in middle and upper middle class neighborhoods than it is in lower income areas.
>
> In fact, when I first started to investigate such gangs in Dallas, I discovered that most of the one hundred or so Skinheads in the area lived in the

Anti-Semitic graffiti like this demonstrates the neo-Nazis' belief that a Jewish conspiracy is to blame for all the problems in the world.

affluent northern section of the city and two surrounding suburbs.[4]

Skinhead gangs, like other gangs, often serve as substitute families for their members. Many join skinhead groups primarily for social reasons—they want to feel a sense of belonging. With the pack, they feel a sense of security. And by degrading others and glorifying violence, they gain a sense of power and self-esteem.

Yet some skinheads break away from the gang, often with the help of counselors, social workers, juvenile law enforcement officers, or other caring adults. One strategy is to help young people learn why they need scapegoats and then guide them away from blaming others to learning self-appreciation and self-worth. Teaching young people that there are alternatives to gang activity and providing experiences for interaction with people different from themselves can also prompt some skinheads to leave the gang, experts say.

Psychologist Raphael Ezekiel, who interviewed young neo-Nazis along with aging white supremacists for his book *The Racist Mind*, pointed out that there were often no sanctions, nothing to stop young people from becoming Nazis—"nothing from family or environment got in the way. Nothing had led them to internalize revulsion about the swastika." But Ezekiel is convinced many did not necessarily have to be members of an extremist group to act out their racism.

> Given . . . an alternative group that offered comradeship, reassuring activities, glamour, and excitement, they could easily have switched their allegiances. They would have remained racist—like

their neighbors who hadn't joined a group—but they would not have needed to carry out racist actions in a group setting. Within four months of beginning my meetings with them, I knew that I could have led the bulk of the membership away if I had had an alternative . . . they quickly built ties to me, despite my clear status as a Jew and a progressive.[5]

In short, Ezekiel has found, as have others who have interviewed or counseled young Nazis, that preventive measures must begin early. In some cases, those measures are educational programs in schools or civic forums that provide opportunities to learn about "other groups, their contributions, the importance of richness derived from various cultures, the satisfactions derived from coopera-tion," as psychiatrist and author Theodore Isaac Rubin stated. In his book *Anti-Semitism: A Disease of the Mind,* Rubin pointed out that familiarity—learning about peo-ple different from oneself—is a good antidote to hate. In his words:

> Humanization, compassion, empathy, and love comprise antihating machinery. . . . By humanization I mean learning and having compassion for the human condition in all of its ramifications, including its tribulations. . . . Camaraderie and communication are the enemies of bigotry.[6]

Educational Programs

Educational programs on diversity and tolerance are part of the mission for such groups as the Anti-Defamation League of B'nai B'rith. Founded in 1913, the ADL, through its national and regional offices, distributes numerous educational materials to increase awareness of prejudice, bigotry, and neo-Nazi hatred. The organization's prejudice reduction program, called A World of Difference, is used in schools and by civic groups and businesses. In addition, the ADL offers sensitivity workshops for teachers and produces TV programs and public service announcements on prejudice reduction.

Another organization, the Southern Poverty Law Center, established a Teaching Tolerance project that distributes a magazine by the same name and several teaching kits, one of the most recent being "The Shadow of Hate." It includes an award-winning video on the history of intolerance in the United States, a companion text *Us and Them,* and a teacher's guide. Tens of thousands of these kits have been sent free to schools, and teachers have reported that the materials have made an impact on their students, helping them to see how victims of hate and intolerance feel.

Along with using educational materials from civil rights groups, some schools have special elective courses to combat intolerance and hatred. One elective class at James Madison High School in Fairfax County, Virginia, is called "Combating Intolerance." To provide some insights into how neo-Nazis indoctrinate their members, a former skinhead, Emily Heinrichs of Pennsylvania, was invited to speak to the students.

When she was about fifteen years old, Emily lived for a year with skinheads in a Christian Identity compound called Christian Identity Comitatus. She broke away from the group in 1994 and now appears on television talk shows and in high schools to try to convince other teenagers not to make the mistake she did. Her story follows the pattern of many young people who join gangs: The skinheads gave her identity. "I was great because I was white," she told the class. The group also taught her antigovernment doctrine, telling her "how the government was out to get everyone—how it was run by all the Jews—and I began to think it might be true," Heinrichs said.[7]

Although her parents tried to steer her away from neo-Nazi involvement, Emily said that only led to arguments. She finally left the compound and returned home after she learned she was pregnant. Now she has a young daughter and has gone back to school, hoping to go on to a career in criminal law.

Some high schools sponsor conferences on diversity, such as the "Walk in My Shoes" conference that has been held since 1989 in Fullerton, California. Nearly five hundred students attended the 1995 conference, where they discussed the frustrations and controversies that divide students of varied backgrounds and also searched for common ground. Organized by the Orange County Human Relations Commission, the conference was needed because of the many changes taking place, according to Rusty Kennedy, the executive director of the commission.

> It's gone from being basically an all-white suburban community to a multiethnic urban area with 2.5 million people. . . . With that comes lots of challenges. Kids are . . . threatened, and nasty things are being said to them. A lot of them are angry and also afraid.

91

Anti-Nazi protesters react to plans by members of the Chicago Nazi party to march in the predominantly Jewish suburb of Skokie.

Through the conference, human relations experts and educators hoped to bring about some changes through workshops that covered topics ranging from "Affirmative Action: Deprivation or Advancement" to "Hate Crimes" to "White Culture Awareness." Some students reported that the conference helped them see that there was more than one side to an issue and that it fostered "better understanding among diverse groups." As one student noted, "It gets everything out in the open."[8]

Community forums that discuss the ideology of neo-Nazis and white supremacists have also been a way to help combat extremism. For example, in Oregon, where neo-Nazis and armed militias have been highly visible since the early 1990s, civic and church groups have sponsored numerous antibigotry campaigns. During May 1995, numerous Oregon groups were host to a guest speaker, a former Aryan Nations member who warned about the dangers of the radical far-right movement in the Northwest. Raised in a foster home, Floyd Cochran joined the Ku Klux Klan when he was thirteen years old, and in 1990, he became part of the Aryan Nation's compound in Hayden Lake, Idaho. As the group's publicist, it was his job to make "hate sound palatable," he said. He left the Aryan Nations when leaders told him his four-year-old son should die because he was born with a cleft palate and was "genetically defective." Now he admonishes parents to be on the alert for the violent-prone radical-right movement, a hate movement that "is out for your children."[9]

Antiextremist Legislation

Although understanding hatred and learning about the neo-Nazi and other white supremacists are essential in efforts to combat hate crimes, most state legislatures have taken additional steps. Nearly all states have passed laws to deal with actual attacks motivated by hate. These hate-crime laws, as they are called, punish criminal action directed against people because of status characteristics—that is, people who are targeted for crimes because of their race, religion, or sexual orientation. According to Klanwatch, "All hate crime laws punish racial, ethnic and religious based crimes, but only about 20 states cover sexual orientation." In some states, laws protect those who are victims of criminal acts because of their gender or disability. And some state laws "punish any criminal act that is based on status. Other hate crime laws are more limited, punishing only certain specific crimes such as assaults or criminal mischief."[10]

At the federal level, numerous members of Congress are convinced that antiterrorism legislation is needed. Bills to combat neo-Nazi and other white supremacist groups were introduced in 1995. But some legislators and civil rights organizations contend that proposed laws would threaten civil liberties and would be unconstitutional. Civil rights groups argue that the better course is being vigilant and exposing extremists rather than passing laws that give government more control over people's lives. In fact, during the 1970s, government officials attempted to stop terrorism by infiltrating some noncriminal dissident groups and filing lawsuits against them, but these actions had little effect. Instead, free speech and civil rights were restricted.

Free speech is certainly an essential part of a democracy, but some federal lawmakers have also proposed legislation that would ban hate messages in written or spoken form. Such laws have been written in some European countries. In the United States, as many neo-Nazi and white supremacists know, their propaganda is usually protected by the First Amendment to the Constitution.

Arguments over free-speech rights have been going on for decades, and over the years, the courts have held that it is unconstitutional to ban political dissent, including far-right messages, some of which may be dangerous or threatening. For example, the Supreme Court decided in a 1969 case (*Brandenburg v. Ohio*) that no government action could be taken against KKK speakers who declared that the Klan might seek revenge against the federal government if it continued to suppress the white race. The High Court ruled that such speech did not specifically advocate an illegal act, so the state of Ohio could not prosecute the Klan. But the Court, like others before it, identified limits to free speech, ruling that free speech is prohibited if it incites or intends to encourage imminent (immediate) illegal acts.

Nevertheless, a major question arises in regard to hate messages in the mass media—whether on the Internet, television, radio, or in print. Should government have the authority to ban messages that advocate violence and killing people? Cass R. Sunstein responds to that question in *The American Prospect* magazine by arguing that "government probably should have the authority to stop speakers from expressly advocating the illegal use of force to kill people. There is little democratic value in protecting [advocates] of murder." He points out that Congress passed a law making it a crime to threaten to kill the president, and the High Court has ruled the law is constitutional. In Sunstein's view, the Federal Communications Commission might be able "to impose civil sanctions on those who expressly advocate illegal, violent acts aimed at killing people." He adds, though, that restricting speech is risky:

> Vigorous, even hateful criticism of government is very much at the heart of the right to free speech. Indeed, advocacy of law violation can be an appropriate part of democratic debate. As the example of Martin Luther King, Jr., testifies, there is an honorable tradition of civil disobedience. We should sharply distinguish, however, King's form of nonviolent civil disobedience from [advocates] or acts of murder. The government should avoid regulating political opinions, including the advocacy of illegal acts. That principle need not, however, be interpreted to bar the government from restricting advocacy of unlawful killing on the mass media.[11]

Arguments over what types of hate message should or should not be legally allowed will certainly continue in the future. "It is never easy to judge what is the most appropriate or effective response to organized hate group activity and acts of bigoted violence," says the Center for Democratic Renewal in its statement of purpose. "But one unfortunate fact remains clear: most situations evoke no response."[12] In other words, too many people of goodwill, people who respect diversity, remain silent when faced with hatred and bigotry in their communities. Yet, countless individual activists have shown over and over again—often in unheralded ways—that neo-Nazis and white supremacists can be challenged and overcome.

8

What Individuals Can Do

Kenneth McVay, who counteracts the neo-Nazi and anti-Semitic postings on the Internet, is a prime example of how one person can have an impact well beyond his own backyard. In fact, McVay has been able to reach computer users worldwide with electronic access to newsgroups, bulletin boards, and the World Wide Web.

Many people, however, do not have the means or resources to conduct a global crusade against hatemongers and hate crimes. But they still can be heard—loud and clear—in their own neighborhoods, villages, or towns.

"Not in Our Town"

In December 1995, numerous cities across the United States took part in week-long campaigns known as "Not in Our Town," coinciding with a television documentary that aired during that month. Sponsored by the

California Working Group of the San Francisco Bay Area and the Institute for Alternative Journalism, the film focused on what citizens can do to stop hate crimes. The documentary is based on actions taken by residents in Billings, Montana, which began with Police Chief Wayne Inman in 1992 when he ordered city workers to paint over racist and anti-Semitic graffiti on hilltop rocks above the city.

As more graffiti and racist leaflets appeared, Inman alerted city political and business leaders to what he perceived as a threat to the community, but the police chief's warnings were not taken seriously—in fact, some people accused him of trying to stir up trouble. Then as anti-Semitic and racist acts escalated, the community began to organize to prevent violence and to help and support victims of attacks.

Labor union members, for example, helped repaint a Native American home that had been damaged by graffiti. After skinheads invaded an African Methodist Episcopal Church to intimidate the congregation, members of predominantly white churches began to attend the African-American church to lend support. When a cement block was thrown through the window of a Jewish home where a Menorah was being displayed, the local newspaper published a full-page picture of a Menorah, and with the encouragement of the newspaper, thousands of Jews and non-Jews displayed the Menorah as a sign of unity. Other signs appeared, declaring, "Not in Our Town. No Hate." More and more citizens protested the violence, marched in candlelight vigils, and formed solidarity groups to combat attacks that were

Some lawmakers seek to ban hate messages, such as the vandalism in the above picture, in both their written and spoken forms.

linked to skinheads, Aryan Nations, and Klan members. Eventually the city residents put an end to the series of hate crimes.

The Billings campaign and the documentary inspired similar events in other cities. For example, high school students in Glenwood, Oregon, helped repair a synagogue that was vandalized and painted with swastikas. In Kenosha, Wisconsin, where African-American students have been harassed by skinheads, schools are confronting the problem, not ignoring it. And throughout southern California, civic groups and human relations organizations are publicly protesting the distribution of neo-Nazi materials and other acts of hatred.

Taking Action

The types of actions that individuals can take alone or with groups varies with the situation, of course, and often the most effective antidotes to neo-Nazi and white supremacist attacks are initiated within the community affected. The Center for Democratic Renewal advises that grassroots groups are the key to fighting extremists because they can "mobilize people block by block." Often those who are mobilized include students who make telephone calls, write letters, send messages via the Internet, take part in fund-raising events, participate in protest marches, or perform other tasks that counter fanatics bent on destruction.

Much information and many suggestions for fighting the Hitlerites and other racists among us are available from many groups. The CDR, for example, offers a guide titled *When Hate Groups Come to Town: A Handbook of Effective Community Responses.*

The basic point civil rights groups and individuals working against extremists make is NOT to give in to neo-Nazi and white supremacist intimidation or their efforts to instigate a race war or "revolution" designed to destroy democracy. Tolerance, compassion, and respect for others can be learned and applied.

Chapter Notes

Chapter 1

1 "Hate Crimes in the Corps," *Newsweek,* December 18, 1995, p. 6; "Racial Slaying Prompts Probe," Associated Press, December 22, 1995. (News posting on Compu-Serve.com)

2. Associated Press, "Three Accused of 'Race War,'" November 6, 1995. (News posting on CompuServe.com)

3. Associated Press, "Germany Seeks Extradition of American Neo-Nazi," *Times Union,* March 24, 1995, p. A4.

4. Raphael S. Ezekiel, *The Racist Mind: Portraits of American Neo-Nazis and Klansmen* (New York: Viking Penguin, 1995), p. xxix.

Chapter 2

1. Kathleen M. Blee, *Women of the Klan* (Berkeley, Calif.: University of California Press, 1991), pp. 12–13.

2. James Ridgeway, *Blood in the Face: The Ku Klux Klan, Aryan Nations, Nazi Skinheads, and the Rise of a New White Culture* (New York: Thunder's Mouth Press, 1990), p. 32.

3. Gene Smith, "Bundersfuhrer Kuhn," *American Heritage,* September 1995, p. 102.

4. Ibid.

5. "Was Lincoln a Bigot?" tract (Arlington, Va.: American Nazi Party, no date).

6. Ridgeway, p. 68.

7. A. V. Schaerffenberg, "Nordic NS Hero George Lincoln Rockwell Battles the Red Rats in Jew York City!" no date. The Independent White Racialists Homepage (site no longer available)

8. "Hate Movement Shifts Tactics in 1994," *Klanwatch Intelligence Report,* March 1995, p. 9.

Chapter 3

1. Loretta J. Ross and the Center for Democratic Renewal, "The Militia Movement—in Their Own Words and Deeds," congressional testimony, July 11, 1995. (On the Internet, July 24, 1995, in pol.right.docs conference/forum on igc.apc.org) This service requires access permission.

2. "White Supremacy in the 1990s," *Center for Democratic Renewal,* June 1995. (On the Internet in pra.reports conference/forum igc.apc.org) This service requires access permission.

3. Alan M. Schwartz, ed., *Extremism on the Right* (United Nations Plaza, N.Y.: The Anti-Defamation League of B'nai B'rith, 1988), p. 21.

4. "Racist Ideology," Center for Democratic Renewal, March 13, 1995. (On the Internet, March 15, 1995, in pol.right.docs conference/forum igc.apc.org)

5. Ibid.

6. Robert Miles, *From the Mountain,* September/October 1987, (newsletter).

7. Jerry Walters, "Inside Extremist 'Theology,'" *The Lutheran,* November 1995, pp. 24–25.

8. Quoted in "First an Oath, Then Alan Berg Must Die," *Rocky Mountain News,* July 24, 1989, p. 126.

9. Ibid.

10. Michael Janofsky, "Aryan World Congress Draws 320 Supremacists to Idaho," *Oregonian,* July 23, 1995, p. A18.

11. "Aryan World Congress Focuses on Militias and an Expected Revolution," *Klanwatch Intelligence Report,* August 1995, p. 1.

12. Ibid.

13. David McHugh, "Hate Rock Adds Gloss to Skinheads' Racism," *Detroit Free Press,* March 31, 1995, p. A1.

14. Ibid.

15. Quoted in David McHugh.

16. Matt O'Connor, "Neo-Nazi Filed Guilty Plea in 1992 Zion Vandalism," *Chicago Tribune,* September 14, 1994, p. 6.

17. Quoted in William Hermann, "2 Held in 'Skinhead' Attack on Hispanics," *Arizona Republic,* June 27, 1995, p. B1.

Chapter 4

1. John Snell, "Metzger's Racism Goes on Trial," *Oregonian,* October 7, 1990, Metro Section, p. 4.

2. John Snell, "Doctor Says Seraw Didn't Fight," *Oregonian,* October 18, 1990, p. C4.

3. White Aryan Resistance Hate Page. (On the Internet at http://www.resist.com)

4. L. R. Beam, "Leaderless Resistance." (On the Internet at http://www.io.com/~wlp/aryan-page/index.html)

5. Chip Berlet, "Armed Militias, Right Wing Populism, and Scapegoating," April 24, 1995. (On the Internet at http://paul.spu.edu/~sinnfein/berlet.html)

6. Daniel Junas, "Rise of the Citizen Militias: Angry White Guys with Guns," *Covert Action Quarterly,* Spring Issue, 1995. (On the Internet at http://MediaFilter.org/MFF/CAQ.militia.html)

7. James Ridgeway, *Blood in the Face: The Ku Klux Klan, Aryan Nations, Nazi Skinheads, and the Rise of a New White Culture* (New York: Thunder's Mouth Press, 1990), p. 20.

8. Quoted in James Corcoran, *Bitter Harvest: Gordon Kahl and the Posse Comitatus: Murder in the Heartland* (New York: Viking, 1990), p. 68.

9. Loretta J. Ross and the Center for Democratic Renewal, "The Militia Movement—in Their Own Words and Deeds," congressional testimony, July 11, 1995. (On the Internet at pol.right.docs conference igc.apc.org)

10. Chip Berlet, "Armed Militias, Right Wing Populism, and Scapegoating," April 24, 1995. (On the Internet at http://paul.spu.edu/~sinnfein/berlet.html)

11. Ibid.

12. Max Baucus, Testimony before the Senate Judiciary Terrorism, Technology, and Government Information Committee, June 15, 1995.

13. Quoted in Dan Yurman, "Update on Militia in Eastern Idaho," April 30, 1995. (On the Internet, May 1, 1995, in pol.right.docs conference/forum on igc.apc.org)

14. Morris Dees with James Corcoran, *Gathering Storm: America's Militia Threat* (New York: HarperCollins, 1996), p. 198.

Chapter 5

1. "White Supremacy in the 1990s," *Center for Democratic Renewal,* August 14, 1994. (On the Internet, October 28, 1994, in DNA pra.reports conference/forum igc.apc.org)

2. "Willis Carto and the Liberty Lobby," *Center for Democratic Renewal,* March 13, 1994. (On the Internet, October 28, 1994, in pra.reports conference/forum igc.apc.org)

3. ADL Research Report, *Liberty Lobby: Hate Central* (United Nations Plaza, N.Y.: Anti-Defamation League of B'nai B'rith, 1995), p. 7.

4. Cecelia Müllermeder, "Primer on Carto and Who is Leon Degrelle?" September 13, 1993. (On the Internet in newsgroups alt.revisionism, soc.history, alt.activism, alt.discrimination, alt.censorship)

5. Ibid

6. "A Few Facts About the Institute for Historical Review," no date. (On the Internet at http://www.kaiwan.com/ ~ihrgreg)

7. "Willis Carto and the Liberty Lobby."

8. "Nizkor QAR Index," Nizkor Home Page, no date. (On the Internet at http://www.almanac.bc.ca)

9. "What is the National Alliance?" no date. (On the Internet at http://www.natvan.com/)

10. David Beard, "Ex-Klan Chief Spews Hate in Internet," *The Atlanta Journal and Constitution,* March 18, 1995, p. C7.

11. "Stormfront White Nationalists Resource Page." (On the Internet at http://stormfront.wat.com/stormfront/)

12. Aryan Crusader, "Overcoming Internet Surveillance," no date. (On the Internet at http://www.io.com/ ~wlp/aryan-page/index.html)

13. Quoted in Arch Puddington, "Black Anti-Semitism and How It Grows," *Commentary,* April 1994, electronic version.

14. *Uncommon Ground: The Black African Holocaust Council and Other Links between Black and White Extremists* (United Nations Plaza, N.Y.: The Anti-Defamation League of B'nai B'rith, 1994), p. 19.

15. Ross, "White Supremacy in the 1990s."

Chapter 6

1. *The Skinhead International: A Worldwide Survey of Neo-Nazi Skinheads* (United Nations Plaza, N.Y.: The Anti-Defamation League of B'nai B'rith, 1995), pp. 77–84.

2. Ibid.

3. James O. Jackson, "Fascism Lives," *Time,* June 6, 1994, p. 50.

4. Stephen Kinzer, "A Climate for Demagogues," *The Atlantic,* February 1994, p. 30.

5. Thom Shanker, "When Neo-Nazis Called, Irish Pub Was Doomed," *Chicago Tribune,* December 4, 1994, p. 10.

6. Ibid.

7. Werner Bohleber, "The Presence of the Past— Xenophobia and Rightwing Extremism in the Federal Republic of Germany: Psychoanalytic Reflections," *American Imago,* Fall 1995, p. 329.

8. Associated Press, "Germany Raids Group of Neo-Nazis," *Chicago Tribune*, November 11, 1994, p. 7.

9. Associated Press, "Rampaging Youths Cause Terror Unrest in England, Portugal, France Laid to Ethnic Tension," *Boston Globe*, June 12, 1995, National/Foreign Section, p. 36.

Chapter 7

1. Quoted in Jann Mitchell, "Why People Hate," *Oregonian*, October 17, 1990, p. E1.

2. Jack Levin and Jack McDevitt, "Landmark Study Reveals Hate Crimes Vary Significantly by Offender Motivation," *Klanwatch Intelligence Report*, August 1995, pp. 7–8.

3. Ibid.

4. Dan Korem, "Neo-Nazi Skinheads: Angry, Violent, Rebellious and Reachable," *Klanwatch Intelligence Report*, March 1994, pp. 8–10.

5. Raphael S. Ezekiel, *The Racist Mind: Portraits of American Neo-Nazis and Klansmen* (New York: Viking, 1995), pp. 158–159.

6. Theodore Isaac Rubin, M.D., *Anti-Semitism: A Disease of the Mind* (New York: The Continuum Publishing Company, 1990), pp. 138–139.

7. Quoted in Leef Smith, "Teen Tells of Her Year as a Skinhead," *The Washington Post*, May 25, 1995, p. D1.

8. Quoted in Diane Seo, "500 Students Mix It Up at Diversity Conference," *Los Angeles Times*, December 1, 1995, p. B1.

9. Quoted in Tom Bates, "Former Aryan Nations Spokesman Takes Aim at Bigotry," *Oregonian*, May 14, 1995, p. C1.

10. "Militia and Extremist Activity Prompts New Legislation," *Klanwatch Intelligence Report*, August 1995, p. 10.

11. Cass R. Sunstein, "Is Violent Speech a Right?" *The American Prospect*, Summer 1995, pp. 34–37.

12. "Mission Statement of the Center for Democratic Renewal," March 13, 1994. (On the Internet, June 28, 1996, at http://www.publiceye.org/pra/cdr.html)

Further Reading

Bornstein, Jerry. *The Neo-Nazis: The Threat of the Hitler Cult.* New York: Julian Messner, 1986.

Corcoran, James. *Bitter Harvest: Gordon Kahl and the Posse Comitatus: Murder in the Heartland.* New York: Viking, 1990.

Gay, Kathlyn. *Bigotry.* Hillside, N.J.: Enslow Publishers, 1989.

Gay, Kathlyn. *A Biographical Dictionary of Twentieth Century Heroes of Conscience.* Santa Barbara, Calif.: ABC-CLIO, 1996.

Karl, Jonathan. *The Right to Bear Arms.* New York: HarperPaperbacks/HarperCollins, 1995.

Lipstadt, Deborah. *Denying the Holocaust.* New York: Penguin, 1993.

Marks, Jane. *The Hidden Children: the Secret Survivors of the Holocaust.* New York: Fawcett, 1993.

Ridgeway, James. *Blood in the Face: The Ku Klux Klan, Aryan Nations, Nazi Skinheads, and the Rise of a New White Culture,* 2nd ed. New York: Thunder's Mouth Press, 1995.

Rubin, Theodore Isaac. *Anti-Semitism: A Disease of the Mind.* New York: The Continuum Publishing Company, 1990.

Segrest, Mab. *Memoir of a Race Traitor.* Boston: South End Press.

Stern, Kenneth S. *A Force Upon the Plain: The American Militia Movement and the Politics of Hate.* New York: Simon & Schuster, 1996.

Watterson, Kathryn. *Not by the Sword: How the Love of a Cantor and His Family Transformed a Klansman.* New York: Simon & Schuster, 1995.

Index